"Dr. Kim's *Social Media Campaigns (2nd ed)* offers a delightful guide for brands and companies to effectively use social media to connect and engage with stakeholders and audiences. Informed by recent research and infused with numerous real-world examples, this text is a must-read primer for anyone who is interested in digital strategic communications or looking to design data-driven social media campaigns."
— **Rita Linjuan Men,** *University of Florida, USA*

"The key strength of this book is its focus on using social media to build communities, cultivate relationships and generate engagement between brands and their followers. It is this attention to two-way communication and relationship-building that is the foundation of any successful social media campaign. Social Media Campaigns demonstrates Dr Kim's expertise as a leader in social media education."
— **Karen Sutherland**, *University of the Sunshine Coast, Australia*

"A go-to book for me and my students for years. In the new edition of *Social Media Campaigns*, Carolyn Mae Kim remains true to what I loved about the first edition: The emphasis on the importance of learning the timeless skill of strategic planning and helping readers develop a social mindset that prioritizes ethics, relationships, and critical thinking. In this text, Dr. Kim masterfully looks beyond the surface of changing trends and tools ... Bravo, Dr. Kim!"
— **Matthew J. Kushin**, *Shepherd University, USA*

"A great balance between research and practice in social media, which is refreshing and wonderful to see. I highly recommend adding this new edition to your library – it's a must have."
— **Karen Freberg**, *University of Louisville, USA*

Social Media Campaigns

This new edition continues to give students a foundation in the principles of digital audience engagement and data metrics across platforms, preparing them to adapt to the quickly evolving world of digital media. It takes students through the processes of social listening, strategic design, creative engagement, and evaluation, with expert insights from social media professionals. Thoroughly updated, this second edition includes:

- new strategies to guide students in the initial campaign planning phase
- added content on influencers, social care teams, and newsjacking
- coverage of research evaluation, the implications of findings, and articulating the ROI
- expanded discussion of ethical considerations in campaign design and data collection and analysis.

The book is suited to both undergraduate and post-graduate students as a primary text for courses in social/digital media marketing and public relations or a secondary text in broader public relations and marketing campaign planning and writing courses.

Accompanying online resources include chapter reviews with suggestions for further resources; instructor guides; in-class exercises; a sample syllabus, assignments, and exams; and lecture slides. Visit www.routledge.com/9780367896201

Carolyn Mae Kim is an associate professor of public relations at Biola University, USA. Her research specialties include credibility, digital strategy, media ecology, and public relations education.

Social Media Campaigns

Strategies for Public Relations and Marketing

Second Edition

Carolyn Mae Kim

Routledge
Taylor & Francis Group

NEW YORK AND LONDON

Second edition published 2021
by Routledge
52 Vanderbilt Avenue, New York, NY 10017

and by Routledge
2 Park Square, Milton Park, Abingdon, Oxon, OX14 4RN

Routledge is an imprint of the Taylor & Francis Group, an informa business

© 2021 Taylor & Francis

The right of Carolyn Mae Kim to be identified as author of this work
has been asserted by her in accordance with sections 77 and 78 of the
Copyright, Designs and Patents Act 1988.

First edition published by Routledge (2016)

Library of Congress Cataloging-in-Publication Data
Names: Kim, Carolyn Mae, author.
Title: Social media campaigns : strategies for public relations and
marketing / Carolyn Mae Kim.
Description: 2nd Edition. | New York : Routledge, 2021. | Revised
edition of the author's Social media campaigns, 2016. | Includes
bibliographical references and index.
Identifiers: LCCN 2020031483 (print) | LCCN 2020031484 (ebook)
    | Subjects: LCSH: Internet in public relations. |
Internet marketing. |
Social media. | Public relations.
Classification: LCC HD59 .K558 2021 (print) | LCC HD59 (ebook)
    | DDC 658.8/72--dc23
LC record available at https://lccn.loc.gov/2020031483
LC ebook record available at https://lccn.loc.gov/2020031484

ISBN: 978-0-367-89629-4 (hbk)
ISBN: 978-0-367-89620-1 (pbk)
ISBN: 978-1-003-02019-6 (ebk)

Typeset in Bembo
by KnowledgeWorks Global Ltd.

Visit the eResource: www.routledge.com/9780367896201

This book is dedicated to the colleagues and students who have made my experience working in and researching social media both rich and rewarding. I am grateful for the opportunity to provide a second edition and hope that it will give something meaningful back to the community of people who have made my experience in social media so impactful.

Contents

Figures

Author's Biography

Carolyn Mae Kim, Ph.D., APR, is an award-winning scholar, educator, and public relations (PR) professional. She is an associate professor at Biola University and has a background working with global charities and national non-profits, developing creative PR and marketing campaigns. Her research interests include credibility, digital strategy, social media, and PR education. She is an accredited public relations (APR) professional and a speaker who regularly addresses audiences on the topics of social media, credibility, and digital communication.

Professor Kim's research has been published in several peer-reviewed journals, including *Journalism & Mass Communication Editor, Public Relations Journal, Public Relations Review,* and *Teaching Public Relations Education.*

During her time at Biola University, Dr. Kim designed and launched public relations degrees at both the undergraduate and graduate levels. Her teaching has gained national attention, receiving the Ginger Rudeseal Carter Miller Teacher of the Year award in 2014 from the Association of Educators in Journalism & Mass Communication (AEJMC) Small Programs Interest Group thanks to her effective engagement in the classroom and innovative teaching projects.

Maintaining an active role in the profession, Dr. Kim has served in numerous leadership roles within the industry. She has served as the chief research editor for the Institute for Public Relation's Digital Media Research Center. In addition, she is an active member of the Public Relations Society of America (PRSA) and is also engaged with the local Orange County PRSA Chapter, where she served on the board of directors for 3 years. She has held leadership positions in PRSA's Educators Academy executive committee, the AEJMC Public Relations Division, and AEJMC's Small Program Interest Group. She was selected multiple times by the Arthur W. Page Center as a legacy scholar and has served with the Commission on Public Relations Education, focusing on standards in public relations online education.

Identifying her significant contributions to the profession, the Orange County PRSA Chapter presented her with a Distinguished Service award in 2016. In addition, in recognition of her work to rebuild the PR program at Biola, she received the Award of Excellence at the prestigious Silver Anvil ceremony for the PRSA in 2016, as well as a PROTOS award from the Orange County PRSA (OC PRSA) in 2015 and the Award of Excellence for Community Relations and Institutional Programs in 2012 from OC PRSA.

Professor Kim received her Ph.D. in communication from Regent University, writing her dissertation on organizational credibility within social media. She received her Master's and Bachelor's degrees from Biola University.

Preface

The world of social media changes rapidly, with updates constantly happening as new platforms launch and tools are developed. For professional communicators, social media competency is now an entry-level expectation, and seasoned professionals are expected to possess the skillsets needed to provide high-level analysis, planning, and strategy for digital communication. Each year, as I teach the future public relations professionals of our industry, and as I consult with clients on their digital needs, I notice something that seems to happen consistently: the latest trends in social media often seem to obscure strategic planning. In other words, in a quest to stay up-to-date, we forget core principles of how social media leverages relationships, expands communication, and emboldens our publics to maintain connection.

This text was never about showcasing the latest trends, tools, or apps. In all honesty, what is current as I write this will likely have changed by the time you are holding this book. But what I believe is going to remain relevant, and has a tangible impact on professionals and brands, is the foundational structure of social media and relationships that we can then *adjust* to whatever the latest applications in social media may be. With the writing of this second edition, there have been updates to particular parts dealing with statistics and some references to new brand activities in social media. However, what makes me most excited in this text, and what I hope you find most beneficial, is the examination of deeper elements of social media. For example, we've seen a change to the overall approach of social media, with people going to dark social and messaging as ways to interact, versus public engagement (which is why Mark Zuckerberg talks about the future of social being private). This transformation also helps highlight why *social care* is a growing structural and behavior change that brands are adopting as social media becomes more intertwined with every element of organizations. There's also a need more than ever before for brands to be strategic in stakeholder relationship management, viewing campaigns as part of a stewardship process, rather than stand-alone communication efforts to reach the public. We've also seen organizations embracing new habits such as newsjacking in order to break into conversations that are trending, or the efforts to use influencers (from macro to nano) in order to expand engagement. These are significant shifts not simply in a tool but in a *behavior* that have pivoted the entire approach people take to social media.

As I wrap up writing this second edition, my hope is that it will help all of us professional communicators to humanize communication in digital spaces by ethically and strategically creating dynamic conversations in social media with our stakeholders. After all, it's all about people. We should do this well.

CHAPTER 1

Introduction: Social Influence

Understanding the Development, Value, and Role of Social Media for Organizations

> Organizations are operating in a new social paradigm. Brands can no longer expect to control, dictate to, or push a conversation onto the public. Rather, they must engage with the public, creating a two-way, relevant conversation in order to thrive in today's social world.

Out of the world's 7.8 billion people, the internet has 4.54 billion users, with 3.72 billion active social media users.[1] To help give context to the power and reach of social media, between October 2018 and October 2019 there was an average of 10 new social media users every second.[2] In the world of public relations (PR), marketing, and communication, it is more important than ever that professionals have a strategic understanding of how to utilize social media effectively. There is, however, a significant difference in how the public perceives organizations engaging on social media and how the brands themselves perceive social media engagement. Despite nearly 90% of social media users indicating that they have used social media to personally communicate with a brand, there is a gap in the perceived quality of interactions. Whereas 80% of companies indicated that they provide "exceptional customer service," only 8% of their customers agreed.[3] Social media is a critical component of brand communication, particularly given the amount of time people invest not only online, but in social media specifically. That's why it is so important that brands get it right when it comes to developing social media communication and thriving brand communities.

Having a purposeful design for social media has the potential to ignite powerful conversations among key stakeholders. As social media has developed as a communication channel, and organizations have matured in their approach to social media community engagement, the methodology for using social media as a platform also needs to change. Although every organization, online community, and social media campaign will have its own unique flavor, there is, nevertheless, a unifying model that underlies social media campaigns, fostering strategic engagement. This model provides a framework in which all the creative, individualized approaches to social relationships can take shape. Organizations that are the most successful users of social media campaigns, however, not only understand the process of a social media campaign, but also the way social media should be integrated into the entire organization's ethos.

SOCIAL ORGANIZATIONAL CULTURE

There is a significant difference between brands that infuse social strategies into the entire organization and those that use them only in social media campaigns for communication purposes. Michael Brito[4] differentiates these two concepts as a "social brand" versus a "social business strategy." Whereas a social brand uses social technologies to communicate with its key audiences, a social business strategy is a "documented plan of action that helps evolve and transform the thinking of an organization bridging internal and external social initiatives resulting in collaborative connections, a more social organization, and shared value for all stakeholders."[5] Figure 1.1 illustrates what a historical approach to a business model looks like. Each department in the organization is separated by its individual roles, responsibilities, and objectives. While they all jointly support the success of the business, they individually specialize in only their specific purpose.

Today's business environment, however, is not a static one in which key stakeholders can be approached in a mechanical way, with each department solely responsible for only its area. Departments can no longer function in a silo without interacting with each other to support the needs of key relationships. Publics expect brands to be holistic, connecting across multiple departments and with multiple people in order to provide the best solution for each stakeholder's need. For example, if someone contacts the brand through Twitter about a concern with billing or with a product, it is important that the social media team communicates *with* the other department in order to get an answer and response to the individual. Research indicates that 83% of people who reach out on Twitter and get a personal response back from the brand report that they felt better about the company, which is key to maintaining a positive reputation, and are likely to continue doing business in the

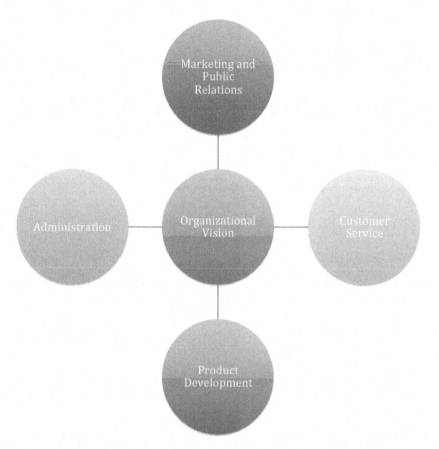

Figure 1.1 The Historical Business Model

future, resulting in loyalty among stakeholders.[6] However, simply giving the phone number or email address of the other department to the person on Twitter, instead of providing the answer, gives the impression that interaction between departments does not occur. The message that is being sent, then, is that the business is not actually relational *internally*, but simply wants to give the impression that it is relational. Today's social business is all about connecting and relating, both *internally* with others in the organization and externally with audiences and their needs. This model is illustrated in Figure 1.2, which shows how the various departments not only surround and support the vision of the brand, but also help each other. *Social organizations* are brands that recognize social interaction as a *core approach* to business, rather than social media as a *tool* to accomplish business, and thus experience the power of authentic relationships with key stakeholders.

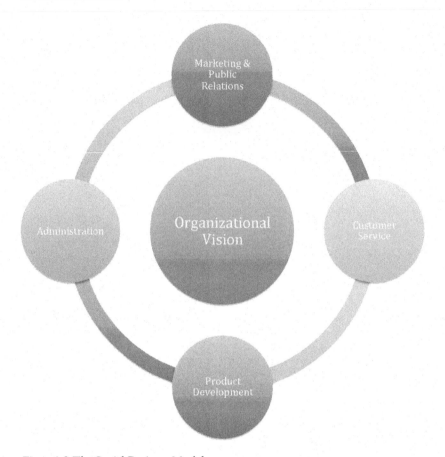

Figure 1.2 The Social Business Model

For a brand to be social requires an entire paradigm shift in business and structure. Jay Baer[7] points out that organizations now need to operate with a "friend-of-mine awareness," recognizing that, in today's world, people do business with brands with which they have relationships. "Like never before in the history of business, our personal and commercial relationships are merging and entangling, line for line, pixel for pixel."[8] He goes on to describe an approach that he has named "Youtility":

> Youtility is marketing upside down. Instead of marketing that's needed by companies, Youtility is marketing that's wanted by customers. Youtility is massively useful information, provided for free, that creates long-term trust and kinship between your company and customers. The difference between helping and selling is just two letters. But those two letters now make all the difference.[9]

In order to achieve this Youtility approach to an organization, Baer[10] suggests that organizations have to recognize that publics want self-serve information, allowing them to get all the details they need whenever they are looking for them. In addition, they expect brands to operate with radical transparency, giving answers and information before they are asked for, and real-time relevancy, which utilizes technology and engagement to connect with key stakeholders in meaningful ways.[11] Essentially, the new paradigm of business in today's social world is all about people. We need to go back to the basics, valuing and investing in relationships with people connected to our brand. For a brand to be truly social, therefore, people have to matter: At every level and in every decision. Social organizations do not just use social media as a tool to communicate. Social organizations operate in an entirely different framework than historical models, they operate in a *social paradigm of business*, placing people and their needs/desires/values front and center in business operations and decisions. Social media, then, should serve as an indicator of the relational priorities of the brand within the digital world, not as the only source of relational interaction that occurs within the organization.

The Crisis of Trust

People do business with organizations that they trust—with *people* that they trust. In a world with more competition than ever before, and thousands of options for people to choose between, relationship becomes the defining factor in business. Unfortunately, despite trust being the cornerstone for ongoing relationships with key stakeholders, there are countless examples of organizations that have defrauded and lied to the public. We've seen this across sectors such as NGOs, for-profit organizations, governments, and the media. The multiple examples of broken trust between organizations and the public have helped create an environment with a dramatic decline in trust, leading Edelman to declare a global *crisis of trust*.[12] This broken trust and lack of transparency within business have led the public to have a deep-seated distrust of organizations.

The crisis of trust can be defined as the developing belief that organizations are deceitful or inauthentic in their communications and relationships with the public. Rohit Bhargava[13] identified this issue as the believability crisis. Bhargava traced the development of our "society of distrust" by exploring the role of propaganda, unethical marketing and PR, and the introduction of mass communication to overwhelm marketplaces with those who could pay the most having the loudest voice. This method, ultimately, ended up treating people like commodities rather than valued relationships. With trust in all institutions at an all-time low, "people are less likely to trust anyone or anything."[14] He suggests that, when communication is humanized, focusing on individuals and relationships, three important elements are reintroduced: purpose, empowerment, and appreciation. The development of this personal relationship through those three elements has the power to rebuild trust between brands and the public.[15]

In the last several years, there have been strong indicators that brands have an opportunity like never before to rebuild trust with the public. In 2019, almost three out of every four people believed that CEOs of organizations should lead the way in making change for society rather than waiting for the government.[16] In addition, PR scholars have increasingly identified publics who actively change behavior, communication, and engagement based on social issues.[17] As brands leverage social media to humanize communication with their brand communities, providing an opportunity to connect on issues that matter to their stakeholders and also on ways the brand itself is contributing to society, organizations have the potential to turn the tide on the crisis of trust.

In conclusion, while brands today are operating in a time of deep mistrust among the public, owing to the unethical and harmful practices that have come to light in the last several decades, social organizations are able to directly counter the believability crisis by building meaningful and authentic relationships with individuals. This commitment to relationships that provide value and are built on trust is the heart of the social principle.

THE SOCIAL PRINCIPLE

A key tenet of social media engagement concerns relationships. Social engagement is driven by connection and community. When organizations enter the social environment, they must keep these facts in mind to be effective in social spaces. Social media is not just a tool—it is a tangible expression of an organizational commitment to trust and value in relationships that is the heart of the social principle. The *social principle* is simply this: The fluid nature of social media is designed for and sustained in *relationships* through two-way communication around topics of mutual interest that is initiated, created, and driven by users. When organizations realize that social media is not a publicity tool used to plaster information in front of users, but rather a dynamic communication platform to foster two-way relationships in an unscripted environment, they are positioned to truly ignite their social communities.

In order to fully explore the social media model in today's organizational environment, it is helpful to understand how online communities developed. Equipped with an understanding of the background and history of how brand communities and organizations on social media have advanced, as well as what has led to developing relationships in social spaces, the full value of this book's proposed social media model will take on much more meaning.

EXPERT INSIGHT

Karen Freberg, Ph.D.

What brands do you see as leaders in the social media world and why?

I have been a fan of the brands that have really been invested in engaging with their fans. Aviation Gin has become one of the top brands for me—which is funny since I am living in the bourbon capital of the world here in Kentucky! They really do great things for their fans on and off social media—speaking to the level of investment they have on the relationships they have with their community. I also have to say the work Steak Umm, Applegate, Cinnabon, and Chipotle have been doing have been tremendous as well. All are food brands—but they really create exceptional online and offline experiences with their content.

What do you think is one hallmark competency social media professionals need to succeed?

Writing is absolutely key. However, it's not just about writing on one platform, but evolving your writing skills to fit the platforms as they change. Plus, we have to look at writing in different circumstances and timing. Social media is a real-time form of media, so we have to be able to write content effectively in a few hours to a few seconds.

What are some key considerations for brands on social media who want to be effective?

Planning and strategy are still at the heart of what makes brands successful on social media. You do not have to be on all platforms, but you want to be there to engage on the platforms where your audiences are located and communicating on. It's about preparing for various situations and being creative yet strategic in how you approach each situation.

With the constantly changing landscape of social media, how can organizations stay relevant?

Social media is a living, breathing platform, and brands have to continue to educate themselves to be on top of the growing changes and shifts we are seeing in the field. Building a strong community of influencers and educators to help share knowledge and trends with each other is essential to stay ahead of the game as well.

Why do you think social media is so powerful in today's culture?

Social media has allowed the individual user to bypass gatekeepers to formulate their own media channel. We are able to share content and connect with people in real time and break down the traditional barriers of communication that have been around for decades. While there are lots of great opportunities that make social media powerful, we also have to consider the challenges it has raised and how it is a powerful, and sometimes dangerous, platform and community. It's about understanding the balance of what makes social media powerful—the positives and the negatives.

What are some of the biggest challenges for brands when they build brand communities in social media?

I'd say trying to be something you are not. It's about being true to your values and unique characteristics as a company and brand that is appealing to people. Audiences want brands who are authentic and transparent with their actions and communication. It's not all about promotion and one-way communication; rather it's really about being active, engaged, and listening to be part of the dialogue. Social media is interactive, so if brands establish themselves on a particular platform, they have to be engaged and invested in formulating and developing the community. Also, brands have to recognize if they are on social media platforms, they are essentially on rented property (e.g., FB, IG, Twitter, Snapchat). We have to follow the rules, terms of service agreements, and changes that follow on the platform. Engaging on these platforms is one thing, but realize you have to have an integrated approach that balances shared/earned media along with owned and paid media.

What do you see as the next big thing for social media and brands?

The next big thing for social media will not necessarily be a new platform, but perspective. We are still thinking social media will either solve all of our problems, or be the death of our work. Social media is all about community building and relationships—and those who do not understand the long game for being successful in social will lose. Sure, you will still be getting people to create content to get their 15 seconds of fame—but those who understand how and why we use social media will be successful in the future. Platforms will change, but the mindset of understanding human behavior, motivations, and attitudes will not.

What does it take for a brand to truly be social?

Social media is indeed a lifestyle, and a brand that embraces this throughout their company and among their employees is going to be successful. I have seen brands that are as engaged online as they are offline. This is one thing I do look for when it comes to strong social media communities and examples to share with my students in the classroom. It comes down to the time, effort, and investment digital and social media managers have embraced in the social landscape. I have to say there are several brands who excel in this arena like Hootsuite, Sprout Social, GM, Skype, and Under Armour. However, sports organizations and teams are ones who I look to as strong examples of embracing social throughout the organization, community, and team. Teams like the Dallas Mavericks. Team USA, Golden State Warriors, USA FIFA Women's World Cup team, XGames University of Nebraska, and Oklahoma Sooners are pretty exceptional in how they have embraced this.

How can social media teams work to minimize crisis or brand risk within social media?

Great question! I think it comes down to crisis prevention and planning. Social media is changing, and we have to look at the potential good and challenging situations that can arise online. There are some situations we can't always plan for, but there are others we can, so it is important to educate, train, and implement these proactive practices before an issue transforms into a crisis online.

Connect with Karen: @kfreberg; www.linkedin.com/in/karen-freberg; www.facebook.com/karen.freberg

Karen Freberg is an assistant professor at the University of Louisville and adjunct instructor for the Integrated Marketing Communications Graduate Online Program for West Virginia University

DEVELOPING AND DEFINING ONLINE COMMUNITIES

The online world has brought in a new focus for PR and marketing—social media communities. Unlike previous types of publics or stakeholders, communities on social media are non-geographically bound groups of people connected through a common social media platform. Much of the world is now connected within and across online communities through various social media platforms.

In one of the first studies dealing with online communities, Rheingold[18] pointed out that the concept of a virtual world is nothing new. In fact, in 1968, researchers for the Department of Defense's Advanced Research Projects Agency (DARPA) initiated what would become the first online community and the internet: ARPANET. These DARPA researchers speculated that communities in the future would not depend on geographic location but rather on common interests.[19] This is exactly what the current culture of social media embodies. People can create online communities, or what Seth Godin[20] coined as "tribes." A tribe is "a group of people connected to one another, connected to a leader, and connected to an idea ... A group needs only two things to be a tribe: a shared interest and a way to communicate."[21] With the internet, the ability to connect and have shared interests and ideas is easier than ever. There is no longer a need to depend on a physical, geographic location in order to form communities of people interested in a common focus. Instead, webs of connections form virtually as people interact in social environments on the internet.

Rheingold[22] defines virtual communities as "social aggregations that emerge from the Net when enough people carry on those public discussions with sufficient human feeling, to form webs of personal relationships in Cyberspace."[23] This is an important definition as it focuses on the idea that the very fabric of an online community is the development of personal relationships. Social media's power emerged from and is sustained through personal connection. Bagozzi and Dholakia[24] further clarify the term virtual communities with the definition of "mediated social spaces in the digital environment that allow groups to form and be sustained primarily through ongoing communication processes."[25] As with the previous definition, this articulation of a virtual community highlights engagement and sustained two-way communication. Many similar definitions hit on the main concepts of the internet being a space utilized by individuals to form relationships and communicate with others in the social community.

While brands recognize that social media is a place to share information and to build connections within a community, there often seems to be confusion on what qualifies specifically as *social* media. Before one can strategically design a campaign *for* social media, one must be able to define social media. This places limits and parameters on what will be included within a *social media* campaign, as it specifies the type of technology, platform, and communities that social media campaigns will engage.

Social Media Defined

To help differentiate what qualifies as *social* media, versus *new* media or *emerging* media or *wearable* media, it is helpful to refer to a definition given by Boyd and Ellison.[26] They defined social networking sites (social media) as:

> Web-based services that allow individuals to (1) construct a public
> or semi-public profile within a bounded system, (2) articulate a list
> of other users with whom they share a connection, and (3) view and
> traverse their list of connections and those made by others within
> the system.[27]

Similarly, Kaplan and Haenlein[28] provided an abbreviated definition of social media as "a group of internet-based applications that build on the ideological and technological foundations of web 2.0, and that allow the creation and exchange of User Generated Content."[29] The core assumptions regarding social media, therefore, are that (1) content is user generated, user controlled and user shared, and (2) that this exchange takes place via a platform on an internet site.

Development of Social Media

The first social media platform that matched the description given earlier began in 1997 with the launch of Sixdegrees.com. Although this platform was unable to sustain business and closed in 2000, it was the catalyst for the start of LiveJournal, Ryze.com, Friendster, and many other similar services.[30] In the years that followed, popular platforms such as Myspace, Facebook, Twitter, Instagram, Snapchat, and TikTok have emerged. Each offers a unique flavor and approach to online community building.

In the last several years, social media technology has created new ways for individuals to interact and share information, such as by using stories, tweets, posts, and messages in a variety of in-app communication options. These new methods of interacting and sharing have altered the way that organizations or brands engage with publics. On a daily basis, "billions of people create trillions of connections" through social media.[31] It's helpful to give some context to this statement in order to really understand the gravity for brands and social media communities. While the average user spends 142 minutes on social media daily, those who are 16–24 tend to spend closer to 3 hours every day on social media.[32] The most common reason people give for being on social media is that they are looking for entertainment.[33] With videos being the top social media content in 2019,[34] three out of four people watch videos online weekly, and 55% report watching daily.[35] Estimates suggest that, by 2022, more than 80% of customer internet traffic is going to be driven by videos—which makes sense, as nearly 92% of mobile users opt to share videos with others (and, thus, have a likelihood of sharing engaging, branded content with their networks).[36] When we say people are connected, though, it's not just thanks to watching videos or sharing them with friends. Messaging is a significant part of social media. Facebook owns the two largest messaging platforms in the world: Messenger and WhatsApp. People are using messaging apps to send 41 million messages every minute, and, on Messenger specifically, 5 billion emojis are sent daily.[37] In short, when we say "people are connected" on social media, we're talking about the fact that people are creating and sharing content with their networks at staggering rates every minute of every day.

Building conversations in social media with brand communities so that individual users are discussing the brand and its value is particularly effective because people are "more trusting of their own opinions and the opinions of their peers" as a result of the social media landscape.[38] This focus on "bottom–up," or user-generated, conversations, as opposed to organization-dictated messaging, is reflected in the fact that publics have become active participants in the creation of brand messages, products, and causes. Users, therefore, are no longer merely consumers—they are invested publics who help shape the organizational culture and conversation.

It is the experience individuals have through social media that organizations need to focus on and understand in order to best connect with their social brand communities. To successfully interact with publics' social media experiences, Kietzmann, Hermkens, McCarthy, and Silvestre[39] suggest looking at seven key parts: (1) identity, (2) conversations, (3) sharing, (4) presence, (5) relationships, (6) reputation, and (7) groups. These seven parts are directly tied to either individuals (identity and reputation), functions of social media (conversations and sharing), or formations of publics within the social media sphere (presence, relationships, and groups). Bringing these areas together in one brand community necessitates a strong commitment to the purpose of *social* media: relationships.

The truth is, discussions taking place about brands through social media highly influence public perceptions of an organization or brand. In fact, today's media landscape makes the old adage "perception is reality" truer than ever before. The impact of perceptions received via social media is why both intentionality and consistency are essential to reaching publics in a noisy world. No longer are brands solely concerned with people who are in close physical proximity to the organization—rather, publics are diverse groups who actively engage in the online world, transcending traditional geographic boundaries and time-zone limitations. Developing a platform in the digital environment requires constant focus on publics who are non-geographically bound, creating dynamic engagement that initiates in the social community itself.[40] This also makes Godin's[41] concept of tribes foundational for understanding of social media publics. Remember, Godin defines an online public, or tribe, as "a group of people connected to one another, connected to a leader, and connected to an idea … A group needs only two things to be a tribe: a shared interest and a way to communicate."[42] Groups' shared interests are core components of online communities. By finding a way to use social media platforms to reach these tribes, social media professionals enhance relationships and build credibility.

Brand Communities

The term "brand community," originally used in relationship marketing theory,[43] refers to the formation in the digital world of a group of people around a brand, organization, or cause. Whereas some online communities are unified around topics or mutual interests, brand communities unite around joint loyalty to an organization as their mutual interest. The main idea behind brand communities and management of digital relationships is that organizations need to sustain strong relationships by utilizing technology to meet publics' desires and needs in order to thrive.[44] It is within this effort that brand communities are sustained.

Muniz and O'Guinn[45] describe a *brand community* as a "specialized non-geographically bound community, based on a structured set of social relationships among users of a brand."[46] Again, relationships are a key component of any online community. Brand communities are made up of the relationships not only between publics and an organization or brand, but also between individuals who are affiliated with the brand community.[47] This means there is great value not only in the brand-to-public relationship, but also in the relationships of various online community members with *each other* within a brand community. In the digital world, brands are able to develop a more robust "brand personality" that allows users to be more engaged with, and attached and attracted to, the brand.[48] Additionally, activities that take place within a brand community can generate value and energize the relationships around a brand.[49] Building commitment in social media communities is critical for relationships between brands and organizations to thrive.

Commitment in Brand Communities

Previously, many organizations considered power and persuasion key functions of interacting with publics.[50] In today's networked world of social media, however, it is committed relationships that are the key. Morgan and Hunt[51] pointed out that, "commitment and trust is central to successful relationship" building.[52] Every organization needs relationships to thrive, and every relationship needs commitment and trust. They described commitment as an "ongoing relationship with another [that] is so important as to warrant maximum efforts at maintaining it."[53] This is very similar to Moorman, Deshpandé, and Zaltman's[54] definition that says, "Commitment to the relationship is defined as an enduring desire to maintain a valued relationship."[55] The main idea, then, is that commitment in brand communities is the dedication of both the public and the brand to the value of the relationship and an intentional effort to maintain it. The end goal is not simply a transaction or bottom-line financial gain. The goal of social media commitment is to sustain the valued relationships developed in the brand community. Commitment, however, is dependent upon trust in an organization or brand, something that is more difficult thanks to the crisis of trust, which was previously discussed.

Trust in Brand Communities

Organizational interaction with publics should be founded on trust, with the goal of creating mutually beneficial relationships.[56] Gundlach and Murphy[57] suggest that trust is the cornerstone of all long-term relationships between organizations and publics. Without trust, relationships erode and eventually disappear. Many additional studies have found that trust is the primary determining factor for a long-term committed relationship with an organization or brand.[58] This is why Berry[59] says that, "the inherent nature of services, coupled with abundant mistrust in America, positions trust as perhaps the single most powerful relationship marketing tool available to a company."[60] Trust is the crucial ingredient for relationships to last.

Essentially, trust is a belief that the organization or brand is reliable and has integrity.[61] Without that belief, relationships will fail. Social media has incredible potential to allow individual users to spread the message of an organization or brand, including the integrity and dependability of that brand, to a large number of people by simply sending a tweet, posting a photo, or uploading a video. The kind of power that individuals exert through social media makes it all the more important for organizations or brands to build and *maintain* publics' trust. This trust directly enhances the organization's credibility. When this happens, the potential for effective social media engagement is established.

Listening in Brand Communities

Developing a thriving brand community in social media also necessitates a commitment from brands to authentically listen to stakeholders. This is the first step in increasing dialogue between organizations and stakeholders, or developing engaged brand communities. However, this kind of dialogue needs to break the traditional paradigm many employ on social media that is focused primarily on communicating organizational information and instead shift to engaging in listening, which will allow organizations to identify and effectively respond to the beliefs of their publics.[62] Macnamara[63] suggests that we need to actually develop an "architecture of listening" instead of the "architecture of speaking" that seems to be what most brands are adopting, which is an idea that Chapter 2 will explain further. When brands, instead, focus on ethical and purposeful listening to their stakeholders *prior* to jumping into the conversation, they have the opportunity to really model what Taylor and Kent[64] suggested as the core components of engagement which "assumes accessibility, presentness, and a willingness to interact."[65] In summary, any thriving brand community that is seeking to build trust and commitment must first be built on the foundation of listening.

DEVELOPING ENGAGEMENT WITH SOCIAL MEDIA COMMUNITIES

Social media professionals have dedicated considerable resources to understanding how to develop engagement in social media communities. With so many functions and measurements available in social media, understanding what makes engagement powerful is critical in campaign development. In other words, rather than simply getting people to see a post or view a story, brands want to have people *interact* with the content. The greater effort required of a person to interact will equate with a quality of "engagement" (which influences social algorithms that are discussed later in this book). For example, beyond simply seeing a post, when someone comments on it or reposts, the brand community has a more robust dialogue. When brands use campaigns that involve personalized interaction (such as using a particular hashtag on a post), they can leverage the true value of engagement as people are creating user-generated content instead of simply consuming brand-made content.

Social media clearly has had a dynamic impact on organizations. As a result, the way social media professionals approach relationships, dialogue, and credibility has been the focus for many scholars and practitioners. In 2010, Smith proposed a "social model" of interaction for social media and PR:

> In this social model, public relations-related activities are initiated by an online public, facilitated by the communication technology, and based on user interactivity (or the searching, retrieval, and distribution of information online). Whereas other online models consider the organization as source, in the dialogic web model (Kent et al., 2003), social public relations are based on user-initiation, and comprise three concepts: viral interaction, public-defined legitimacy, and social stake.[66]

In other words, PR in the social media world rests on the understanding that conversations, activities, and dialogue are driven by publics and not organizations. This is, as mentioned earlier, the core fabric of what drives and sustains social media communities.

Realizing that developing relationships through social media is pivotal to the growth of trust, relationships, and the perception of an organization's credibility, many professionals have proposed theories to support social media interaction. For example, Kerpen[67] identified that listening, authenticity, transparency, and honesty are key factors in succeeding in the world of social media. Penenberg[68] developed the term "viral loop" to describe the value of customer dialogue, activity, and interaction on social sites. This loop is what Penenberg suggests businesses must develop not only to survive, but also to grow in the new digital world. This theory supports the overall development and historical nature of social media. In addition, Shih[69] argued that organizations must understand the "flattening effect" of social media which gives voice to publics that might have been less vocal or less likely to engage in a relationship with the brand previously.[70] These studies, as well as many others, have found that, just as was the case with traditional media and with organizational spokespeople, social media has specific dimensions that enhance relationships between an organization and their publics. Transparency, two-way dialogue, expertise, and consistent interaction, for example, are factors of social media that directly impact the development of organizational relationships. Additionally, the way an organization develops a presence and the process used to engage publics through social media are crucial. This includes determining which platforms are best for the organization's or brand's specific goals and audience, creating engaging content for the platforms, and understanding how to correctly use and analyze data from the digital environment to further develop and enhance relationships.

Social Media Tactics

Social media tactics tend to be what people most often think of when considering how brands can use social media. Thoughts such as "launch a contest" or "show a behind-the-scene video" often quickly surface in conversations. That is because tactics can often be the most visible part of a campaign—they are what brands *do* in social media. The focus on tactics and the approach to using social media is an important area of study both for professionals and academics. Expertise in social media, however, is when brands recognize that tactics must be born out of specific strategies and objectives set by the organization. It is not a haphazard string of activities, but rather a specific engagement fueled by the research and design of the overall campaign.

One way brands develop tactics is by understanding how the culture of a social media community influences existing and new members in order to create engagement. Schau, Muniz, and Arnould[71] found that, "If firms give consumers the opportunity to construct brand communities and the freedom to modify their products," the organization "should foster or sponsor social networking practices to build and sustain the community and to inspire further co-creation."[72] In other words, the *ways* that online communities develop around an organization or brand can create patterns of interaction that contribute to publics' perceptions of the organization or brand. When this happens, not only does the brand gain value, but value is also given back to the publics. An example of this can be seen in Starbucks' classic example with the #ProTip social media campaign. They regularly post tips and insights on how to order drinks or get the most out of a Starbucks experience using #ProTip They have shared things such as "#ProTip: Your local Starbucks can grind coffee for almost any brewer and filter. And it's free!"[73] and "#ProTip: Add a pump of caramel to your #icedcoffee, sing, dance, have an awesome day."[74] What happens with these types of tweets, however, is the real value. Members of the brand community add their own tips, such as "#ProTip: When the sun is out, add a pump of vanilla syrup to your iced coffee. #CoffeePairings."[75] Starbucks as a brand created value by providing tips that the community wanted. This ignited conversations within the community, causing users to generate their own content and create value for other users by sharing useful tips. This creates value for the brand and for the community.

THE NEED FOR MORE THAN JUST TACTICS

The growing focus on interactivity and customer care via social media may be why there are so many resources based on tactical approaches to maintaining a strong business presence in social media. A key ingredient in truly leveraging the power of social media for organizations, however, is to move beyond tactical understanding and into a paradigm of process. This was the point Jonathan Becher, CMO of international software provider SAP, made when he argued that social media is an *enabler*, but not the goal itself.[76] Often, organizations are eager to jump into the social media world because it is what people expect, because there is the potential to create engagement, or simply because it is "the thing to do." The reality, however, is that social media should be approached more holistically, with careful consideration given to the vision of the organization and the potential of social media to enhance its vision.

In the last decade, multiple resources have provided counsel on how to capitalize on social media to build relationships, foster business return on investment (ROI), and develop social communities. This focus on social communication is indicative of not only the opportunity available to organizations in the social world, but also the expectation from publics that businesses will utilize social media channels. This expectation aligns with many brands, as 91% of retailers use two or more social media platforms, and 81% of small and medium business are also found on social media.[77] The world of social media is also highly lucrative, with brands investing $90 billion in social media advertising in 2019. With the rise in the number of brands on social media, the public has also increased its expectation and understanding of that interaction—one study found that four out of five people think that social media has provided greater accountability for businesses, and 55% of people have used social media to call out a brand in order to gain a response or resolution to an issue.[78] Just as brands are working to create brand community engagement in social media, the public expects that organizations will also engage with questions, criticism, feedback, and comments. This two-way dialogue is critical to meet relational expectations between a brand and the public.

Strategic social media plans involve much more than simply linking together tactics that other organizations have found effective. They are about the art and science of weaving together a brand community and an organization into a thriving, growing conversation in the social environment.

DEVELOPING A SOCIAL MEDIA PROCESS

Some may think that the dynamic nature of social media creates an environment that really cannot be mapped or placed in a planned process. After all, social media is about fluid conversations and relationships, not controlled propaganda or behavior. Because of this, it may seem contrary to the essence of social media to consider a model that would structure approaches to social media. The concerns regarding maintaining the flexibility and interactive nature of social media are real and important. However, while it is true that social media, by its very nature, is a vibrant environment with publics generating and driving the conversation, it does not follow that a model cannot be proposed by which professionals can strategically design campaigns for social media that support the overall organization's vision. Social media is no longer a new platform or an "arriving" way for organizations to communicate. It has arrived. What we see now in the social landscape, therefore, is a developing and maturing of frameworks that organizations can use to fully engage with social media communities.

Social media's very fiber is that it enables dynamic conversations based on relationships. But the truth is, if an organization is not intentional about being present in those conversations, developing meaningful connections with key publics, it is very likely that the two-way dialogue and relationship will never thrive. Business is busy. Deadlines must be met. Without a dedicated focus on relationships within social media, the essence of the platform (relationships) gets altogether lost. It becomes an afterthought rather than the primary focus. When that happens, the value of social media to support the vision of the brand also diminishes.

In light of this, not only does a framework, or model, for social media campaigns allow professionals to better plan, prepare, and align their social media campaigns with the larger vision of the organizations for which they work, it also enables them to enhance the quality and value of social media within a business context. In the early days of social media, many perceived it to be of little bottom-line value in helping a business succeed. In recent years, however, organizations are requiring that social media professionals prove that the social initiatives help business objectives and relationships. A model that strategically outlines approaches to social media engagement by organizations empowers professionals to have a framework within which they can illustrate the value of social media for a brand. Research, design, engagement, and evaluation are all key components of a model for social media campaigns. Otherwise, social media activity becomes simply that: activity. It is not a uniquely crafted plan that has a strategic purpose. This is what Gary Vaynerchuk, founder of VaynerMedia, highlighted when he said, "There is no ROI in anything if you don't learn how to use it."[79] We must know *how* to strategically leverage social media, not just the ways we can string together numerous tactics.

In addition to providing a framework to show the value of social media to an organization, a model also helps establish a framework within which brands can operate in ethical and transparent ways. Individuals in social communities expect personal, transparent, and genuine engagement. Sometimes, these expectations can seem to hinder organizations' primary interest in social media: to succeed as a brand. There are limited time and resources, leaving brands appearing inauthentic or uninterested in two-way connections in social media. This tension is precisely why social media experts are needed! It is the ethical responsibility of a social media strategist to harmonize the commitment to an organization's vision, resources, and capabilities with the staunch dedication to authentic and trusted engagement within a brand community.

Four-Step Process

The aim of this book is to explore a model for social media campaigns that provides a blueprint for professionals. Although the reality of the social world dictates a certain level of fluidity and uncertainty, sometimes even chaos, when engaging in social media campaigns organizations that utilize a strategic process to develop an effective framework for campaigns have a stronger capacity to leverage the potential of social media.

This book proposes a four-step process, which should guide social media campaigns. Although every campaign needs to have its own creative flair and original engagement, genuine expertise also recognizes that there are key elements, or steps, in social media campaigns. The four steps used to develop structure in a way that professionals can purposefully design and engage with audiences around organizational objectives are: (1) listening, (2) strategic design, (3) monitoring and interaction, and (4) evaluation (see Figure 1.3).

Listening

The first step in any social media campaign is to listen. Think of this step as the *research* phase of the campaign process. In this phase, it is important to understand not only *how* to listen in the social media environment,

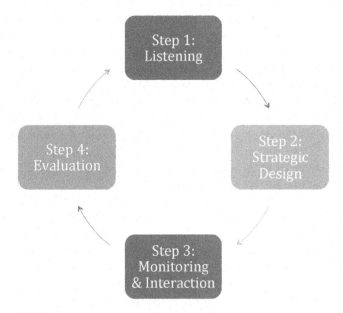

Figure 1.3 The Social Media Four-Step Model

but also to *what* one should be listening. The world of social media is littered with content. Expertise in social media, therefore, extends past one's ability to listen and into the ability to proficiently determine what to listen for and how to interpret that information in a meaningful plan for the organization.

Strategic Design

After listening, the second step is to design the campaign. The goals, objectives, strategies, and tactics are all directly related to the information gathered in listening. During this step, professionals map out the entire social media campaign. The functionality and capabilities of certain platforms, as well as key business considerations that must go into every campaign, are considered. The strategic design and focus are then married in creative engagement pieces designed to ignite connection and conversations within brand communities. In addition, ethical foundations to guide strategic design are crucial to developing strong plans, ensuring that interaction is not dissected from a commitment to the quality and value of relationships.

Monitoring and Interaction

Once a strategically designed campaign is created out of solid research, the next step is to implement the campaign. As with any marketing or PR campaign, however, one cannot simply activate it and walk away. Professionals must fully monitor and engage with the campaign throughout its life cycle. Within this step, it is vital that professionals interact and monitor so that campaign adjustments can be made, accountability of the value of social media within the organization is strong, and, ultimately, the two-way dialogic nature of social media is protected. The process of monitoring and engaging relates directly to our social principle—social media is about relationships, not preprogrammed content that is pushed out without any live-time interaction.

Evaluation

Although analysis will naturally happen throughout the course of the campaign delivery (Step 3), it is important to clearly assess the effectiveness and growth opportunities of a campaign when it is complete. Evaluation requires measurement across social media platforms and a solid attribution strategy to be established for the value of social media in an overall digital campaign. The opportunity to evaluate a campaign is truly where social media professionals can highlight the value to the organization. It allows for the clear articulation of ROI and contribution to the organization's vision.

KEY CONCEPT SNAPSHOT

1. Today's brands operate in a society that has deep mistrust of organizations. In order to address this, brands must build authentic, committed relationships based on trust.
2. The historical development of social media as a communication platform is uniquely poised to address the issue of mistrust by facilitating two-way dialogue between organizations and key stakeholders. This communication is most powerful when purposefully designed, yet placed in a framework that allows freedom for interaction to be adapted and customized.
3. The social principle: The fluid nature of social media is designed for and sustained in *relationships* through two-way communication around topics of mutual interest that is user-generated, created, and driven.
4. When organizations embrace the paradigm that social media is not simply a tool for publicity, plastering information in front of users, but rather a dynamic platform to foster two-way relationships in an unscripted environment, they are positioned to truly ignite their social communities.
5. Brands can use the four-step social media model to build dynamic campaigns that truly leverage the power of a social community: (1) research, (2) strategic design, (3) monitoring and interaction, and (4) evaluation.

NOTES

1   Smith, 2019, "Social Media Statistics."
2   Ibid.
3   Mangles, 2017, paras. 3–4.
4   2013.
5   Brito, 2013, p. 44.
6   Coats, 2020, "Twitter Statistics."
7   2013.
8   Baer, 2013, p. 27.
9   Baer, 2013, p. 3.
10   2013.
11   Baer, 2013, p. 44.
12   Edelman, 2017.
13   2012.

14   Bhargava, 2012, p. 17.
15   p. 25.
16   Edelman, 2019.
17   Dodd, 2018; Kim & Austin, 2019.
18   2000.
19   p. 9.
20   2008.
21   Godin, 2008, pp. 1–2.
22   2000.
23   Rheingold, 2000, p. 5.
24   2002.
25   Bagozzi & Dholakia, 2002, p. 3.
26   2007.
27   p. 211.
28   2010.
29   p. 61.
30   Boyd & Ellison, 2007, pp. 214–216.
31   Hansen et al., 2011, p. 3.
32   Cooper, 2020, "Time Spent on Social Media."
33   Cooper, 2020, "Social Media Is Interwoven."
34   Kolowich, 2020.
35   Ahmad, 2019.
36   Ibid.
37   Spajic, 2019.
38   Hanna et al., 2011, p. 267.
39   2011.
40   Hyatt, 2012.
41   2008.
42   pp. 1–2.
43   Webster, 1992; Morgan & Hunt, 1994.
44   McKenna, 1991.
45   2001.
46   p. 412.
47   McAlexander, Schouten, & Koenig, 2002.
48   Aaker, 1997.
49   Schau, Muniz, & Arnould, 2009.
50   Webster, 1992; Morgan & Hunt, 1994.
51   1994.
52   p. 22.
53   p. 23.
54   1993.
55   p. 316.
56   Morgan & Hunt, 1994.
57   1993.
58   Tax, Brown, & Chandrashekaran, 1998.
59   1996.
60   p. 42.

61   Morgan & Hunt, 1994, p. 23.
62   Macnamara, 2018; Place, 2019.
63   2018.
64   2014.
65   p. 387.
66   p. 333.
67   2011.
68   2009.
69   2011.
70   p. 52.
71   2009.
72   p. 41.
73   Starbucks, 2015a.
74   Starbucks, 2015b.
75   OCTA Wise, 2015.
76   Hong, 2014.
77   Smith, 2019, "Social Media Statistics."
78   Sprout Social, 2017.
79   Wong, 2014.

SUGGESTED READING

Baer, J. (2016). *Hug Your Haters: How to Embrace Complaints and Keep Your Customers.* New York: Portfolio.

Kerpen, D., Greenbaum, M., & Berk, R. (2019). *Likeable Social Media: How to Delight Your Customers, Create an Irresistible Brand, & Be Generally Amazing on All Social Networks That Matter* (3rd ed.). New York: McGraw-Hill Professional.

Schaefer, M. (2012). *Return on Influence: The Revolutionary Power of Klout, Social Scoring, and Influence Marketing.* New York: McGraw-Hill.

REFERENCES

Aaker, J. L. (1997). Dimensions of Brand Personality. *Journal of Marketing*, 34(3), 347–356.

Ahmad, I. (October 30, 2019). *Video Marketing Statistics for 2020* [Infographic]. Retrieved from: www.socialmediatoday.com/news/video-marketing-statistics-for-2020-infographic/566099/

Baer, J. (2013). *Youtility: Why Smart Marketing Is About Help Not Hype.* New York: Portfolio/Penguin.

Bagozzi, R. P. & Dholakia, U. M. (2002). Intentional Social Action in Virtual Communities. *Journal of Interactive Marketing*, 16(2), 2–21.

Berry, L. (1996). Retailers with a Future. *Marketing Management*, 5(Spring), 39–46.

Bhargava, R. (2012). *Likeonomics: The Unexpected Truth behind Earning Trust, Influencing Behavior, and Inspiring Action.* Hoboken, NJ: John Wiley.

Boyd, D. & Ellison, N. (2007). Social Network Sites: Definition, History and Scholarship. *Journal of Computer-Mediated Communication*, 13(1), 210–230.

Brito, M. (2013). *Your Brand, the Next Media Company: How a Social Business Strategy Enables Better Content, Smarter Marketing, and Deeper Customer Relationships*. Indianapolis, IN: Que.

Coats, E. (June 2, 2020). *77 Essential Social Media Marketing Statistics for 2020*. Retrieved from: https://blog.hubspot.com/blog/tabid/6307/bid/23865/13-mind-bending-social-media-marketing-statistics.aspx

Cooper, P. (February 20, 2020). *140+ Social Media Statistics that Matter to Marketers in 2020*. Retrieved from: https://blog.hootsuite.com/social-media-statistics-for-social-media-managers/

Dodd, M. (2018). Globalization, Pluralization, and Erosion: The Impact of Shifting Societal Expectations for Advocacy and Public Good. *The Journal of Public Interest Communications*, 2(2), 221.

Edelman. (2017). 2017 Edelman Trust Barometer. *Edelman*. Retrieved from: www.edelman.com/trust2017/

Edelman. (2019). 2019 Edelman Trust Barometer. *Edelman*. Retrieved from: https://www.edelman.com/research/2019-edelman-trust-barometer

Godin, S. (2008). *Tribes: We Need You to Lead Us*. New York: Portfolio.

Gundlach, G. & Murphy, P. (1993). Ethical and Legal Foundations of Relational Marketing Exchanges. *Journal of Marketing*, 57(4), 35–46.

Hanna, R., Rohm, A., & Crittenden, V. L. (2011). We're All Connected: The Power of the Social Media Ecosystem. *Business Horizons*, 54(3), 265-273.

Hansen, D., Shneiderman, B., & Smith, M. A. (2010). *Analyzing Social Media Networks with NodeXL: Insights from a Connected World*. Burlington, MA: Morgan Kaufmann.

Hong, P. (2014, Sept. 8). SAP's CMO Shares 7 Ways Brands Can Create Powerful Connections. *Momentology*. Retrieved from: www.momentology.com/302-saps-cmo-shares-7-ways-brands-can-create-powerful-connections/

Hyatt, M. (2012). *Platform: Get Noticed in a Noisy World*. Nashville, TN: Thomas Nelson.

Kaplan, A. M. & Haenlein, M. (2010). Users of the World, Unite! The Challenges and Opportunities of Social Media. *Business Horizons*, 53(1), 59–68.

Kerpen, D. (2011). *Likeable Social Media: How to Delight Your Customers, Create an Irresistible Brand, and Be Generally Amazing on Facebook*. New York: McGraw-Hill.

Kietzmann, J. H., Hermkens, K., McCarthy, I. P., & Silvestre, B. S. (2011). Social Media? Get Serious! Understanding the Functional Building Blocks of Social Media. *Business Horizons*, 54(3), 241–251.

Kolowich, L. (February 25, 2020). *16 Video Marketing Statistics to Inform Your 2020 Strategy* [Infographic]. Retrieved from: https://blog.hubspot.com/marketing/video-marketing-statistics

Macnamara, J. (2018). Toward a Theory and Practice of Organizational Listening. *International Journal of Listening*, 32(1), 1–23.

Mangles, C. (December 5, 2017). *Why Social Media Customer Care Is Important in Retaining Loyal Customers and Positive Brand Awareness*. Retrieved from: www.smartinsights.com/customer-relationship-management/customer-service-and-support/rise-social-media-customer-care/

McAlexander, J. H., Schouten, J. W., & Koenig, H. F. (2002). Building Brand Community. *Journal of Marketing*, 66(1), 38–54.

McKenna, R. (1991). Marketing Is Everything. *Harvard Business Review*, 69(1), 65–79.

Moorman, C., Deshpandé, R., & Zaltman, G. (1993). Factors Effecting Trust in Market Research Relationships. *Journal of Marketing*, 57(1), 81–101.

Morgan, R. M. & Hunt, S. D. (1994). The Commitment Trust Theory of Relationships Marketing. *Journal of Marketing*, 58, 20–38.

Muniz, A. M. & O'Guinn, T. C. (2001). Brand Community. *Journal of Consumer Research*, 27(4), 412–432.

OCTAWISE (OCTA Wise.). (2015, May 29). #ProTip: When the sun is out, add a pump of vanilla syrup to your iced coffee. #CoffeePairings [Tweet]. Retrieved from: https://twitter.com/octawise/status/604201327523061760

Penenberg, A. (2009). *Viral Loop: From Facebook to Twitter, how Today's Smartest Businesses Grow Themselves*. New York: Hyperion.

Place, K. R. (2019). Listening as the Driver of Public Relations Practice and Communications Strategy Within a Global Public Relations Agency. *Public Relations Journal*, 12(3), 1–18.

Rheingold, H. (2000). *The Virtual Community: Homesteading on the Electronic Frontier*. Cambridge, MA: MIT Press.

Schau, H. J., Muniz, A. M., & Arnould, E. (2009). How Brand Community Practices Create Value. *Journal of Marketing*, 73(5), 30–51.

Shih, C. (2011). *The Facebook Era: Tapping Online Social Networks to Market, Sell, and Innovate*. Upper Saddle River, NJ: Prentice Hall.

Smith, B. G. (2010). Socially Distributing Public Relations: Twitter, Haiti, and Interactivity in Social Media. *Public Relations Review*, 36(4), 329–335.

Smith, K. (December 30, 2019). *126 Amazing Social Media Statistics and Facts*. Retrieved from: www.brandwatch.com/blog/amazing-social-media-statistics-and-facts/

Spajic, D. J. (2019, December 11). *Text, Don't Call: Messaging Apps Statistics for 2020*. Retrieved from: https://kommandotech.com/statistics/messaging-apps-statistics/

Sprout Social. (2017, August 22). *The Sprout Social Index, Edition XII: Call-out Culture*. Retrieved from: https://sproutsocial.com/insights/data/q3-2017/

Starbucks [Starbucks Coffee]. (2015a, April 22). #ProTip: Your local Starbucks can grind coffee for almost any brewer and filter. And it's free! [Tweet]. Retrieved from: https://twitter.com/starbucks/status/590947495053631488

Starbucks. [Starbucks Coffee]. (2015b, May 26). #ProTip: Add a pump of caramel to your #icedcoffee, sing, dance, have an awesome day [Tweet]. Retrieved from: https://twitter.com/starbucks/status/603183820888625154

Taylor, M. & Kent, M. L. (2014). Dialogic Engagement: Clarifying Foundational Concepts. *Journal of Public Relations Research*, 26(5), 384–398.

Tax, S., Brown, S. W., & Chandrashekaran, M. (1998). Customer Evaluation of Service Complaint Experiences: Implications for Relationship Marketing. *Journal of Marketing*, 62(2), 60–76.

Webster, F. E. (1992). The Changing Role of Marketing in Corporations. *Journal of Marketing*, 56(4), 1–17.

Wong, K. (2014, May 13). What Is the Value of Social Media Engagement? *Forbes*. Retrieved from: https://www.forbes.com/sites/kylewong/2014/05/13/what-is-the-value-of-social-media-engagement/#128314d45951

CHAPTER 2

Step 1: Listening

Developing Research, Discovering Data, and Applying Meaning

> Social media expertise stems from informed decisions leading to strategic design. The ability for a social media professional to discover needed information, determine how to understand the context of that data, and provide meaningful application into a social media campaign is paramount.

The first step in developing a social media strategic campaign is to *listen*. This *listening* or formative research phase is where social media strategists collect the data required to make informed decisions that will form the foundation for a campaign. There are two primary areas involved in the listening stage: the foundational background and the social landscape. Both will be addressed in this chapter.

Before we explain how to use listening as a research function, however, it is equally important to explain the ethical and foundational role of listening in PR and strategic communication. Once the foundation is established (or the *why* brands should listen), then understanding the tools and process (or *how* the technical side of listening in social media occurs) will come much more naturally.

LISTENING IN ORGANIZATIONAL STAKEHOLDER RELATIONSHIPS

PR and marketing scholars suggest that trust is the cornerstone for all long-term relationships—the kind we want with the public for our brands both online and offline.[1] But, as was noted in the previous chapter, trust in institutions is declining globally, leading to what many have called a crisis of trust.[2] It has been suggested that organizations can overcome this crisis and rebuild trust through the act of authentically listening to stakeholders and key publics.[3] The issue is, however, that most organizations seem to not understand what a genuine posture of listening is. Rather, listening is used simply as a tool to figure out how best to *speak*, *interact*, and *engage*. This is why Macnamara suggests that many organizations are using an architecture of *speaking* rather than an architecture of *listening* as their foundation for interacting. In fact, research suggests that organizations are using an 80:20 (and some a 90:10) ratio of speaking to listening.[4]

When considering how much emphasis is put on communicating, it is surprising that brands (and education for future professionals) often place so little emphasis on not only how to listen but why we *should* be listening. Listening can be defined as "the practice of giving recognition to others' right to speak, acknowledging and understanding others' views, paying attention to others, interpreting what others say fairly, and responding appropriately."[5] Thus, professional communicators need to understand that listening is other focused. It is about the public and understanding, rather than about the organization and positioning future communication.

To clarify, understanding the societal expectations of PR professionals and strategic communication leaders is helpful. While PR has undergone several models of practice,[6] the modern application positions the discipline as part of a profession that has a social contract with society.[7] This social contract brings responsibilities regarding ethical behavior, contributing towards good in society, and serving as an organizational conscience.[8] Thus, in the world of social media, listening helps professionals understand the public's values, beliefs, needs, and opinions. This knowledge is used to help build relationships. The focus is on the *relationship* rather than on manipulating behaviors to align with organizational needs. Being a scientist of people and artisan of relationships in the world of social media is not an easy task—it is far easier to treat listening as some practice that is all about gathering data on a stakeholder in order to reach the persuasive end of communication. Keeping the act of listening as a deeply human function, however, is a skill that organizations need. Brands in today's environment need professionals who can ignite brand communities and develop authentic relationships, and it all starts with genuine listening. This kind of dialogue needs to break the traditional paradigm of being primarily about communicating organizational information and instead shift to engaging in listening that will allow organizations to identify and effectively respond to their publics.[9]

FOUNDATIONAL BACKGROUND

In preparing to craft a social media campaign that truly enhances an organization's goals, it is vital to have a strong understanding of the organization itself. This is because separating the vision of the organization from social engagement will significantly limit the full potential and influence social media provides as a relationship-building platform. Social media is an extension of communication from the organization toward its publics—it is rooted in a commitment to relationships and dialogue. To segregate social media from the rest of the organization, making it a tool that only gets used each time a brand wants to publicize information, reveals a deep misunderstanding about the purpose of *social* media. Thus, a truly powerful approach to social media requires brands to connect the vision of the organization to its social media efforts. An organization's social media strategy, therefore, should be born out of the organization's mission and value. If an organization leverages social media well, it can be a natural extension of the organization into the social media world, uniquely planned to support the brand's needs.

Mission Statement

Before developing a plan to build relationships and engage with the communities that are connected to the business, it is crucial to first understand why the organization exists. The first step, therefore, in formative research is to review the brand's mission or vision statement, value commitments, and even strategic plans. It is helpful to analyze and apply these to the social media process as this will provide the direction for the social media strategy. After understanding the purpose of the organization, it is also important to evaluate how the organization functions in order to truly leverage the power of social media within the brand's structure.

Key Data Application: Social strategists recognize that all campaigns, strategies, and tactics in social media should relate to the brand's vision. Informed social media engagement relates to the core essence, or mission statement, of the brand.

Organizational Structure

After developing a solid understanding of what the organization is about and what differentiates it from any other business, the next step is to identify the structure of the organization. When it is time to develop key messaging and communication maps that include all relevant participants from the organization, knowledge of how management is set up,

Foundational Background

Mission Statments

- Social strategists recognize that each campaign, strategy and tactics in social media should relate to the brand's vision. Informed social media engagement relates to the core essence, or mission statement, of the brand.

Organizational Structure

- Strategists use data from the organizational structure research to determine the level of support for social media integration into the core processes of a brand, as well as the appropriate type of social media team to create in order to help a brand thrive in the social environment.

Communication Audit

- Data from communication audits display the tapestry of ways that key publics are being communicated with, informing key elements of message structure and timing within a campaign's design.

Policies & Procedures

- Employee handbooks, brand guides, crises response plans, market research, and SEO & Web Analytic reports all provide key information into the ways that an organization communicates its values and engages with key stakeholders. Applying this information to a campaign design is critical to ensuring that the social initiatives are consistent with the brand's business model and values.

Figure 2.1 Foundational Background for Research

how departments are structured within the organization, and who is responsible for each component will be important. Be sure to pay special attention to the marketing, PR, communication, and information technology (IT) departments' structures. All of these departments tend to be required in developing an effective and integrated social media campaign.

Discovering Support for Social Media Team Structure

Part of what occurs during the listening phase of a social media campaign is the process of gathering information on what kind of social media team or structure would thrive within the organization. To gather the best information possible on what kind of social team structure will work, it is important to look at: leadership, key players, and required skills.

Leadership

Organizations that truly desire to engage the powerful potential of social media to build key relationships must recognize that this starts at the top of the organization. It needs to be presidents and CEOs that lead the organization into a social culture. Jim Claussen,[10] Senior Strategy Manager for Social Business at IBM, identifies the kinds of leaders that organizations need today as "blue unicorns." He defines blue unicorns as "the rare leaders who are transforming their leadership for today's connected social economy."[11] Although some brands may argue that having leadership that is social is not a necessity, Ted Coiné and Mark Babbitt[12] suggest that, in the future, "An engaging presence on social media will not just be 'nice to have,' it will be considered a leadership competency."[13] In recent years, both stakeholders and key leadership have recognized the value of social media. Research into active social media use for CEOs indicates that 82% of employees and 71% of consumers indicate a higher trust in organizations that have leaders who are active on social media. Additionally, research also indicates that senior leaders understand the value, with 76% of CEOs who use social media indicating that it helps display brand innovation and 69% believing that it enhances the organization's credibility.[14]

Part of the organizational structure research on leadership should reveal whether the top leader(s) in the organization are active on any social media accounts and review what level of engagement they seem to have with social media communication. In addition, time should be taken to meet with the leaders to understand their view of the role and value of social media in the life of the brand and their personal dedication (or hesitation) to be involved in social communication. One important concept to get a feel for is whether or not top the leadership is willing and ready to maintain its own social media activity. Although some leaders seem to express commitment to social media by being willing to allow a social media team to run their personal social media presence, this approach to social media engagement for leadership is not advisable. Coiné and Babbitt[15] highlight this kind of approach as an "insincere social leader," likening it to the absurd idea of sending a proxy to a business dinner, dressed up like the CEO, speaking like the CEO, and introducing himself or herself as the CEO, but not actually being the CEO.[16] A brand leader would never embrace that kind of inauthentic communication with publics in face-to-face settings. It should not be acceptable in social media either.

Key Players

The social media team or department of an organization will likely be divided into two groups. The first group is what Michael Brito[17] called the "Social Business Center of Excellence (CoE)."[18] The people who constitute the CoE for an organization need to be individuals who have leadership influence and the ability to apply action to organizational behaviors and who are deeply committed to the integration of social media as part of organizational life. The CoE needs to comprise individuals who play a leadership role in the organization's business behaviors and communication. For example, key people to include would be the head of marketing, the director of PR, the top research analysts, the manager of IT, and the social media director. The CoE's role is to envision the potential for complete social integration within the organization, understanding the power of two-way dialogue throughout the lifeblood of a brand: from employee orientation to customer interaction, from leadership communication to the brand ambassador program. Instead of simply seeing social media as a tack-on to communication efforts or a secret weapon to drive sales, the CoE comprises social visionaries who lead the way for an organization to integrate the power of two-way dialogue in real-time communication via social media into the core practices of an organization. The goal of the CoE is to succeed:

> at changing organizational behavior—the way it thinks, communicates, and markets to customers. In doing so, the members must adapt and change their own behavior at the same time. They must become change agents if they truly want to see the transformation come to fruition.[19]

So that the best people are on a CoE team, it is crucial that research is done to understand which departments within an organization carry out certain responsibilities (such as technology roll-outs, communication with clients, communication with customers, employee relations, etc.). Then, the individuals within those departments who have the capacity, authority, and vision to be part of the CoE must be identified. The second group is made up of the individuals who are tasked with maintaining and engaging the organization's social media platforms. In the research phase of a social media campaign, it is important to identify whether the organization has resources for a team to be employed, the number of positions available, and the skills or qualifications that are needed. In order to identify what kind(s) of people are needed on a social media team, identifying key skills is necessary.

Skills

It is crucial to determine what skills may already be available for the team in existing staff or structures, what skills may be lacking, and what team structure might work for the given organization's long-term approach to social engagement. In describing the skills/staff members needed for real-time marketing campaigns in social media, Chris Kerns[20] suggests the following areas: program lead, creative lead, copy lead, social lead, and analysts. Real-time responses will be covered later, but this structure is a helpful starting point for identifying key areas that a social team needs. The reality is that some organizations may have the resources to employ a team of social media pros, letting extraordinary expertise and specialization be part of each job description. Other organizations may be lucky if they have one or two people working on social media. Whether it is a team of 100 or a team of one, a strong social media team needs people with the following skills:

Leader. Each social media team needs a leader. Whether they are called the program lead, social media director, or some other title, the key responsibilities of this individual are to lead the strategy for social media engagement on behalf of the organization, to advocate for social integration across the brand, and to guide the other members of the social team. People who fill this role need not only key competencies in social media, but also business acumen. This person should have strategic foresight, be able to skillfully articulate the value and need for social media within the CoE and to upper management, and have a strong grasp of team dynamics and people skills. It is their job to develop, lead, and manage the social media strategy and also to encourage the individuals on the social team to develop as professionals.

Word Artisans: Social media should be engaging, punchy, and to-the-point. Word artisans can effortlessly engage in 140 characters and can also weave together a beautiful post to accompany an infographic on Facebook. Grammar, style, and vocabulary are core parts of this skill. Word artisans are the kinds of people that you could listen to all day simply because the *way* they communicate is unique, it catches your ear (or eye) and takes a new approach even when talking about a common topic. In the research phase, take time to identify who should be the word artisan for social media campaigns. If there is not a set position in social media, is there someone on the team who is a natural with words? Perhaps the communication or marketing department has an individual who would take on the responsibility of helping craft messages.

Creative Gurus: Visual engagement is on the rise in social media. Instagram, Snapchat, and TikTok—these are all media that rely solely on the power of images and videos. As was noted earlier, video is significant to the future of social media. Thus, this person should not only understand images, but have the ability to create engaging and relevant video content. Some teams may find that this role is actually one that needs two distinct individuals—one for images and one for videos specifically. It is most likely that more visual-based platforms are on the horizon, poised to be the most prominent social media platforms available. Having a creative guru on the team, therefore, is a must. Sometimes, the creative guru and the word artisan are one and the same person—and other times, someone who is fantastic with the written word seems to struggle with finding that perfect image (or filter). As with the word artisan, be resourceful in identifying who would be a potential fit for this needed skill on the social media team. Additionally, do research on apps, tools, and subscriptions that are available to help the social team succeed. The marketing or PR department may already have a subscription to an image library that is available for use, or perhaps the organization has other processes to develop creative pieces across the brand. Be sure to have done enough research to identify each resource available to help the creative guru succeed.

Social Designer: The social lead is relied upon to marry the power of a post with the potential of a platform. They are tasked with identifying the right type of content and topic for the right platform, working closely with the other members of the team to strategize creative ways to capitalize on certain social media functions (such as a story versus a snap in Snapchat, or the reason one might choose to run a Twitter chat or provide a Facebook giveaway). On smaller teams, this skillset is placed with the social media director, as they formulate the overall strategy and help guide the other members of the team toward success.

Data Analyst: This will be discussed in greater detail later, but each social media team needs an analyst. The ability to gather data, apply that information, and adjust social media initiatives is a must in today's social world. As with other skills that the team needs, the data pro may be combined with some other skills into one job description. Alternatively, the data might come from a variety of other places, such as working closely with marketing research or the website analyst to help interpret the data. Whatever model best serves the size of organization, regular review and application of data is crucial.

Once the skills, positions, and people who should be part of a social media campaign have been identified, the next area to collect data on is the overall communication from the organization.

Key Data Application: Strategists use data from organizational structure research to determine the level of support for social media integration into the core processes of a brand, as well as the appropriate type of social media team to create in order to help a brand thrive in the social environment.

Communication Audit

Social media communication should harmonize with other communication platforms and initiatives from the organization. A *communication audit* is a comprehensive analysis of all the information being communicated by the brand and a review of the intended audience and desired outcome expected from sharing that information. Create a list that identifies all the ways that the public is communicated with by the organization. Be sure to classify the type of communication platform (such as a newsletter, media relations efforts, community events, etc.), the intended audience (employees, consumers, donors, etc.), the frequency of the communication (such as how often the website is updated, when consumer emails are sent, or the timing of speeches by the CEO), and the person or department responsible for developing and managing the specific communication piece. The next step in formative research is to understand any policies that guide organizational activities or procedures developed to structure the communication process.

Key Data Application: Data from communication audits display the tapestry of ways that key publics are being communicated with, informing key elements of message structure and timing within a campaign's design.

Policies and Procedures

Having identified the core vision for the organization, how it is structured, and how it communicates to all publics, it is also helpful to understand any existing policies or procedures that will impact the social media campaign design.

Employee Handbook

Reading through the organization's employee handbook will provide a lot of insight into the culture of the organization. It should also clarify expectations of employees, responsibilities for employees, and, potentially, any information that already exists about how employees are trained on interacting via social media. Ideally, social media training will be part of every new employee training seminar, as well as incorporated into a regular rotation for existing employee training to make sure everyone is aware of policies and guidelines. This will be discussed in greater detail in Chapter 3.

Key Data Application: The way in which employees are introduced, trained, and encouraged to share their stories on social media directly influences the brand's voice and influence in social media. Understanding the role of employees in a brand's social media voice provides key insights into designing campaign tactics.

Brand Guide

The marketing or PR department for the organization will likely have this on hand. It will include all the guidelines for colors and font choices with the brand logo, instructions on messaging or positioning, and information on the brand persona. Understanding the brand persona for the organization is crucial in social media. Moving forward with designing a social media campaign, it is important to ensure that the voice and personality that are portrayed in social media reflect the organization in a unified manner, consistent with other communication pieces. People should not experience one kind of organization if they come by the offices and another when they visit the social media profiles. Thorough familiarity with the brand guidelines will lead to a higher likelihood of success in unifying the brand persona both in social media and in other communication outlets. A more detailed process to develop and design specific communication messages for social media in line with the brand persona is discussed in Chapter 3.

Key Data Application: Social media is one way in which a brand communicates, not the *only* way. Familiarity with the brand's requirements and voice allows social media initiatives to enhance branding and connection rather than creating a division between the brand's presence on social media and its presentation on other platforms.

Crisis Response Plan

It is important that a social media strategist has access to the organizational crisis response plan. During a crisis, social media needs to fully align with the larger crisis response of the organization. It may be that the organization has already identified the role and functions social media will fulfill in a crisis, but, if that is not the case, it is important for the social media team to be aware of the entire crisis plan so that a fully integrated social media crisis response document can be developed. The process to develop and design a crisis response is explained in Chapter 3.

Key Data Application: Every organization will face crises, and social media will play a key role. Crisis plans allow social media teams to be prepared and equipped to engage in a crisis, rather than their being forced to respond in the moment, which often leads to increased problems.

Market Research

Reach out to the marketing department to get the latest market research for the organization. This will identify key audiences that should be considered in social media. Although it may be that not all of the audiences identified in the market research apply specifically to social media, the strategic insight gained from reviewing the market research for an organization will save a lot of time in developing a social media campaign that aligns with the overall communication efforts of the organization.

Additionally, within the market research report, or potentially housed in another more specific report produced by the marketing department, specific ROI metrics may be identified for types of behaviors. For example, the marketing department should have a report that clarifies what the value of a name for someone who signs up for a newsletter is for the brand, the value assigned to leads generated for certain types of sales, or the lifetime value of a new donor. Whatever the organization is measuring and assigning value to, be sure to have a full list and details on the exact ROI numbers. These metrics are crucial in the next stage (designing a strategic plan) as they allow the social media strategist to understand any tangible, bottom-line goals that can be linked to social media activity.

Key Data Application: The marketing team will have a wealth of information on key publics. Although not all of it will be applicable, social strategists glean key points from these reports and apply them to the publics who are active on social media in order to create a more effective campaign design.

Search Engine Optimization and Website Analytic Reports

Although it may seem like search engine optimization (SEO) and website analytic reports are not areas social media professionals must be versed in, the reality is that SEO is highly influenced by social media. In addition, social media optimization is a growing focus within the industry as platform algorithms are having a greater influence on social media reach. There is a wealth of information available in both the SEO and the analytic reports. For example, in the SEO report, it is possible to identify the keywords and phrases that drive the most traffic and the top pages that are optimized on the website. These findings are significant to the organization and so allow a social strategist to understand keywords that are important to be integrated into social media and potential webpages that are most effective to link to from social media. Even if in-depth analytics have not been set up, a basic analytics report can provide insight into the demographics of your online audience, typical actions (also known as conversions) such as purchases or sign-ups, the typical online path people follow when exploring the website, and social media traffic sources. This is just a small portion of what is available in these reports. In order to effectively create a strong listening strategy and develop a strategic campaign that relates to the larger goals of the organization, be sure that a thorough review of both documents is completed in the formative research phase as it provides a strong platform to move forward with social media design. After all the information available on the organization's background and processes has been gathered, it is now time to develop formative research in a social media context.

Key Data Application: The SEO and web analytic reports provide key details regarding the online behaviors of audiences. Social strategists apply this information to the unique needs of social media brand communities in order to design engaging and effective digital tactics.

SOCIAL LANDSCAPE

Having completed the foundational research as preparation, it is now possible to effectively survey the social landscape in the context of its application to an organization. In this phase of the listening (research) stage, the goal is to identify what conversations are taking place on social media that may be relevant to the brand, who is having those conversations, and ways that the organization might engage with that dialogue. It is important to remember that even in listening, which can often seem removed and objective rather than relational and engaged, social media

Social Landscape

Key Listening Phrases	Conversation Platforms	Brand Community Dialogue	Influencers	Competition
• The key listening phrase list will provide valuable data into what topics are most meaningful and the many types of words that people use when joining these conversation. When it comes time to craft messaging, this information informs content design.	• Key listening phrases revealed *what* conversations are taking place and the Conversation Platform research reveals *where* those conversations are happening. These data help in crafting the appropriate type of content for the right kind of platform in a campaign.	• Audience analysis, content evaluation, community interaction and brand dialogue provide key insights into the way two-way interaction is driven and sustained within a brand community. This information should be applied when crafting campaign messaging in order to ensure robust engagement is created in campaign tactics.	• Within each brand community, there are key individuals who drive conversations forward and truly ignite connection. These influencers should be identified and specifically encouraged to participate within a campaign.	• Competition analysis allows brands to identify what type of content is generally the most effective across an industry, to identify engaging profile creation, and ultimately to evaluate the brand's Share of Voice and sentiment score within the social landscape. This information can then be used to inform specific tactical creation within a campaign as well as serving as benchmarks to evaluate the success of campaign messaging.

Figure 2.2 Social Landscape Research

is about humanizing communication. Listening, then, is not cold and mechanized, but rather about understanding and seeing the people who are important to the brand. Dave Kerpen advocates for the power of social listening, saying,

> Listening is the single most important skill in social media, and one that's easy to forget once you get started with all of the sexier, more exciting things you can do. So, whatever you do, once you start, never stop listening.[21]

Key Listening Phrases

The first step for this stage is to identify all the categories to listen to on social media. Some people identify these as "keywords." A keyword is more than simply a single word, however. It can be an entire phrase. The idea is to write out what words or phrases someone in social media may be using to discuss topics that pertain to the organization or brand. Keywords will fall in to two categories: specific and generic. The SEO report gathered earlier will likely have a list of keywords already used by the organization. This can be very useful in creating a social media list as it will save time and a great deal of research. Identify specific words to search for that will open up opportunities to join social conversations. In addition, keywords are concepts that people type into a search bar in social media in order to find conversations related to things they care about. When making a keyword list, it is important to consider not only what the organization thinks are important conversations, but also what social media users would think of when trying to reach information available from your organization. Remember, organizations are not starting a conversation on social media—they are *joining* the conversation. This means they must be able to find out where the conversation is taking place and who is participating. This is where specific and generic keywords come into play.

Specific

Specific keywords are those words or phrases that are unique to the organization. They may include the names of key people, such as the president or CEO, the name of a specific product or service, or the company's tagline or slogan. If the brand has launched any specific PR campaigns or marketing initiatives, it is also useful to include those phrases or keywords in this list. Keep track of every keyword in a document to apply to later strategy.

Generic

Keywords or phrases that fall into the generic category are a goldmine for many brands. However, organizations often forget to create a generic keyword list and only focus on the specific terms that apply only to the brand. Thus, they miss out on some very relevant and vibrant social conversations. When developing a generic list, identify categories that publics connected to the organization deeply care about. For example, a coffee company could identify generic keywords such as "coffee brewing," "coffee beans," and "coffee grains." Although these are not specific to any individual coffee brand, people who drink coffee would likely engage with those topics.

The goal is to identify what online communities care about and want to be discussing. The brand is joining a conversation with people who have a mutual interest. What brought the social media community that the brand cares about together into a virtual tribe and provides a commonality that connects? When those areas are identified, the generic keywords are developed. Think through words and phrases that relate to the industry, services, products, and vision.

Key Data Application: The key listening phrase list will provide valuable data on what topics are most meaningful and the many types of words that people use when joining these conversations. When it comes time to craft messaging, this information informs content design.

Conversations on Platforms

Having developed a robust list of what phrases and words are relevant to the organization in the social media landscape, it is now time find out *where* these conversations are taking place. There are a number of tools that are available to do this. Many may choose to listen to platforms by using the search functions available on each social media site. For example, it is possible to use the advanced search on Twitter to find specific conversations. Social strategists may also choose to do a similar search on Facebook, narrowing the conversation by top posts or people or even photos. Carefully analyze the data to ensure that the data are not simply a review of information from people that the organization is somehow connected to through social media (people that the brand likes, friends, followers, etc.). Do a public, or all-user, search.

Many people prefer to use tools that aggregate data from several platforms to ensure a more robust analysis and save time. Hootsuite is one of the leading platforms for this type of research. Several other platforms (at the time of this book's writing) include Social Mention, Topsy, and Tweet-Deck. The value of having a place that analyzes multiple social channels at once is that it allows identification of not only the genres of conversations

Figure 2.3 The Social Conversation Checklist

taking place on social media with specific keywords, but also the quality of the conversation, who is participating, and how it compares with other platforms, in an expedited fashion. The goal is to use these real-time data to make informed decisions in building a strategic campaign.

Using these tools, go through all the relevant conversations that are taking place on the social platform. By adding a column next to each of the keywords previously identified, keep a list of which platforms have the largest conversation around a given topic or keyword. For example, it could be that, on Twitter, people are more interested in certain topics than they are on Facebook. These data can provide key insights that can help in the development of a stronger message map. In addition to the platforms and conversations taking place, identify who participates in the conversations and who has the largest impact when they interact. These people are known as influencers and are key individuals to connect and interact with throughout social media initiatives. Finally, be sure to note the tone of the conversations. People may have a positive tone, generally, when talking about a specific brand name but a negative tone with some of the generic topics. Again, this will come in handy in developing messaging for social media.

Key Data Application: Key listening phrases reveal *what* conversations are taking place, and the conversation platform research reveals *where* those conversations are happening. These data help in crafting the appropriate type of content for the right kind of platform in a campaign.

Brand Community Dialogue

When it is understood what conversations are taking place and who is participating in the general social media landscape, it is time to examine the online communities for the brand. There are several steps to take when evaluating the climate of social media communities.

Key Data Application: Audience analysis, content evaluation, community interaction, and brand dialogue provide key insights into the way two-way interaction is driven and sustained within a brand community. This information should be applied when crafting campaign messaging in order to ensure robust engagement is created in campaign tactics.

Audience Analysis

The very first place to begin is to understand who is involved in the organization's social media communities. In an *audience analysis*, brands create a profile of key publics by providing basic demographic and behavioral information that helps brands to identify the appropriate platforms and methods for engagement. The previous reports from the marketing department on market research will be helpful with this step. That report will detail the general audiences for the organization, usually identifying the primary and secondary audiences for a brand. In addition, the reports should provide general information about key audiences, including details such as demographics, which communication channels are most effective for reaching specific audiences, and the behavioral analysis of the audience.

It is also helpful to review the website analytics report that should be able to identify which social media sites are sending visitors to the organization's website; what those visitors are doing once they reach the website; whether they complete an action that is valuable to an organization, which is a concept known as converting individuals (sign up for a newsletter, purchase a product, etc.); and any other online trends that are monitored by the organization. All of this information should be compiled to provide a complete analysis of the audiences on social media.

Key Data Application: Having reviewed the general audience research for the organization, compare those findings and data with the current social media community in order to understand what values and content are most meaningful for the social media community. There are several ways to analyze a social media audience, including:

* Comparing the geographic region of the various platforms' online communities to the geographic regions of the general audience analysis from the organization. Next, dive deeper into the marketing analysis regarding behaviors and communication preferences for individuals from those various regions identified as active in social media to apply that information into message design within the campaign.

- Analyze the demographics such as age and gender from the website analytic report for all users who arrive at the website from social media platforms. Determine the typical needs of those users (which pages were they going to, what content was available) and the behaviors of those users (whether they converted, stayed on the page, shared any content). This information will pinpoint some of the key values for the brand's social media community and how those can be highlighted within a campaign.
- Review the user paths, or the order of pages that users view on a website, of the individuals coming to the website from social media channels. Do they seem interested in specific sections of the website? If so, that may identify specific information needs of the social media audience. Do they seem to jump from page to page rather quickly, but eventually take an action? If so, that may indicate that social media posts prepared them in advance to convert, and the users are more interested in a behavioral objective once they reach the website.

It is important to remember that, although detailed analysis of the general audience for the organization through marketing will provide analysis of online community behavior, a social strategist's ability to integrate that understanding of typical online behaviors with the brand's social media community will be crucial. The social media community will be unique. *Through audience analysis, identify which people from the general audience of the organization are using social media, what they are using it for, and what actions they take or behaviors they demonstrate as a result of that interaction.*

Content

The next area to review is the kind of content that has previously been posted in the social media channels. Develop an in-depth understanding of each platform. Review whether there is a rhythm to the split between original content in posts and curated content, whether posts are from partner organizations, and how often content is discussing topics other than the brand itself. Identify how frequently content is posted, and whether there seem to be specific genres that are typical on the platform. Keep note, as this will clarify previous social media engagement approaches that will help inform future action.

Key Data Application: Social media campaign development needs a historical understanding of how information was shared previously with the brand community. Each platform's historical content and data distribution plan need to be analyzed in order to effectively design a content calendar that resonates with the brand community.

EXPERT INSIGHT

Stephen Waddington

What do you think is one hallmark competency social media professionals need to succeed?

Professionals need to be actively engaged in using social forms of media. A basic understanding of theory is important, but there is no better way of understanding how content, conversations, and networks work than creating content and being active on networks.

What is the value, if any, of listening in social media before launching into a campaign?

It is absolutely critical. Social media activity should start with listening. Whatever your market, product, or service, you'll almost certainly find relevant conversations taking place around the social web. These will provide useful information for your organization.

Are there areas you've identified as the bread–and–butter for brands to focus on when doing research before a campaign?

Start with Google. There is then a huge third-party market of tools that you can use as the entry point to understand where the conversations relevant to your organization are taking place and what people are talking about related to your organization, brand, or market.

Do you have any tips or strategies for how social media professionals should sort through the data gathered in social media listening in order to make meaningful application to campaigns?

Surface the key issue relevant to your organization, its market, products, and services. Rank these by topic pulling out the top three to five issues. Then, for each topic, determine how your organization can add value to the conversation. These are the areas that you should focus on when developing content.

How can brands identify which influencers are most important for their social media efforts?

A network typically consists of content creators (1%), curators or editors that share content (9%), and consumers (90%). There's a burgeoning third-party tool market to help map and understand the make-up of networks and identify creators, curators, and editors. Typically, individuals are ranked for context, reach, and resonance.

What's something that is often overlooked but could provide a lot of value for brands in the listening phase of social media?

There's often a lack of rigor to planning in public relations. Practitioners jump directly to a network without properly interrogating whether it is the most appropriate form of media for their public. My recommendation is always to follow a formal planning process.

Is there some example of the power of listening in social media that you've experienced as a professional?

There are lots of excellent case studies, but my personal favorite is the Harry Potter franchise. Listening by W20 Group identified 43 influencers responsible for conversation and content sharing online. Its work now focuses promotional activity on this community.

What are the trends that you see in how brands are listening to stakeholders in social media and analyzing those conversations?

Progressive organizations use social media to listen and engage with their publics as an always-on activity. This provides useful insight and an early warning of issues arising among key stakeholders, including customers and staff.

What do you see as core standards and practices for brands' research practices in social media?

Start by mapping your social media footprint and determine how listening could help your organization. Social media listening can be used for research, customer insight, product development, crisis, issues management, and to identify influential stakeholders.

Connect with Stephen: @wadds; https://uk.linkedin.com/in/stephenwaddington

Stephen Waddington is Managing Director at Metia and a visiting professor at the University of Newcastle

Community Engagement

As the entire point of social media is to be *social*, evaluate whether the brand community is interacting with the content in any way. Keep in mind that different types of engagement carry different "values" in the social world. For example, when someone likes a photo on Instagram, it is a fairly easy action to take and, therefore, carries less weight or value. When someone comments, however, it takes a little bit more work on his or her part and, therefore, carries more weight. Actions that take more work on the part of a brand community in social media tend to indicate a deeper commitment to or passion for the topic, brand, or conversation. These actions by community members influence algorithms on many social media platforms and impact whether content will be shown to the larger social media community.

Understanding Social Algorithms

There are many factors to consider in brand engagement. But it is absolutely critical to understand the way social algorithms work and how they influence social media strategy. The *social algorithms* are mathematical equations designed to evaluate the quality of content posted by brands and determine which content receives more prominent placement in social media streams. Social media expert Rohit Bhargava[22] illustrated the importance of social algorithms when he pointed out that 90% of Facebook users do not return to a fan page once they click the 'like' button, and only about 16% of a page's updates are seen by the page's fans. The goal of social media campaigns is to fully engage a brand community with relevant and thriving conversations in which they want to participate, and brands can only do this well if content is optimized and performing well according to social algorithms.

In order to understand social algorithms, we should first review the basic premise of SEO, which established the foundation for today's modern social media algorithms. Google, as one may expect, was the vanguard search engine to implement SEO algorithms.[23] The goal of Google was to sift through the millions of indexed web pages and provide a qualified result to people who were searching for information on Google.com. Strictly from a business standpoint, this was an extremely successful strategic move for Google. Search engines have one commodity: to provide the best, most accurate results for what a user wants. If they are unable to do that, people will migrate to a different search engine. Google's algorithm revolutionized digital communications and caused industry professionals to begin a quest to understand SEO and its impact on online organizational communications. Bruce Clay, a leading SEO expert, defines SEO as: "the science/art of increasing traffic to a website by helping it rank higher in organic (non-paid) search results."[24] Applying this same concept to social media, *social media optimization involves the science and art of engaging online communities effectively to build strategic conversations on social media platforms among a brand community, causing organic (non-paid) content to show in the general streams of information for users.*

So, what is included in the algorithm for social media? It is impossible to know all of the factors. For example, there are more than 100,000 factors included in determining what shows in an individual's news feed on Facebook.[25] Each user will have different stories showing in their news feeds. Why so many factors? It is an indication of the maturing of the social media sites.

In 2009, Facebook first launched the news feed feature for users but quickly found that the sheer amount of information was overwhelming. It contained every update, post, and status in the news feed for each user. This led Ari Steinberg, a Facebook engineer, to introduce the idea of news feed optimization (NFO) using an algorithm called EdgeRank. It had three main factors: $\Sigma = U_e W_e D_e$:[26]

1. U_e = affinity, or the score of the connection between the user and the creator of the content.
2. W_e = weight, or the value for the type of action users take with the content. As previously mentioned, something like a comment would have more weight than a like.
3. D_e = decay, or the measurement of the time between when content is created and when the individual may see it.

Over the years, Facebook has made many changes to the algorithm in order to be more competitive in how users engage with content on the platform. Changes include adjustments such as privileging links to quality news sites in December 2013, increasing the exposure of text updates by friends of users in January 2014, expanding the reach of tagged content among the connections of those who were tagged in February 2014, penalizing brands who posted content with little context in August 2014, highlighting trending content in the news feed in September 2014, and penalizing overly promotional posts by organizations in November 2014.[27] In addition, in 2015, Facebook further adjusted its NFO to help reduce hoaxes and to push content from friends of users higher in the news feed.[28] All of these are part of what Lars Backstrom, engineering manager for news feed ranking at Facebook, views as increasing the maturity of the algorithm:

> The easiest analogy is to search engines and how they rank web pages. It's like comparing the Google of today with Alta Vista. Both Google and Bing have a lot of new signals, like personalization, that they use. It's more sophisticated than the early days of search, when the words on a page were the most important thing.[29]

Another "maturation" occurred in 2018 when Facebook announced that it would prioritize "posts that spark conversations and meaningful interaction," and it also openly committed to prioritizing posts from family and friends of people instead of content owned by brands.[30] This change set the tone for other major platforms. Although every platform will have its own factors, there are similarities to keep in mind. For example, TikTok has an emphasis on *user interactions*, such as whether people are liking, sharing, or commenting on posts.[31] Instagram places a strong emphasis on the relationship of the user to the post, interest in the type of content that the post contains compared with past user interaction with content, and timeliness.[32] Similarly, YouTube is customizing its algorithm around user experiences—accounting for not only the videos users click and watch, but the length of time spent watching and the videos they do not watch. Ultimately, this information, alongside factors such as the video title and description, all play a part in the algorithm.[33]

Although social media strategists cannot know each factor in an algorithm, as these are closely protected by social platforms and search engines, there are many indicators that give insight into what is important in social media content. Essentially, content that is relational and engaging tends to yield the highest impact in algorithms. Social media platforms become successful when people are encountering the type of content they want each and every time they use the app. Thus, algorithms will increasingly use data points related to tracking and monitoring whether the content you post is not only appropriate, but also wanted and interesting to particular individuals. The world of social media is consistently customizing the experience for each user based on their past interaction (likes, comments, posts) and their relationships to others in the social media community.

It is very important to recognize the value of algorithms. If a social media campaign is being developed for an online community that has previously experienced a very poor interaction rate, thus having a low score in social algorithms, it will take some time to rebuild the brand's status in the social media platform's performance. That is highly relevant to note, as it will influence the kinds of strategies and timing for content when a social media campaign is created.

Returning to the evaluation of the brand community's engagement, it is now possible to evaluate the interaction with greater expertise. Evaluate both the kind of engagement users have within a brand community and the genres of content that seem most valuable. One way to do this is by looking at the platform's analytics.

Understanding Platform Analytics

In-depth understanding of analytics for social media will be covered in the chapter on evaluation, Chapter 6, but it is helpful to highlight a few brief components that are particularly useful in the listening phase of a social media campaign. The goal in evaluating platform analytics at this stage is to understand which content has had the highest quality and quantity engagement. For example, in Facebook Insights, available to every official page on Facebook, it is possible to review key measurements. Identify if there has been a day with particular growth in the number of likes or, potentially, a decrease in the number of likes. Then, review the content posted that day to see what may have triggered those behaviors. It is also possible to review individual posts to see which ones led to the most likes, comments, or shares. In YouTube, review which videos have the highest estimated minutes watched or subscriber content, which can identify which videos are building subscribers and which ones may be driving traffic away. In Twitter's analytics, evaluate which tweets have the highest impressions and engagement and what the interests of the brand's followers are in order to customize content even further.

Go through each one of the organization's existing platforms and analyze the information available. By the end of this analysis of community engagement, it is possible to identify what content is more valuable to users on each platform and what kinds of content are disengaging a brand community.

Key Data Application: Understanding of a brand community audience and knowledge of historical content distribution are only valuable when integrated with expertise in recognizing *how* the brand community responds to communication. Engagement is crucial in order to evaluate the impact of social algorithms, implications for why content may or may not be appearing in prominent locations, and an overall assessment of the likelihood that certain kinds of content effect weightier or more valuable engagement by the brand community.

Brand Dialogue

Another helpful component to review prior to developing a campaign is the brand's dialogue with the community. Beyond posting content, does the organization interact with users, respond to questions, or share content from the community? If so, how often, and what is the time gap between when a community member posts and the organization responds. It may seem surprising, but people expect an organization to respond within 1 hour.[34] Although that may be unrealistic, particularly for organizations that do not have a dedicated staff member working on social media, it is helpful to determine if there are long gaps between engagement. This may be an indicator of why users are less likely to re-engage with social media content.

Today's social media communities do not simply desire to consume information from organizations. Rather, they want to actively participate in and produce information as well.[35] Those who fall into this category of desiring to produce rather than just be a consumer are known as "prosumers."[36] Susan Gunelius[37] describes the prosumer phenomenon like this: "Rather than simply 'consuming' products, people are becoming the voices of those products." She goes on to point out that, "Prosumers are the online influencers that business leaders and marketers must not just identify but also acknowledge, respect and develop relationships with" to thrive in today's social world.[38] Clearly, if brands are not interacting with online communities that have a deep desire to engage and produce, treating them simply as consumers of whatever content the brand has posted, the opportunity to build relevant conversations within a brand community is drastically diminished.

Key Data Application: Responding to brand community engagement is just as important as the initial social media post. Brand dialogue analysis provides a platform to understand the ways in which the brand has historically interacted and allows for strategists to identify areas to increase, optimize, or develop in two-way conversations.

Influencers

Influencers are the individuals on social media platforms who drive engagement, ignite dialogue around certain topics, and typically would be able to help expand a conversation. This text will cover influencers more in Chapter 4, but it is helpful to understand how influencers play a part in this step of campaign development. To identify influencers, see which users repeatedly show up in results for certain topics and keywords. Use the same listening tools discussed above for identifying keywords and topics in social platforms and then sort the data based on users. There are also several platforms designed with specific functions to easily identify influencers in social media. These platforms are generally based on an algorithm that calculates the engagement with individual users' content and scores them on a level of "influence." Some platforms organizations use include Sprout Social, Brandwatch, Kred, and Traackr.

When developing an influencer list for each platform, create a file or database to easily tag the influencer with the keywords/phrases to which they relate. This will allow one to quickly identify which influencers may be interested in particular content that is being created. Additionally, know which platforms influencers are on, how many followers they have, and any other information or scoring metrics that are available such as other topics do they like to discuss online, whether they are interacting with other brands already, and if the organization has followed/liked/connected with them (if not, be sure to do so). The goal is to have a full profile of these influencers in order to effectively build a relationship with them. Remember, people want to be prosumers—to create content. Influencers are those individuals who are already known for being thought leaders and conversation starters. A great component to keep in mind when laying the foundation for a social media campaign, therefore, is which influencers might be interested in participating in the brand's social initiatives.

Key Data Application: In each brand community, there are key individuals who drive conversations forward and truly spark connections. These influencers should be identified and specifically encouraged to participate in a campaign.

Competition

One of the best things that can be done to strategize effective social media campaigns is to analyze competitors and other leaders in the industry. This gives insight into how organizations of similar vision and focus are performing in the social spaces.

Create a list of key competitors and determine which social media sites they currently use. Go onto each platform and note the audience size and any other pertinent metrics. Consider using similar reviewing strategies for engagement as previously discussed for the brand's own page. There are several areas to note in this analysis. First, identify which platforms seem to be most popular, based on what is widely utilized in the organization's sector or industry. Second, note the type of audience engagement and size that are standard in the industry. Organizations can also purchase subscriptions to third-party analytic apps that allow this type of analysis, sometimes across multiple platforms. This can be a

great benefit to brands. The end goal of these efforts, whether an organization opts for a paid service or manual tracking, is to identify how the
brand's engagement and community compare with those of the competition. Using this information, social media strategists are able to provide
greater context for the decisions that will inform social media campaign
design. Rather than solely looking at the brand's audience engagement
and community reach in a vacuum, compare them with competitive
standards among others in the social media landscape.

Another area to evaluate with competition is the design of their
social media profiles. Consider what pieces of content they provide, the
images they highlight, and their use of rich media. It is useful to see
what the strongest competitors are doing in terms of profile design as
well as how underperforming competitors have set up their social presence. Be sure to compare these competitor findings with the current
social media profiles of the brand in order to identify areas to enhance or
change. In addition, review the kind of content competitors are producing. Previously, the brand's own content was analyzed to calculate the
percentage of originally produced content versus curated content, type
of tone, media type, and other factors. Now review the same categories
for the competition to see what kind of content seems to work the best
for engagement and what patterns are observable in their content use.

Finally, analyze the brand's share of voice (SOV). SOV "essentially
means comparing your crucial performance metrics against those of key
competitors."[39] In short, SOV is a metric that "details what percentage of
mentions within your industry are about your brand, and what percentage is about the competition."[40] For example, this can be accomplished
by identifying key competitors and tracking how often they are mentioned on social media platforms compared with the brand's mentions.
Or, track the organization's main keywords or phrases connected to
the brand, compared with those same keywords or phrases referencing
competition.

To calculate SOV, use an Excel sheet or some other table feature (you
can also find this sheet available in the eResources for this text). When
representing SOV, calculate total mentions as well as create a pie chart
to illustrate findings. First, tabulate all relevant references to the brand in
the last 30 days. Include the tone of the comments, which can be highlighted by many social listening tools. Be sure to review the comments,
as the tone can be ambiguous and easily mistaken. For example, sarcasm
may make a comment appear to have a positive tone when the person
actually was upset with a brand (e.g., "So glad I waited an hour and still
did not get a response from customer service. #FavoriteBrand). Calculate all positive comments, negative comments, and neutral comments.

Social Comments	Positive	Neutral	Share of Voice	Negative
Your Brand	50	15	65	5
Competition 1	48	10	58	10
Competition 2	30	5	35	0
Competition 3	55	15	70	15

Share of Voice Percent	
Your Brand	28.51%
Competition 1	25.44%
Competition 2	15.35%
Competition 3	30.70%
Total	100.00%

Share of Voice

Your Brand, 28.51%
Competition 1, 25.44%
Competition 2, 15.35%
Competition 3, 30.70%

Figure 2.4 Share of Voice Chart

In the final column, calculate SOV mentions by adding the positive and neutral comments together. Finally, develop a pie chart that shows the percentages of SOV broken down by each brand. This will give an idea of how often conversations that relate to the brand's industry or sector reference the organization and the brand's competition.

Next, perform the same activities for the top competitors. When all the numbers are gathered, create another chart that will show total *positive* and *neutral* mentions as SOV. Although the negative comments will not be useful in determining a positive share of the conversation being attributed to your brand, it may give insight into a change over time that reveals a better SOV for your brand. To calculate the percentage of SOV, divide the positive and neutral mentions each organization received by the total mentions for all brands that you assessed.[41]

Next, create an average sentiment chart. A *sentiment score* is a metric that communicates the strength or level of positive communication in social media from key publics regarding a brand. To calculate the sentiment value for each brand in the SOV report, use the following equation from Jay Baer:[42]

$$\text{(number of positive posts for the brand} \times 5) +$$
$$\text{(number of neutral posts for the brand} \times 3) +$$
$$\text{(number of negative posts for the brand} \times 1)$$

Take the number and divide it by the total number of mentions for all brands to arrive at a number between 1 and 5. The closer the number is to 5, the better a sentiment score is. From the average sentiment, it is possible to analyze what type of content competition may be using to yield a higher SOV, and this also provides a benchmark to use as a comparison after a social media campaign.[43]

Social Comments	Positive	Neutral	Negative	Total
Your Brand	50	15	5	70
Competition 1	48	10	10	68
Competition 2	30	5	0	35
Competition 3	55	15	15	85

Sentiment Score (Positive X 5) + (Neutral X 3) + (Negative X 1) / Total	
Your Brand	4.29
Competition 1	4.12
Competition 2	4.71
Competition 3	3.94

Figure 2.5 Sentiment Score Chart

Having gathered a large amount of data on the organization's background, mission, and communication processes, as well as a robust analysis of the social media landscape for the brand, the social media strategist must *apply* the information purposefully and deliberately for a campaign.

Key Data Application: Competition analysis allows brands to identify what type of content is generally the most effective across an industry, to identify engaging profile creation, and ultimately to evaluate the brand's SOV and sentiment score within the social landscape. This information can then be used to inform specific tactical creation within a campaign as well as serving as benchmarks to evaluate the success of campaign messaging.

SENSE-MAKING

Once there is a robust understanding of the organization, audience, platforms, and competition, it is important to move into strategic use of those data. Sense-making is the final, crucial component of the listening phase. Often, people are eager to jump into developing a campaign after gathering so much data. But, unless the data are mined for information and that information is applied in meaningful ways to the context of a brand's social media needs, organizations will be unable to effectively leverage the power of social media for their brand.

Listening Analysis Steps—Understanding the Data

In order to visualize how all the data gathered in the listening phase are helpful, it can be useful to put the data into three larger sections. Each of these sections should be informed by your knowledge of the organization—the commitments of the mission/vision, the structure of the organization and its ability to support social media efforts, and the communication framework already in place that you identified through the communication audit. These data pieces should always shape the recommendations and insights you bring, as it is critical that the data are shaped based on the unique needs and requirements of the particular brand.

1. *Audience*: Always start with what you know about the public. Just as the chapter began with an examination of the ethical obligation to listen authentically, your analysis and sense-making should be rooted in the publics you are seeking to engage with through social media. Never assume that larger trends are relevant to your particular audience until you have completed specific analysis for your stakeholders.

Consider the values, opinions, beliefs, and behaviors of your audience and how those inform when, how, and where your brand should interact with these stakeholders via social media.

2. *Relevant Conversations*: Having analyzed the specific and generic keywords, and the key platforms for those words, analyze which conversations are most relevant to your brand. You do not want simply to calculate which keywords have the highest engagement or which conversations are most prevalent—rather, look for an intersection between top keywords, platforms, and the essence of what you learned about your own brand during your communication audit (looking at conversations they are already having on channels) and the heart of your brand (the mission/vision statement). In light of all of this, what are the most salient or applicable conversations to join? You might identify macro and micro conversations. Consider macro conversations as the top ones that will yield high engagement, are particularly important based on a platform or keyword, and uniquely appropriate for the brand. Micro conversations can be considered ones that are less about volume and impact, but may have arisen through social listening as you discovered your key publics' particular needs, feedback, or desires. These micro conversations may seem less relevant in terms of impact, but may actually be incredibly important for maintaining trust and loyalty in your stakeholders.

3. *Competitors*: This portion of your data should not simply summarize where your competitors are active and how they are engaging, but also provide a deeper analysis and connection of that information for you to consider. For example, always ask "why is that?" when you make an observation. For example, "Our top competitor is gaining incredible momentum in TikTok and posting regularly to that platform"—"Why is that?" The *why* question is really where the deeper analysis begins. This is when you analyze what is causing your competitor to invest in particular platforms or conversations, why audiences are responding to that, and whether it is, in fact, an appropriate area for your own brand to consider based on existing knowledge about your publics, the goals of the organization, and current communication capabilities.

SWOT Analysis

A SWOT analysis is a common tool that assesses an organization's strengths, weaknesses, opportunities, and threats. It will also develop a framework to understand how these four areas relate to each other. An example of how to set up the chart is provided in Figure 2.6.

SWOT ANALYSIS

Figure 2.6 SWOT Matrix

When considering what items to place in each box, there are a couple of dimensions to keep in mind. First, think about the organizational strengths and weaknesses and write them down in the first two boxes. These are the two *inward*-facing or organization-facing categories, relating to factors over which the brand has direct control or influence. For example, a strength could be that the management team is very supportive and invests resources in the social media efforts. On the other hand, a weakness might be that the organization has little online analysis available from the website or other initiatives to inform actions. Another example of a strength would be that the brand has highly loyal audiences who are already engaged online. Another weakness may be that, despite a highly loyal audience, the brand itself is relatively unknown, resulting in a rather small, though loyal, audience. Making a list of these factors will be the first step. Next, the opportunities and threats relate to external factors, or areas that are not under the direct control or influence of the brand. For example, there might be a significant opportunity in social media to provide real-time engagement with audiences. However, a threat could be that a competitor already has a strong social media presence and a majority of the SOV.

Once the data have been categorized in a SWOT diagram, make meaningful applications by using the quadrants. Each quadrant can be related to the others to help analyze the data and apply them in meaningful ways to strategic design. For example, examining strengths in relation to opportunities provides the potential to develop strategies that take full advantage of the potential in social media. It is possible to also evaluate the weaknesses identified in the organization's social media use

Figure 2.7 SWOT Tactic Matrix

to determine steps that can be taken to ensure that threats do not inhibit the social media campaign's potential. Figure 2.7 is a diagram showing how to convert the raw data from a SWOT analysis into a meaningful application for a social media campaign.

Problem/Opportunity Statements

After all the key pieces of background necessary have been identified, the social landscape has been surveyed, and those findings have been applied in a SWOT analysis, it is now possible to create a problem or opportunity statement. This statement will help guide the social media campaign. In one or two sentences, capture the essence of what is going on with social media and why, at this time, the brand is setting about creating a social media campaign. Write it in the present tense (because it is happening now) and simply state what is going on—do not provide a solution or answer to the current problem/opportunity. This statement is an assessment of the current status in the brand's social media world.

Sometimes these statements fall into the genre of a "problem" statement. For example: "Current social media engagement with our online community is severely diminished resulting in customer complaints." However, sometimes brand research identifies opportunities that are untapped in social media. For example, an opportunity statement might be written such as:

> Social media platforms currently provide 25% of the traffic to the website but result in 50% of the conversations for online traffic. There is opportunity to grow social media as a traffic source for our website beyond its current 25%.

Whether writing a problem or opportunity statement, remember to keep it short. Make it present tense. Do not infer blame or indicate an "answer." Now that a refined problem/opportunity statement has been developed, based on in-depth research, it is possible to move into strategic design. This is the part of the campaign process where social media strategists propose data-informed solutions or responses to the current social media environment that the organization is experiencing.

KEY CONCEPT SNAPSHOT

1. A social media strategy directly relates to organizational vision and purpose. Be sure to do a complete review of the organization's key documents prior to developing a social media campaign.
2. While strategy is a conduit to express the organization's vision, social media is a direct connection- and relationship-building process with key stakeholders. Understand the needs, values, interests, and conversations that are taking place among social media publics.
3. Craft an opportunity or problem statement that specifies the intentionality of the organization's social media activities. This statement guides the campaign development.

To download an SOV template you can use for brand social listening, visit ⬇ www.routledge.com/9780367896201

NOTES

1   Gundlach & Murphy, 1993.
2   Edelman, 2017.
3   Macnamara, 2018.
4   Place, 2019.
5   Place, 2019, p. 2.
6   Grunig & Hunt, 1984.
7   Fitzpatrick & Gauthier, 2001; Khurana & Nohria, 2008; Neill & Drumwright, 2012.
8   Neill & Drumwright, 2012; Place, 2019.
9   Macnamara, 2018; Place, 2019.
10   2015.
11   para. 3.
12   2014.
13   p. 128.
14   Tourville, 2019.

15 2014.
16 p. 128.
17 2014.
18 p. 60.
19 p. 60.
20 2014, pp. 158–160.
21 2011, p. 24.
22 2012.
23 Page, 2015.
24 Bruce Clay Inc., n.d., "What Is SEO?" in "Search engine optimization—SEO
    tutorial."
25 McGee, 2013.
26 Patterson, 2015.
27 Ibid.
28 Lee, 2015.
29 As quoted in Page, 2015.
30 Mosseri, 2018, para. 3–4.
31 Hutchinson, 2020.
32 Cooper, 2020.
33 Chi, 2019.
34 Gesenhues, 2013.
35 Kaplan & Haenlein, 2010.
36 Toffler, 1980.
37 2010, para. 4.
38 para. 6.
39 Weintraub, n.d., para. 1.
40 Torr, 2015, para. 2.
41 Dunham, 2015.
42 n.d.
43 Dunham, 2015.

SUGGESTED READING

Lipschultz, J. H. (2019). *Social Media Measurement and Management: Entrepreneurial Digital Analytics.* New York: Routledge.
Quesenberry, K. A. (2018). *Social Media Strategy: Marketing, Advertising, and Public Relations in the Consumer Revolution.* Lanham, MD: Rowman & Littlefield.
Place, K. R. (2019). Listening as the Driver of Public Relations Practice and Communications Strategy within a Global Public Relations Agency. *Public Relations Journal,* 12(3), 1–18.

REFERENCES

Baer, J. (n.d.). "How to calculate a share of voice report." *Convince and Convert.* Retrieved from: www.convinceandconvert.com/social-media-strategy/how-to-create-a-share-of-voice-report/

Bhargava, R. (2012). *Likeonomics: The Unexpected Truth behind Earning Trust, Influencing Behavior, and Inspiring Action.* Hoboken, NJ: John Wiley.

Brito, M. (2013). *Your Brand, the Next Media Company: How a Social Business Strategy Enables Better Content, Smarter Marketing, and Deeper Customer Relationships.* Indianapolis, IN: Que.

Bruce Clay Inc. (n.d.). "Search engine optimization—SEO tutorial." *BruceClay.com.* Retrieved from www.bruceclay.com/seo/search-engine-optimization.htm

Chi, C. (2019, October 30). *Youtube Algorithm: The Constantly Updated Guide to YouTube's Updates & Changes.* Retrieved from: https://blog.hubspot.com/marketing/youtube-algorithm

Claussen, J. (2015, Feb. 9). "Are you a social leader? Finding your blue unicorn." *ShoCase.com.* Retrieved from: http://corp.shocase.com/2015/02/social-leader-finding-blue-unicorn/

Coiné, T. & Babbitt, M. (2014). *A World Gone Social: How Companies Must Adapt to Survive.* New York: AMACOM, American Management Association.

Cooper, P. (April 20, 2020). *How the Instagram Algorithm Works in 2020 (and How to Work with It).* Retrieved from: https://blog.hootsuite.com/instagram-algorithm/

Dunham, K. (2015, June). "The beginner's guide to social media metrics: Share of voice." *UberVu.* Retrieved from: http://blog.ubervu.com/beginners-guide-social-media-metrics-share-voice.html

Edelman. (2017). 2017 Edelman Trust Barometer. Edelman. Retrieved from: www.edelman.com/trust2017/

Fitzpatrick, K. & Gauthier, C. (2001). Toward a Professional Responsibility Theory of Public Relations Ethics. *Journal of Mass Media Ethics,* 16(2–3), 193–212.

Gesenhues, A. (2013, Oct. 30). "Study: 72% of consumers expect brands to respond within an hour to complaints posted on twitter." *Marketing Land.* Retrieved from: http://marketingland.com/study-72-of-consumers-expect-brands-to-respond-within-an-hour-to-complaints-posted-on-twitter-63496

Grunig, J. E. & Hunt, T. (1984). *Managing Public Relations.* New York: Holt, Rinehart & Winston.

Gundlach, G. & Murphy, P. (1993). Ethical and Legal Foundations of Relational Marketing Exchanges. *Journal of Marketing,* 57(4), 35–46.

Gunelius, S. (2010, July 3). "The shift from CONsumers to PROsumers." *Forbes.* Retrieved from: https://www.forbes.com/sites/work-in-progress/2010/07/03/the-shift-from-consumers-to-prosumers/#41244daf33df

Hutchinson, A. (June 18, 2020). "How TikTok's Algorithm Works—As Explained by TikTok." Retrieved from: www.socialmediatoday.com/news/how-tiktoks-algorithm-works-as-explained-by-tiktok/580153/

Kaplan, A. M. & Haenlein, M. (2010). Users of the World, Unite! The Challenges and Opportunities of Social Media. *Business Horizons,* 53(1), 59–68.

Kerpen, D. (2011). *Likeable Social Media: How to Delight Your Customers, Create an Irresistible Brand, and Be Generally Amazing on Facebook.* New York: McGraw-Hill.

Kerns, C. (2014). *Trendology: Building an Advantage through Data-Driven Real-Time Marketing.* New York: Palgrave Macmillan.

Khurana, R. & Nohria, N. (2008). It's Time to Make Management a True Profession. *Harvard Business Review,* 86(10), 70–77.

Lee, K. (2015, July). "Decoding the Facebook news feed: An up-to-date list of the algorithm factors and changes." *BufferSocial*. Retrieved from: https://blog.bufferapp.com/facebook-news-feed-algorithm

Macnamara, J. (2018). Toward a Theory and Practice of Organizational Listening. *International Journal of Listening*, 32(1), 1–23.

McGee, M. (2013, Aug. 13). "EdgeRank is dead: Facebook's news feed algorithm now has close to 100K weight factors." *Marketing Land*. Retrieved from: http://marketingland.com/edgerank-is-dead-facebooks-news-feed-algorithm-now-has-close-to-100k-weight-factors-55908

Mosseri, A. (2018, January 11). "Bringing People Closer Together." Retrieved from: https://about.fb.com/news/2018/01/news-feed-fyi-bringing-people-closer-together/

Neill, M. S. & Drumwright, M. E. (2012). PR Professionals as Organizational Conscience. *Journal of Mass Media Ethics*, 27(4), 220–234.

Page, M. (2015, March 11). "Taking advantage of the social network algorithms." *Smart Insights*. Retrieved from: www.smartinsights.com/social-media-marketing/social-media-optimisation/social-network-algorithms/

Patterson, M. (2015, January 26). "Edgerank: A guide to the Facebook news feed algorithm." *Sprout Social*. Retrieved from: http://sproutsocial.com/insights/facebook-news-feed-algorithm-guide/

Place, K. R. (2019). Listening as the Driver of Public Relations Practice and Communications Strategy within a Global Public Relations Agency. *Public Relations Journal*, 12(3).

Toffler, A. (1980). *The Third Wave: The Classic Study of Tomorrow*. New York: Bantam Books.

Torr, D. (2015). "4 ways to increase your share of voice on social media." *Hootsuite*. Retrieved from: http://blog.hootsuite.com/how-to-increase-share-of-voice/

Tourville, S. (2019, August 14). *Why the CEO and C-Suite Should Be on Social Media*. Retrieved from: www.prnewsonline.com/CEO-social+media

Weintraub, M. (n.d.). "The definitive share of voice guide: PPC, SEO, social & multi-channel SOV models." aimClear. Retrieved from: https://www.aimclear.com/the-definitive-share-of-voice-guide-ppc-seo-social-multi-channel-sov-models/

CHAPTER 3

Step 2: Strategic Design Part A

Developing a Data-Informed Social Media Campaign

> Respect for the nature and potential of social media demands that organizations approach engagement with intentionality and data-informed designs to develop trusted and authentic relationships.

After gathering the formative research from the listening phase and going through the sense-making process to develop a data-informed problem/opportunity statement, the next stage involves mapping out the overall strategy for the organization's social media. Before designing individual, shorter-term campaigns, first an organization must solidify the overall purpose of and approach to social media. If this is not already in place, a social media professional should first start by developing a *social media strategic plan* that is the guiding framework for all the brand's campaigns and initiatives in social media.

SOCIAL MEDIA STRATEGIC PLAN

Social Media Goals

With the full weight of the background about the company's vision, the current social media presence of the organization, and potential audience, it is possible to effectively establish the goals for a brand's social media presence. Goals can be defined as "broad, summative statements that spell out the overall outcomes of the program."[1] They essentially state where the brand plans to end up as a result of social media efforts. An example of a social media goal may be: "Become a thought leader in social media for the technology industry." Another example could be: "Be recognized as a premier source for information and resources on non-profit philanthropy." When crafting the goal for social media, keep in mind the organization's overall mission or vision statement. A social media goal should directly relate to the purpose or mission of the brand, extending or enhancing the likelihood that the organization's overall vision will be accomplished. Once the goal is established, move on to specific social media platform plans.

Social Media Vision Statements

Once the goal of a brand's social media is identified, it is important to create *vision statements* for each platform that zero in on the value and purpose of each social media channel for the organization. To do this, identify each social media platform that is beneficial for the organization. This identification comes from research gathered during the listening phase where social media channels were reviewed based on keyword activity. It may have been that certain platforms were identified that did not have conversations relevant for the organization, resulting in few conversations taking place that related to keywords. Or, perhaps, there were others that were highly relevant but not used by the brand yet. Create a list of all platforms that will be incorporated as regular parts of the brand's social media presence. In determining which platforms are important, consider the capabilities of the platform, the general audience it serves, the research regarding conversations on the platform, and details from the competitive analysis.

With identified social media channels in hand, it is important to create social media platform vision statements. In order to fully craft a vision statement, be sure to identify the capabilities of each platform. For example, Facebook has a strong advertising option, video integration, photo albums, and so on. Instagram, on the other hand, has shorter video options and is mainly driven by individual visuals. TikTok has rapidly gained a following, particularly in the younger demographic, for videos. When you identify the potential *uses* of each platform, it is possible to specify how these specific platforms play into the overall goal of the organization and to craft a platform vision statement to guide future strategy.

The vision statements should include "the description of each social media profile's purpose, and how this purpose contributes to your business goals."[2] The value of identifying these areas is to strategically develop social media content and campaigns while unifying the approach to various platforms. Olsy Sorokina,[3] a social media expert, suggests using the model of: "We will use (*social network*) for (*purpose of this social network*) in order to help (*business goal*)." Examples of this could include: "We will use Facebook for advertising to target a specific audience in order to help increase sales"[4] or

"We will use Instagram for promoting and sharing our company culture to help with recruitment and employee happiness."[5] In this way, a vision statement should be developed for each of the brand's social media sites.

Creating SMART Objectives

With an end purpose in view and vision statements for each platform, social media strategists are now ready to create objectives for the social media strategic plan. An objective can be defined as "specific knowledge, opinion, and behavior outcomes to be achieved for each well-defined target publics, what some call 'key results.'"[6] Essentially, an *objective* is what will be measured as a key progress indicator (KPI) showing that a campaign goal is being met. In the context of social media, identify the precise platform and the audience behavior or activities that the brand would like to see displayed as a result of the social media efforts.

It is important to draft these objectives in a way that provides parameters and accountability for social media engagement by using the acronym SMART. This stands for specific, measurable, achievable, relevant, and timely. Each objective that is created should have all of these elements present. For example, a SMART social media objective may be, "Have 30 retweets a week as a result of posting to Twitter twice a day." The "specific" element of this objective is that it applies solely to Twitter. The "measurable" element is that there should be 30 retweets. Knowing how large the current Twitter audience is and

Figure 3.1 SMART Objectives

the engagement history would clarify whether the measurable element is truly "achievable" as part of the objective. This may be an objective the brand will have to build towards achieving, or it may be strongly realistic based on research. "Relevant" will relate to the vision statement for Twitter and evaluation of what should be accomplished by those retweets. For example, it is relevant if the brand's vision statement for Twitter included content that was designed to be shared or develop engagement. It could be that 30 retweets lead to creating awareness in a larger audience or potentially enhancing the likelihood that people are clicking the link in that tweet and going to a website. Whatever the brand's purpose is for Twitter, make sure that the specific objective relates in a tangible way to achieving the vision. Finally, the example is "timely" as it has a 1-week parameter for the retweets. Each week, it should be reset, and the brand can evaluate whether this objective has been reached.

Outcome-Based Objectives

It is important to note that objectives should also be *outcome-based*. This means an objective is about what happens on the platform and within the brand community as a result of social media engagement. For example, in the illustration above, posting twice a week is an *output*. It is something that the organization will do. However, the 30 retweets will be an *outcome*. Those retweets are the result of the social media activities by brand community members. Ensuring that each objective is an outcome allows for higher accountability in social media program evaluation, which will be discussed in the evaluation section later. It is worth noting, however, that evaluation of objectives is used to illustrate the effectiveness and value of a social media campaign. The ability to evaluate a campaign rests heavily on developing SMART, *outcome-based objectives*. There is no authentic measurement of brand communities' engagement in social media when outputs are used as the measurement—they simply indicate that the social media team was very active. What should be measured is the impact, or results, of the efforts on social media platforms. In order to do that effectively, each objective must be SMART and outcome-based.

Social Profile Branding

The next steps to take in a social media strategic plan are to ensure that all the organization's profiles are fully filled in, properly branded, and maintain a strong presence among online communities. The purpose of this is not just to fill in the information and make it look nice. The focus should be on a unifying brand presence as well as optimizing social media accounts. Here are some basic elements to consider:

About Section

The "About" section in each social profile is an opportunity to introduce the brand. Keep in mind the keywords and phrases developed in the social media listening stage, the marketing department's branding guidelines, and the platform's audience. When completing about sections, have a consistent presentation so that audiences feel like the brand is the same organization, no matter which platform they are currently using. In addition, be strategic with wording in order to capitalize on SEO opportunities. With search engines pulling in more content from social media sites, particularly with the partnership between Google and Twitter that began in 2015, using each phrase and posting strategically are vital for brands. Neil Patel,[7] co-founder of Crazy Egg, Hello Bar, and KISSmetrics, explains: "Social and search have intertwined into a squirming nexus of who's-where-and-who's-who."[8] The about section provides a platform to share who the brand is and what it is all about with the online brand communities.

Profile Photos and Thumbnails

It seems like social media profile image sizes are constantly changing. Be sure to regularly review the social channels of a brand to ensure that images are crisp, properly sized, engaging, and branded. Although all platforms do not need the exact same photos, it is helpful to consider the general branding guidelines and applications of images across platforms. On some platforms, such as Facebook, more engagement can be gained when a cover image is regularly changed. It might be something to consider updating with various initiatives or campaigns. But even when rotating those images, be sure to keep the feel of the brand in mind. Users should still recognize each cover photo as being from the brand or organization. Thumbnail images should be easily recognizable as well. Consider using the logo, as that is often the image associated with posts or comments. Have it created and sized specifically for each social media outlet. An easy way to identify the latest size requirements is to quickly search the internet for an updated listing of each platform's image dimensions.

Vanity URLs

Customizing an organization's URL for each platform makes it easy for people to connect. A *vanity URL* is a unique, individualized URL for a social platform. For example, facebook.com/CarolynMaeKim is far easier to remember and share than facebook.com/149272585126883. When creating vanity URLs for an organization's social platforms, keep them consistent. Ideally, have one URL for all social media properties. Twitter tends to have less space, and so it is a good idea to make a vanity URL for Twitter first and then apply that to other platforms. A helpful website to quickly check if a vanity URL is available across the social media landscape is www.Namechk.com.

Company Connections

Some of the weakest points for many organizations are the connections between social platforms, as well as the connection with the organization's website. Be sure to have the correct URL provided for the organization's main site, as well as incorporating the connections to other social profiles within each social media channel. It is helpful at this stage to also review the organization's website and ensure that the social media channels are easily identified on the homepage and other key locations. If they are not, work with the website development team to ensure all channels are properly added on the website. This permits users to easily connect in multiple places, as well as allowing the community to quickly identify where they will be able to engage with the brand. For example, people should be able to get to the brand's TikTok profile from the website's home page, or they should be able easily to share a blog from the website to their Facebook news feed. On Facebook, users should be able to connect to the Instagram profile or YouTube channel. It should be a well-organized and clearly defined web of connections.

Rich Media

When developing social profiles, also consider the inclusion of rich media. For example, on Twitter, there are six locations for images or video that show on the main profile. It is advisable to add at least these six pieces of rich media to the Twitter profile before it goes live so that the brand's profile presence appears complete. Instagram has a regular rotation of images across the profile background. It is helpful to make sure the brand has enough images that, as they rotate in and out, it appears diverse and interesting, rather than underdeveloped. Review each platform to understand how it displays, what media are needed, and where they are used. After this, develop branded pieces that can meet those needs to fully utilize each platform. If the brand is unsure what kinds of media-rich content pieces to create, it can be helpful to reflect on the brand community conversations and keywords for the organization. Find images, video, infographics, and other rich media that involve these topics of mutual interest. That is what the brand community cares about and with which they will engage. Remember, the social principle is about identifying topics of mutual interest with a brand's audience and engaging in a conversation.

Content Distribution

After each profile has a mission statement and the profile design is fully up to speed, consider the content distribution strategy for the organization. The first step in a distribution plan is to create a content topic guide. Hootsuite's senior director of social media, Jaime Stein, provides a model for organizations on social media that essentially allocates various percentages of social media content to specific focuses of the organization.[9] Hootsuite's free online template, "How to create a social media strategy in 8 easy steps" illustrates this:[10] "50% of your content will drive back to the blog; 25% of your content will be curated from other sources; 20% of your content will be lead generation; 5% of your content will be company culture." The percentages identified in the example are just that—an example. Each organization needs to create content distribution guide percentages based on the brand's objectives and social media purpose. However, some organizations may not be well placed to know how to develop such defined metrics yet. It could be that more time is needed in social media before that can be solidified. If that is the case, brands may opt for the rule of thirds. The rule of thirds is essentially that one third of the content will be about the brand, one third will be shared from industry thought leaders, and one third will be dedicated to individual interactions with a brand community on social media.

Beyond the base allocation of percentages for content information, it is also helpful to create a general content calendar. A general content calendar guides the overall social media communication pieces and allows for harmonization across platforms. Much more specific content calendars are developed for each campaign. However, the general content calendar provides a framework to develop specific campaigns and also to align communication with the overall brand's other communiqué pieces for audiences. A general content calendar should include:

* Platforms
* Day, and if possible, time of posts
* Keywords or topic of the post
* Category of content topic design
* Any media needed (images, photos, etc.)
* Team member responsible for post.

If the organization already uses a master content calendar for communication across all platforms (such as newsletters, website blogs, press releases), it is helpful to coordinate in order to ensure that social media complements the overall organizational communication patterns. Knowing what the organization is communicating in general will help social media strategists tailor content that is appropriate for each social channel.

Social Media Voice

With a general content distribution guide in place and a calendar created, develop the social media voice for the brand. This will include key messages and a message map that will guide how the organization interacts on social media and ensure that the brand persona is highlighted in all types of engagement. Before determining *what* to say and how to say it, having a strong brand persona is crucial. The *social media voice* is composed by understanding the brand's persona, the appropriate tone for a message, and the intentional language needed to effectively communicate in each post.

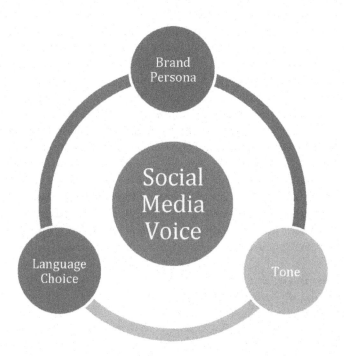

Figure 3.2 Developing a Social Media Voice

Understanding Brand Persona

Style guides and brand voice are often captured in marketing style guidelines. The reality, however, is that many organizations have trouble translating those marketing guidelines into social media or, perhaps, they simply choose not to consider those guidelines. This becomes quite problematic. A brand's presentation on social media intricately influences key publics' perceptions of the brand itself. It is not just a "social media" activity—it directly impacts the organization's reputation and perception. It is, therefore, crucial that the brand persona and style are maintained so that all social media efforts support the overall vision of the organization. Brian Solis,[11] social media guru, points out:

> In social networks, the brand and how it's perceived, is open to public interpretation and potential misconception now more than ever. Without a deliberate separation between the brand voice and personality and that of the person representing it, we are instantly at odds with our goals, purpose, and potential stature.[12]

Strategic social media messaging involves more than just coming up with the right words. It is about understanding what the brand symbolizes and the persona of the brand in the digital sphere.[13] When identifying a brand's persona, consider what kind of person the brand would be if it came to life. The organization may have a thoughtful brand persona, or, perhaps, the brand persona would be more appropriate to the organization if it was somewhat playful or adventurous. Perhaps the organization's brand is lighthearted or maybe academic. Determine what the brand's persona is before developing key messaging. Keep in mind that, no matter what the persona, it still needs to be a humanized concept. Paul Armstrong,[14] emerging technology expert, says "Brands need to be human (in some form or another) if they want to succeed online."[15]

Tone

After identifying the brand's persona, establish the kind of tone that should come across in communication. Tone can be defined as "the underlying vibe that emanates from your brand's communications."[16] The tone should reflect the brand persona and be uniquely appropriate to the specific audience the brand is engaging. Some brands might have a more personable tone, where others might take on a more direct or academic tone. When developing the key traits of a brand's social voice tone, consider not only the brand's current type of communication tone, but also where the brand would like to see the social media conversations develop. Perhaps the tone will be quiet and humble if the brand is on a new platform, but, after gaining credibility, will develop into more of an authoritative or scientific tone in the future. Understanding where the brand is today, where the brand hopes to be tomorrow, as well as the long-term objectives of the brand in social media will determine the proper tone in the right context.[17]

Intentional Language

Keeping in mind the brand persona and tone, consider the purpose, or reason, for the communication. This should relate back to the social media campaign objectives. Recognizing the purpose of the social media content, think of the specific language that will be used. This concept will be developed further in the key messages and message map creation. Stephanie Schwab,[18] CEO and founder of Crackerjack Marketing, describes the challenge of developing language to match a social media voice, writing:

> Although your brand may be the expert in its field, coming off
> sounding like you're smarter than your customers could turn people
> off pretty quickly. Establishing appropriate brand language will
> give you a foundation for the types of words, phrases and jargon
> to be used in social media communications. Want to sound very
> exclusive? Use insider language and acronyms. Want to sound hip?
> Stay up-to-date on the latest slang. But be careful—if you make a
> misstep in slang it'll look like you're trying too hard.[19]

Learning to craft appropriate content is part of designing a strong social media voice. The key to effectively crafting appropriate content is remembering to design it based on the brand's persona and tone, as well as applying insight from the formative research on what causes audiences to engage and what the purpose of social media for the brand is.

Finally, before moving on to create social media campaigns, ensure that certain policies and procedures are in place. The four that will be discussed in this section include: (1) A social media community policy, (2) an employee social media use policy, (3) a policy for the social media teams in an organization, and (4) a crisis plan for social media.

Social Media Community Policy

The goal of having a social media user policy is to protect the online community and the quality of conversations that take place in social media. A *community policy* is a document that outlines the kinds of behaviors that are welcome in the brand community, as well as identifying negative behaviors and the consequences of those. Obviously, the nature of social media is such that a brand cannot control all conversations, nor should it try. However, it is important to have a policy in place that addresses certain kinds of interaction or communication that may be harmful to social media engagement and communities. A good place to start would be to reference whether the organization's website has a user policy in place for comments on blogs and other locations online.

Craft a social media community policy with the values of the organization and online brand community in mind. There are three main parts to include: (1) the values of the online community and the type of behavior that creates an environment where those values are seen, (2) behaviors that may conflict with the values of the community, and (3) actions that will be taken if comments, posts, and so on violate those values.

Values of the Community

As with anything in social media, the goal of the brand should be to inspire and engage—not dictate. With that in view, it is important that the beginning of a social media community policy focuses on what the purpose of the community is and how it can be accomplished. For example, remind people that, every day, thousands of users are having conversations about mutual interests that engage, connect, and inform. Next, clarify the vision for the brand's platform and how that vision will enhance and expand the conversations that are meaningful to the community. For example, the brand may identify that the purpose of the Twitter account is to provide answers and resources for the brand community. Perhaps the value of the Facebook page is to provide a community where brand advocates can connect, share stories, and provide feedback for the brand. Whatever the goal is, it should be identified for users. Then, connect how that goal can be achieved with specific platform behaviors. For example, the brand might identify that, because the specific social site is a place to share stories, users are welcome to share their experiences and feedback. It would also be good to note that the brand might be unable to respond to each and every post owing to the volume, but that the brand values the conversations and wants the platform to be a place where that type of feedback takes place. There are a number of strong examples of social media user policies available online for easy reference.

Types of Behavior that May Inhibit the Values

The next area to address in a user policy concerns the kinds of actions that may inhibit the values and purpose of the online community. In other words, are there certain kinds of engagement that the brand would delete if they are found in places such as comments on Facebook posts or on a YouTube channel? Comments may include such things as racial slurs, explicit or inappropriate language, or personal threats against other users. Identify the *exact* kinds of behaviors that are not appropriate and why those behaviors directly conflict with the platform's values and purpose. Ultimately, the focus of a community policy, also sometimes called a social media user policy, is to foster a strong environment within the social media platform. If community members are threatening that goal, they need to understand how their behavior is harmful and why it does not support the values of the community. A great example can be seen in the Mayo Clinic's participation guidelines.[20] After establishing some basics about the platforms and encouraging participation in the online conversations, the Mayo Clinic says: "We also expect a basic level of civility; disagreements are fine, but mutual respect is a must, and profanity or abusive language are out-of-bounds."[21] The idea is that, while conversation is encouraged, there are certain behaviors that would actually limit the overall communication climate of the online community.

Consequences of Behavior

Finally, specify how the organization will respond when behaviors do not foster the values of the community. Be very clear in this section. The reason is that it allows everyone to be on the same page if the brand does, in fact, end up needing to delete comments, block users, or report content. Having a policy in place early means that, if the brand has to respond to content in one of these ways, the organization cannot be accused of censoring or being biased against certain views. Rather, it will be clear to everyone in the social media community that, from the very beginning, the organization had set values, identified behaviors that support those values and specific behaviors that are not appropriate on the social media platforms, and set responses to inappropriate behaviors.

EXPERT INSIGHT

Matt Prince

What do you think is one hallmark competency social media professionals need to succeed?

Being a storyteller. This is one of the most powerful aspects to any brand and/or individual. Fundamental human behavior has not changed when it comes to marketing, but the way we do it has. Keeping that in mind is key to the underlying importance of connecting on an emotional level and doing it in an authentic way.

What role do brand persona and tone play in developing a social media campaign for a brand?

Good social media campaigns have a developed voice, while great social media campaigns incorporate tone. Voice defines your brand personality, while tone reflects your specific audience.

What are some ways brands can stay engaging and interesting on social media with so many organizations already launching incredible campaigns?

The most important way for brands to maintain interest is to stay relevant and true to their audience. Authenticity is the strongest currency a brand can have. Communications should be grounded in truth and differentiated by the emotional connection. It's important to remember choices by consumers are not made by function alone, but are driven by emotion.

What role should social media advertising play within a campaign?

Social platforms are making it harder and harder for brands to organically reach their audiences. Whether it's through sponsored posts or paid influencers, social media has established itself as a valuable business driver, and its increasing budgets are reflecting that.

Is it possible for organizations to develop employee social media policies that empower? If so, what are those key ingredients?

Companies no longer have a social media team of one or two—it's as big as their entire workforce. Each employee has the ability to share, leak, promote, defend, and deter your brand. Empowered employees can be a remarkable social tool for brands, but that isn't built in the social media policy. It's developed in the company culture and shared through social media.

What are the core elements of a strong social media campaign goal?

Measurability is key to any campaign and social media is no exception. Whether it's sales overnight or brand over time, all social campaigns should have clear objectives that are measurable.

What are the key ethical areas that brands should keep in mind on social media?

Policies and laws are quickly catching up to the dynamic economy of social media. Making sure brands are up to date on influencer promotions, legal repercussions, accuracy, credibility, and privacy is key to ensuring ethical social media success.

What strategies should brands keep in mind to effectively interact with influencers in social media campaigns?

Authenticity is one of the most important things to keep in mind when engaging with social media influencers. Set strict criteria that provide a thorough process to ensure those you're working with align with your brand and its values. Also, ensure you and your teams are up to speed on the constantly evolving world of FTC guidelines and disclosures when it comes to influencer engagement. There's a huge responsibility when it comes to how brands connect with consumers; influencers are an extension of that and add in their own complexity.

What do you see as the future trends brand leaders should be considering in social media?

The business and brand impact we saw with COVID-19 goes to show how quickly trends can shift when it comes to consumer behavior and how brands are adapting. Now more than ever it's important to offer more than just value, but showcase your values.

Today's generation, especially Generation Z, will stand behind brands that clearly and authentically stand for causes and put people ahead of profit.

Connect with Matt: @Matt_Prince; www.linkedin.com/in/mattprince1; www.facebook.com/matthewprince

Matt Prince is the PR + Newsroom Manager at Taco Bell

Employee Social Media Policies

Social media policies for employees are a growing area of focus for organizations. Employees can be a brand's biggest advocates and fans in the social world, and they should be empowered. However, organizations also need to provide some guidance for appropriate social media usage, particularly with the growing saturation of social media use in personal and professional contexts. It is recommended that employee social media policies are added to the employee handbook, incorporated into new employee training, and added into regular employee training meetings to remind the organization about the ways that social media impacts the workplace. A social media policy for employees should empower, build trust, and guide. This kind of policy, however, tends to be the most difficult to write. Beyond working to be sure that the organization is empowering and not stifling, it is also vital to work very closely with the legal team to make sure that the brand is not violating any employee rights.

National Labor Relations Act and Social Media

The National Labor Relations Act has several areas that apply directly to the types of policies an organization can have for social media use. For example, Section 7 says: "Employees have the right to unionize, to join together to advance their interests as employees, and to refrain from such activity. It is unlawful for an employer to interfere with, restrain, or coerce employees in the exercise of their rights."[22] Essentially, this means that communication by employees that deals with matters such as working conditions, their pay, and interest to advance themselves as employees in a joint effort is protected. Businesses and organizations cannot create social media policies that would discipline that kind of communication. In fact, some organizations that fired employees over social media communication that falls into this genre of content have been required to reinstate them. The National Relations Labor Board (NRLB) has also required organizations to adjust their policies because the requirements were overly broad. These kinds of cases are nothing new—in fact, the NRLB began reviewing and providing memos of cases dealing with employees and social media policies in 2011. It identified two main areas to keep in mind: "Employer policies should not be so sweeping that they prohibit the kinds of activity protected by federal labor law, such as the discussion of wages or working conditions among employees" and "an employee's comments on social media are generally not protected if they are mere gripes not made in relation to group activity among employees."[23]

Keeping in mind the protections of employees making concerted efforts in a group toward better working conditions, there are parameters that can be placed. For example, there are legal policies organizations have regarding harassing other employees, releasing proprietary information, and other kinds of behaviors that intersect with existing HR and legal requirements. On April 16, 2015, the NLRB concluded that a social media policy put in place by Landry's Inc. was legal and upheld employees' rights while also providing guidelines on how social media behaviors may influence the organization's existing legal policies. The policy provides an excellent example to consider for employee policy design. Part of the policy stated:

> While your free time is generally not subject to any restriction by the Company, the Company urges all employees not to post information regarding the Company, their jobs, or other employees which could lead to morale issues in the workplace or detrimentally affect the Company's business. This can be accomplished by always thinking before you post, being civil to others and their opinions, and not posting personal information about others unless you have received their permission. You are personally responsible for the content you publish on blogs, wikis, or any other form of social media. Be mindful that what you publish will be public for a long time. Be also mindful that if the Company receives a complaint from an employee about information you have posted about that employee, the Company may need to investigate that complaint to ensure that there has been no violation of the harassment policy or other Company policy. In the event there is such a complaint, you will be expected to cooperate in any investigation of that complaint, including providing access to the posts at issue.[24]

As has been illustrated, it is highly advisable to work closely with HR and the legal team to compose an employee social media policy. As the policy is shaped, keep in mind the goals: empower, build trust, and guide.

Empower

The first thing to do in a social media policy for employees is to empower them. Ideally, they will love where they work and want to share the great things in which they are involved. Coca-Cola, for example, created its social media principles to help employees be empowered. After noting that there are more than 150,000 associates in 200 companies that may be engaging in the social media world, Coca-Cola writes, "Have fun, but be smart. Use sound judgment and common sense, adhere to the Company's values, and follow the same Company policies that you follow in the offline world."[25] Leading by example, Coca-Cola then identifies the values that will guide the brand's social media interaction including: Transparency of communication, protection of privacy, respecting rights of others, responsible use of technology, and monitoring their behavior for appropriate records of interaction. Coca-Cola also has five key points for its employees on social media, including reminding them about policies that influence employee behavior, disclosing their work status if they are promoting information regarding the company on social media, and being conscientious about their personal social media use while at work.[26]

Another great example of an employee social media policy comes from Kodak's "Social Media Tips" document.[27] Kodak provided these tips to empower strong use of social media by organizations. It identifies ten rules that help guide its employees' use of social media in two general areas: reputation and privacy.[28] In addition to the guides for its employees, it also created details on each platform and some basic Q and A sections to assist users who may be less familiar with the platform. This is a great way to empower employees not only to understand *how* to share but also to know the functionality of the platforms themselves.

Build Trust

Social media policies for employees are not about a brand's attempt to control those who work for them, but rather about creating online communities that are positive experiences for everyone. It is important, therefore, that your employees recognize the intention behind a social media policy. To build trust, it is helpful to include the values of the organization itself on social media, perhaps even referencing the overall goal of why the organization is in social media in the first place. It can also help to remind people about what will *not* be required—for example, the organization should not require that employees become their managers' "friends" on Facebook or that all employees have to follow the brand on Instagram or Twitter.

In addition, create specific things to help encourage employees on social media—perhaps highlight the top "brand advocates" in an employee meeting or recognize outstanding contributions to community conversations in the social world. Employees are an incredibly valuable part of any organization—both in the online and offline worlds. Building trust requires not only that the organization empower employees to be brand ambassadors on behalf of the organization, but also that it recognize the employees' value and contribution to the online community in the same way that any other brand influencer would be recognized. It all goes back to being relational and human, not coercive and dictatorial.

Guide

The guide part of the social media plan helps employees to connect their workplace policies and how they may impact online interaction. For example, although there is a certain level of free speech allowed and concerted employee activity, disclosure of confidential information may also be harmful. If an organization is an educational institution, there are legal requirements established by the Federal Education Rights and Privacy Act (FERPA) that prohibit disclosure of student information. This Act applies online in the same way it would in person. To help, an organization may want to give examples in the employee guidelines that illustrate appropriate ways to celebrate and recognize students they work with and inappropriate ways that may violate FERPA. There may also be organizations that have products in development that require employees and contractors to sign non-disclosure documents. Again, employees need to understand how that non-disclosure agreement applies not just to in-person conversation settings, but online as well. For example, employees may not realize that their location can be disclosed when they upload to certain social media sites. It is helpful to remind them of that function if the organization has any work in undisclosed locations. These types of examples depend highly on the kind of organization. That is why it is helpful to be sure to customize an employee social media policy specifically for the organization itself.

Social Media Brand User Policy

The final type of user policy that needs to be in place is the social media policy for the individuals who will actually be running the brand's social media account. There are countless examples of brands that have had disasters with their own social media accounts. The goal of an internal social media brand user policy is to prevent these kinds of situations.

When creating a brand user policy, it is extremely important to have buy-in from all parties that will be involved. It is advisable to work with the groups together in creating the policy so that all needs are met and everyone involved supports the process. Within any organization, there will be many parties interested in getting information out via social media. There may be a marketing team, a sales team, a PR team, a community relations team, and management. The social media strategists will also likely need to consult with leadership, HR, and, at times, legal on what is posted. The brand user policy should account for the needs and requirements of all these groups.

Roles

An internal brand user policy should clearly identify roles. For example, who will be the main contact for social media questions that need to go to legal? When multiple groups need to get information onto social media channels, who is the lead on collecting those requests and getting back to the various groups? Will HR be involved with all posts that involve anything around an employee, or only specific ones? Working together with all parties on addressing these questions will allow everyone to feel comfortable with and committed to the social media process. It also will incorporate the expertise of each of these areas, which will enhance the effectiveness of the policy.

In addition to points of contact, a social media team also needs to identify the roles of content creation and delivery. Be clear about who is responsible for posting the content and on which channels, who will be responsible for monitoring and reporting on the content interaction, and who will be the lead social media person. The director or manager may be tasked with the strategy behind campaigns and content, allowing them to be the decision-maker when multiple requests come in simultaneously. It will be their responsibility to harmonize the needs of groups into one communication message on social media and to manage the other team members who are implementing the actual components of a campaign in the social media world.

Branding and Platforms

Although already identified, it is helpful to include a consolidated explanation of branding requirements and logo use in the social media brand user policy. It allows anyone who is involved with the brand's social media to understand what is and is not the appropriate application of colors, fonts, slogans, and trademarks. It is also important to incorporate the social media voice in this portion so that people understand the tone and approach to use when interacting on social media. In this document, list the platforms the brand is on and the usernames and vanity URLs associated with those accounts. The document should not, however, include passwords, as the social media director will want to restrict access to the individual directly responsible for posting on that platform. It is also advisable to include the content distribution strategy so that all users understand the genres of content and ultimate goals for the platforms. Although these sections will be abbreviated versions from the larger social media strategic plan, discussed above, it is helpful to reference each area for familiarity. Also provide access to the entire social media strategic plan to establish a more robust understanding of the organization's approach to social media, as well as the policies that guide activities when working for the brand's social media team.

White Papers

A final part that is highly recommended for a brand's social media user policy is white papers. These are often not included in the official social media brand user policy but can be kept in the same area. White papers can be created on each platform the brand is currently using, addressing current platform basics such as audience size and known functionality, proprietary information such as traditional performance and the audience profile, and any platform-specific guidelines such as partners on the platform used for cross-promotion, advertising policies, and so on. White papers can easily be updated as platforms change and develop. This is helpful, as updating the official social media brand user policy is much more involved and requires representatives from various departments. White papers, on the other hand, should be more fluid as they require constant updating to reflect platform specifications and requirements. The white papers do not incorporate approval processes, responsibilities, and other areas that require joint agreement. Rather, they simply provide guidance based on specific social media properties.

Crisis Plan

The approach to dealing with a social media crisis will be addressed later, but it is important to note that every social media team needs to have a crisis plan on file. This crisis plan should have a direct connection with the organization's overall crisis plan. Usually, the PR department will already have created a crisis plan. Meeting with them to discuss specific applications, roles, and approval processes for social media posting during a crisis is important. Key areas to identify include: how social media will be used during a crisis that was created outside of social media, and what roles or approval processes will involve the PR team for crises created as a result of something happening in social media. Often, crises arise external to social media and are caused as a result of something internal with the brand. Perhaps there were mass lay-offs, maybe a product caused harm to someone, or potentially a natural disaster impacted the brand. But, at other times, social media is the direct cause of the crisis itself, such as an employee posting an inappropriate picture or a customer's tweet about a negative experience going viral. A crisis plan will need to address both types of situations.

One thing to keep in mind when drafting the plan is having a process in place for approval of content during a crisis. Often, in a crisis, legal and HR may be involved. However, the nature of social media is that it moves extremely quickly, and so a brand cannot afford to simply be quiet for hours on end in a social context while teams go through numerous approval processes. In addition to understanding approval processes and time lines for specific crisis information that could be released during an event, a team must also develop a plan for the kinds of social responses that can be posted quickly without causing legal problems. It is helpful to consider creating pre-approved crisis posts that can be both customized for the specific situation and used to direct people to a set platform for updates, such as a company blog, which would be maintained by the PR team during a crisis. In addition, most organizations have a crisis team that will be called during any major event. Consider asking if the social media director may be part of the team, or if the social media strategist can have direct access to a key decision maker on the crisis response team who will be able to give approval for social media content.

If a crisis is caused as a result of social media, it is also helpful to have a key group of people in place that can be called on for advice and direction. These contacts and their roles and titles should be identified in the crisis plan. When a crisis erupts as a result of social media, brands need to respond quickly. If it was a rogue post accidentally sent from the company's personal profile, a situation that has become all too familiar, be sure to quickly remove the post and provide an explanation for what happened. If the crisis arises from a poor experience of a key stakeholder who has taken to social media to air their grievances, be sure to quickly engage with them and directly connect them with someone who can resolve the problem. Always make sure to follow up to ensure it was handled appropriately. Key considerations for engagement and response to social media crises will be addressed in Chapter 5.

At this point, a goal has been established for the purpose of social media, which relates to the organization's main vision; each platform has a vision statement associated with it, and SMART, outcome-based objectives have been created; all the brand profiles are optimized; and the brand has a content distribution model and general content calendar outlined. It is now possible to create individual social media campaigns that support the larger role of social media in an organization.

SOCIAL MEDIA CAMPAIGN DESIGN

Each individual campaign will have elements similar to the larger social media strategic plan. A social media campaign allows an organization to strategically design a shorter-term engagement plan around specific topics on social media. The creation of a social media strategic plan will be the unifying and guiding parameter for all campaigns that are produced by an organization.

Developing Campaign Goal(s)

As with the strategic plan, a social media campaign goal will be the broad end purpose of the campaign. Unlike the strategic plan, however, the campaign's goal may be shorter-term in nature. For example, a campaign goal might be: "Be a leading choice for summer vacation destinations." Or perhaps it might be something along the lines of: "Be a top charity to donate and engage with during Giving Tuesday." Social media campaign goals directly relate to the organization's vision and, more specifically, to the social media strategic design goals. They are ultimately born out of the formative research collected in the listening phase. These goals may also have been identified from the SWOT analysis. For instance, an example of a SWOT application for a temp agency's goal on social media may have been that there is significant opportunity to engage with potential new hires via LinkedIn. That opportunity relates to the vision of the organization being accomplished (finding people to fill positions) and supports the social media goals (the organization's desire to take advantage of social media as a way of finding potential hires). As a result, it may be determined that there is a need to create a specific social media campaign that pursues this opportunity and it should take place between April and June in order to target new graduates. Remember, any goal for a social media campaign should be driven by data—not just reactions. Be sure to thoroughly review all areas of research and needs for an organization prior to establishing the social media campaign goal.

Audiences

After establishing a campaign goal, identify which audiences are most important to the success of this particular campaign. An organization may have a variety of primary and secondary audiences, and each campaign should be tailored to the most appropriate audience for the given goal. An audience can be defined as: "people who are somehow mutually involved or interdependent with particular organizations."[29] In this context, consider which audiences or platform communities are especially involved with the success of the given campaign goal. The audience analysis that was conducted during the listening stage is particularly helpful during this point. The analysis specifies information such as user demographics, key behaviors of certain stakeholders, and important communication background (such as other places the audience is receiving information, and how often). Be sure to clearly identify the values, opinions, beliefs, and behaviors of each audience and then select those that are most related to the success of the campaign goal. Create an audience profile for each of the key publics involved in the campaign. An easy way to create this kind of audience profile is to use PIPP: public, important segment, profile, priority.[30] An example of an audience profile chart can be seen in Figure 3.3. These audience profiles will help develop the rest of the social media campaign.

Public	Important Segment	Profile	Priority
College Students	Freshmen	Typically 17–18 years old; prefer Snapchat and Instagram as platforms; value entertainment on social channels.	Primary
Parents of College Students	Moms of Freshmen	Active on Pinterest and Facebook; value information on helping their students and resources for college funding.	Secondary

Figure 3.3 PIPP Chart for Audience Analysis

Campaign SMART Objectives

As with the strategic plan, create SMART outcome-based objectives for the campaign. These objectives must directly support the goal created for the campaign and be related to the specific audience or platform community that was identified in the audience analysis section. For most audiences, brands may have one specific objective. However, some campaigns necessitate multiple objectives for an audience in order to achieve a goal. If the audience is first identified and its profile is developed, the SMART objectives can be much more strategic and precise. This also provides a clearer understanding of who the audience is, what it values and wants from the organization, and what behaviors are typical. This information gives data to develop "achievable" and "relevant" goals that are appropriate for the campaign.

Finally, be sure each objective supports the goal. Sometimes, there are some fantastic social media objectives, but they do not lead to the goal being reached. Social media strategists should consider the following question: If each of these objectives is met, does that mean the goal has been reached? If the answer is yes, move forward with developing campaign strategies. If the answer is no, it is important to evaluate which objectives may need to be removed or refined, and whether there are additional objectives that should be added.

Strategies

With the goal, audiences, and objectives in place, it is now possible to move into the "what" stage of planning by creating strategies to achieve those campaign objectives. Strategies are defined as the "overall concept, approach, or general plan for the program designed to achieve an objective"[31] or the "how and why campaign components will achieve objectives."[32] Essentially, *strategies* are the ways or approaches in which a campaign will effectively work toward reaching objectives. For example, a strategy might be: "develop a photo contest to highlight the new product in use by fans." This is a concept that may lead to an objective being met. Another example could be, "launch a quarterly Twitter chat to provide thought leadership in education." The idea behind strategies is that they are *what* will be done as part of the campaign in order to achieve an objective. It is likely that there will be between three and five strategies for each objective, though that may vary depending on the campaign and specific needs. This is where creativity starts coming to life as strategists intentionally identify the kinds of activities and initiatives that would be beneficial in the campaign and required for the success of objectives.

Tactics

After the "what" of the campaign has been identified, the various parts to accomplish those strategies, also known as tactics, are needed. Tactics can be defined as "The nuts and bolts part of a plan."[33] *Tactics* are the specific activities and tasks that must be completed for a strategy to be fulfilled. List all the specific pieces and actions that need to happen in order to make a strategy successful. For example, one strategy from above identified a photo contest. In order to accomplish this, many tactics must be in place. Rules must be developed. Prizes must be identified and secured. Media and posts must be created for the specific platform that is hosting the contest. Each strategy can only be accomplished if specific *tactics* take place. Just like before, at the end of making the list of tactics, consider the following: "If all of these tactics happen, will that make the strategy successful?" If so, move forward. If not, it is time to reassess the tactics.

Key Messages

When key messages are created, the words and content must be based on the individual audiences to which the brand will be communicating. A *key message* is the core concept, or elevator pitch, that is used to develop other communication pieces. Think of one or two sentences that capture the heart of the campaign, designed with the brand persona,

Goal
• Broad, end-goal of the campaign.

Audience
• Key publics that are most crucial to the success of the campaign's goal.

Objective
• SMART, outcome based statement of what will be accomplished.
• Generally 3-5 in a campaign, but number adjusts based on the goal.

Strategies
• Roadmap for how the objectives will be achieved.
• Usually at least 2-3 per objective.

Tactics
• The actual activities or tasks to make strategies happen.

Figure 3.4 Social Media Campaign Elements

tone, and language in mind, and strategically match the unique needs and values of the audience that the campaign is designed to reach. For example, when crafting a key message to engage new moms in relation to a product that recently launched, a key message might be: "The [new product] is a safe and effective way to help you care for your child." When developing a key message, consider the following:"

- What does the audience value?
- What unique benefit does this brand, cause, product, service, or event offer in relation to the audience need?
- Which keywords or topics capture this issue?
- What would be most important in this topic for the audience to know?
- How would our brand persona and tone strategically articulate this concept?

After crafting a key message of one to two sentences for each audience in the campaign, it is time to develop a social media message map.

Message Map

A message map will guide the communications on social platforms. It can be defined as, "a framework used to create compelling, relevant messages for various audience segments and for organizational alignment"[34] or a "compass that guides all of your communications."[35] Essentially, it is a way to extrapolate how to communicate in meaningful ways with each audience. The word communication is a term derived from the Latin word *communis*, which means "common." This is applicable as common knowledge and experience lead to connections that intertwine communities. As a message map is developed, identify the commonalities, or mutual interests, between the brand and key audiences to make the connection through communication stronger.

First, when developing a social message map, create a guide for how to communicate the key messages in various settings. For example, perhaps there will be a key message for an audience followed by several longer, supporting messages that could be used to craft posts for various platforms such as Facebook, Twitter, and LinkedIn. Keep in mind that a message map is not a copy-and-paste place to put all social content. It is a place to model how to effectively communicate the key message in the various places for the campaign.

Second, consider creating supporting messages in ways that engage a variety of people, such as articulating key messages with facts, statistics, or logical points *(logos)*, using stories and anecdotes *(pathos)*, and

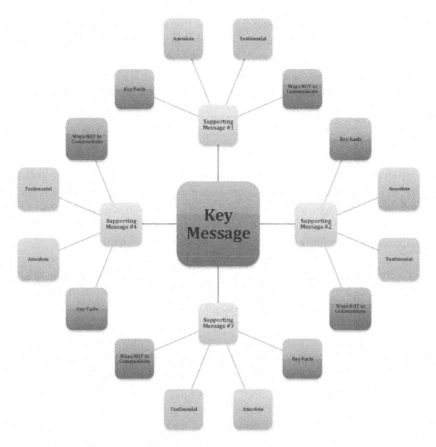

Figure 3.5 Social Media Message Map

testimonials or endorsements and success stories *(ethos)*. This will help the messages truly resonate with a variety of perspectives and brand community members. Also consider examples of how *not* to communicate the key message. This could be a secondary part of a social media message map to help provide specific guidelines and examples of ways that the brand persona or tone would not be applied to a concept.

Budget and Resources

A final component when designing a campaign is identifying the budgetary needs and resources that will be required to accomplish the campaign. Social media is not free. It takes staff hours, money for giveaways, time to create graphics, and any number of other elements to make it successful. A social media professional should be able to identify those needs and document them for the campaign. The first step is to create a list of all resources needed. This should include things such as social media interns (if applicable), staff time, creative design, and so on. Next, add a column beside each of these items and list their cost. This will calculate the total expenditures expected for the social media campaign. It is also important, however, to list income.

Calculating Potential Social Media Income

Although some argue that it is impossible to attribute income to social media, many businesses have found that it drives revenue in some remarkable ways. A vast amount of social media value comes in the form of development of stronger relationships, increases in the brand's credibility, and two-way dialogue. However, social media strategists should be able to harmonize the return on investment both in monetary, bottom-line terms as well as in some of the intangible dimensions of social media value. This section will focus on the first type of calculation: bottom-line dollars.

In order to calculate the potential income, review the campaign objectives. Each objective has a specific, measurable outcome. Coordinate with the marketing and IT department to ascertain the value of that outcome. For example, if one of the objectives was to have 25 sign-ups for a free giveaway in the month of May, ask the marketing team for the value of each name that is collected. In the budget, identify the value per name and multiply it by the 25 potential sign-ups identified in the SMART objective to determine the potential income associated with the objective. Some of the social actions merely contribute to larger organizational objectives. For example, it could be that the value of a sign-up for the free giveaway needs to be split between the SEO team, which is optimizing the landing page for the giveaway, and the social media team, which drives traffic to the page. The social media objective, therefore, is considered a secondary or complementary driver to the bottom-line conversions. It is helpful to discuss with the marketing department and management what percentage of value can be agreed upon to attribute to the social action so that a specific dollar amount can be assigned to the behavior objective in a campaign. When those values have been determined, subtract the total costs from any total income that can be attached to an objective to determine the monetary value of the campaign.

It is worth noting that much of social value is found in developing healthy relationships and communication with key stakeholders, not driving bottom-line business revenue. There is strong precedent in the PR and communication fields to establish objectives that are based on increasing credibility, developing trust, and influencing the predispositions of audiences. These interactions still provide value for the organization by benefitting the continued health of relationships that are key to the organization's success. If a social media objective relates to a category that is more PR or communications rather than marketing-specific, it may be helpful to add a note at the bottom of the budget regarding the non-monetary value that will be added to the organization through relationship efforts and the implications for the success of the organization as a result.

Finally, before concluding the discussion on the elements of strong social media strategic plans and campaign designs, consideration must be given to ethics in the social media context. With the increased use of social media by organizations, a new capacity to engage and maintain two-way communication has become the norm for brands. However, these social platforms have also posed ethical concerns that include activities such as ghost blogging, responses to negative comments online, organizations' transparency, privacy issues, and coercive communication efforts.[36] The heart of social media has always been about relationships—and that is why it is crucial for organizations to develop a strong ethical framework that supports social media activities. Each social media strategic plan and campaign should be reviewed to ensure it upholds the highest ethical standards for organizations engaging in social media.

SOCIAL MEDIA ETHICS

Organizations that use social media face a multitude of ethical questions: Some are significant, and others may seem rather small. Social media strategists need to be able to identify areas of ethical concern and apply an ethical framework to social media decision-making in order to best serve their organizations and the social media community. Brian Solis explains the concept like this:

> At its very core, social media is not about technology, it's about people. Connections, emotions, expression become the souls and personalities of online communities. The ties that bind them together are relationships. Without value, mutual benefits, the quality of the relationship erodes.[37]

A core commitment to the well-being of the relationships developed in social media should be a primary ethics consideration for organizations in social spaces. In order to accomplish this commitment to relationships and ethics, many suggest using the "ethics of care" principles when interacting in social media. This can be defined as "doing what is right using the principles of care and concern."[38] Stoker and Walton[39] suggest that, "The ethic of care moves beyond thinking about the relationship in terms of organizational or personal rights and places an emphasis on relationships and an organization's responsibility to relationships created under its care."[40] In other words, "the ethic of care's focus on interdependence, mutuality and reciprocity mirrors our perspective on public relations … We cannot choose to ignore a relationship with a stakeholder simply because it is not important to us."[41] *Ethics of care* is when decisions and interactions are guided by a deep commitment to the inherent value of relationships and the responsibility to protect those relationships as the primary guide for the brand. To provide a framework to approach social media campaigns with an ethic of care, this chapter will explore several key considerations for social media strategists.

Defining Ethics

In order to understand a proper application of ethical approaches to social media, one must first understand what is meant by the concept of ethics. Scott Rae,[42] a well-known ethicist and researcher, points out that often there is confusion between morality and ethics:

> Most people use the terms morality and ethics interchangeably. Technically, morality refers to the actual content of right and wrong, and ethics refers to the process of determining right and wrong. In other words, morality deals with moral *knowledge* and ethics with moral reasoning. Thus, ethics is both an art and a science. It does involve some precision like the sciences, but like art, it is an inexact and sometimes intuitive discipline. Morality is the end result of ethical deliberation, the substance of right and wrong.[43]

Ethics, then, involve determining a course of proper behavior based on existing standards, not simply reacting to a tense moment in social media. Brian Solis suggests that, "without a strong ethical foundation, you unintentionally make perilous decisions driven by what's right … right now, rather than what's truly right."[44] In other words, ethics help identify right actions by what we should do and wrong actions by what we should not do.[45] But the question still remains of what standards can help guide the process of determining proper behavior and inappropriate behavior. In order to address this, there are several ethical principles that social media professionals can use as they develop campaigns.

The first principle stems from the idea that ethics involve making decisions that can be justified to another person, not just to the brand.

This is what Bok[46] would call "public justification."[47] Essentially, the "test of publicity"[48] involves being capable of justifying, to a reasonable audience, that the communication was ethical.[49] Rather than relying on a justification that can fall down an ethically slippery slope when only the organization's goals are considered, social media professionals should consider every social media post through the lens of how the public would perceive the interaction. This consideration should be based on a fierce commitment to protecting and sustaining relationships, not to reaching bottom-line goals for a company. For example, ethically, organizations should disclose when employees or professionals are being paid to endorse the brand online. Otherwise, it is a deceptive practice, because the social community is unaware of the financial incentive associated with the content posted.

Ethics will come into play on a daily basis—sometimes forcing social media teams to make significant decisions, and other times surfacing in the seemingly typical interactions that happen when responding to tweets, comments, and mentions. "Many decisions you will make on a day-to-day basis involve questions of right and wrong, some of which may have easy answers but are difficult to carry out. Ethics provide the basis on which you make those decisions."[50] A key component of the basis for making ethical decisions in social media is understanding of the goal and purpose of *social* media: relationships.

Dialogic Communication Ethic

As previously identified, a key component of organizations' social media initiatives is the development of relationships with their online communities. Although social media can be used to support overall business objectives and, at times, yields direct business profits, it often is used to support the long-term value of strong relationships with key audiences. It is helpful, therefore, to examine historical approaches to relationship building and theories that would apply to social media, in order to create an ethical schema for social media professionals.

Grunig and Hunt[51] proposed four models for how PR processes, or the act of building mutually beneficial relationships, have been practiced throughout history. They conclude that a two-way symmetrical model is the best approach, as it "uses research to facilitate understanding and communication rather than to identify messages most likely to motivate or persuade publics. In the symmetrical model, understanding is the principal objective of PR rather than persuasion."[52] The idea of mutual understanding and communication fits perfectly into the core purpose of social media. Thus, using a two-way symmetrical theory to analyze social media communication is important. In addition, using a two-way symmetrical theory for relationship building also allows for a co-creational perspective of communication, which is in line with the idea previously addressed of social media communities being composed of "prosumers" not consumers. Botan and Taylor[53] point out that, "the co-creational perspective sees publics as co-creators of meaning and communication as to what makes it possible to agree to shared meanings, interpretations and goals."[54] Social media is uniquely designed to support this model of relationship building, being contingent on the public and organizations interacting to pursue mutual understanding by co-creating the conversation within the social environment. It is a two-way, joint dialogue around a conversation of mutual interest. The commitment to dialogue, which should be "ethical, honest, forthright and honest,"[55] is what gives dialogic communication ethics a foundation to be applied in social media.

Dialogic communication can be defined as "any negotiated exchange of ideas and opinions."[56] In other words, when organizations develop strategic plans to engage in conversation with online communities, a dialogic communication approach is being used. However, for authentic dialogic communication to occur, a two-way process must happen: Online communities and organizations interact, rather than organizations just pushing content. Essentially, "this requires that both parties are willing to be open and listen to the other even if there is disagreement and the communication should be focused on intersubjectivity."[57] The focus on this authentic, two-way dialogic communication should guide strategies in social media campaigns. The focus needs to remain on the conversation and relationship, not just publicity for brand messages. Kent and Taylor[58] suggest that,

> for a dialogic relationship to exist, parties must view communicating with each other as the goal of a relationship. Communication should not be a means to an end, but rather, as Kant's Categorical Imperative suggested, communication should be an end in itself.[59]

An interesting challenge that brands are facing, however, is the presence of echo chambers online. Over the last several years, fake news has grown rapidly and caused a growing concern about echo chambers.[60] Echo chambers can be understood as "ways that social media (the chamber) allows users to isolate themselves into conversations that only verify (echo) ideas they already believe."[61] As people continue to insulate themselves in conversations only with others online who repeat and enforce existing ideas, it becomes challenging for individuals (or brands) to enter a conversation unless they also repeat the same ideas. This is a very important factor for organizations to consider, particularly as social media strategists create campaigns designed to engage *new* people in a brand community.

A commitment to dialogue is particularly helpful when trying to break out of echo chambers in social media. While, traditionally, organizations have more power and voice than the average person in the public, social media helps equalize the communication environment. It facilitates a one-to-one engagement that allows the social media dialogue in a brand community to be "participatory, collaborative, personal, and simultaneously communal, thus allowing organizations to engage publics in constant conversations."[62] Through these constant conversations, people move to being "co-creators of meaning and communication."[63] Although echo chambers potentially insulate individuals from outside conversations, organizations that are committed to dialogue open the door to engaging these stakeholders by creating an environment that invites interaction from the user in order to create conversations together (rather than to simply "receive" a message from the brand). This invitation to collaboration has the potential to draw people out of echo chambers as they move toward an opportunity to share ideas, opinions, and perspectives. Particularly in the context of an individual connecting with a brand or brand community, this type of opportunity is appealing as it can feel empowering for someone to have their voice join conversations that have more amplification or participants in an online environment.

Whether seeking to break through echo chambers or simply designing a campaign that is for an existing audience, it is critical that all communication maintains ethical standards. In order to understand what it would look like to make ethical decisions based on communication itself, rather than as a tactic to force a certain behavior, Baker and Martinson[64] proposed a five-step process: TARES.

The TARES Ethics Model

Baker and Martinson[65] suggest that there are five principles that can help guide communication efforts. These five duties are: truthfulness of the message, authenticity of the organization, respect for the people being communicated with, equity of the message and social responsibility.[66]

Figure 3.6 TARES Ethical Test

Truthfulness of the Message

The concept of truthfulness within the TARES test incorporates a broad approach to accurate information. As previously mentioned, trust is a cornerstone in relationships. When it is harmed, the value of the relationship is diminished. Bok[67] went so far as to describe the value of truthfulness in relationships by saying "trust is a social good to be protected."[68] In other words, truthfulness in the TARES test goes beyond simply sharing literal truth and to the heart of the idea of trust: Does the information provided give transparent content, not designed to deceive, allowing individuals to make informed decisions. In an effort to further define what "transparent" messages would include, Rawlins[69] suggests that transparent means:

> The deliberate attempt to make available all legally releasable information—whether positive or negative in nature—in a manner that is accurate, timely, balanced, and unequivocal, for the purpose of enhancing the reasoning ability of publics and holding organizations accountable for their actions, policies and practices.[70]

For communication in social media to pass the truthful principle in TARES, it must not only be accurate but also be transparent, providing complete information that is capable of allowing publics to make the most informed decision and choice possible, rather than attempting to hide, remove, or limit information that may be less than positive for the organization. Bok[71] suggested that, when information is intentionally left out of communication with a public, it is a harmful act against people, similar to violence, as it inhibits their ability to make informed choices "by preventing people from adequately understanding a threatening situation, from seeing the relevant alternatives clearly, from assessing the consequences of each, and from arriving at preferences with respect to them."[72] With this in view, truthful communication is more than just putting messages that are accurate on social media. It involves providing complete and transparent information that gives audiences all the information available to make an informed decision.

Authenticity

Authenticity of communication in an organization requires that there is a commitment to personal responsibility and a deep concern for the value of others.[73] In other words, "The Principle of Authenticity requires persuaders to evaluate the motivations, intentions, and attitudes that drive their persuasive activities, and to act nobly."[74] In addition, the concept of authenticity requires genuineness and sincerity when interacting in relationships. It is important to position a brand appropriately and engage in social media around topics of mutual interest, but this must come from a communication virtue that focuses on the genuine belief that the organization makes a positive contribution to the online community. While social media teams fiercely represent the organizations that they serve, they also have a deep commitment and dedication to the good of their online communities. Balancing the needs of the organization with the needs of the online community is part of being authentic.

Respect

This principle requires that the brand's communication and actions on social media illustrate that the brand recognizes that each community member is "worthy of dignity, that they not violate their rights, interests, and well-being for raw self-interest or purely client-serving purposes."[75] In other words, it should be clear that the people with whom the organization has relationships are incredibly valuable, simply because they are real people. Jaksa and Pritchard[76] argue that people "should not be treated merely as a means to an end; they are to be respected as ends in themselves. Human beings are 'beyond price.'"[77] This principle is a cornerstone for the TARES model as it is the motivation that informs the other tenets—the inherent dignity and value of each person.

Equity

The concept of equity is that all parties involved in the communication will be treated fairly. The idea is to consider the other person and identify if they are being taken advantage of or being coerced owing to the form of communication. The goal is that "the interests of some are not sacrificed to the arbitrary advantages held by others,"[78] such as organizations who hold a great deal of power using propaganda on social media to take advantage of a situation. Each time a strategy or tactic is designed for social media, consider whether the primary audience of the strategy or tactic is being approached with equity, being given not only accurate and truthful information, but information presented in a legitimate way that is free of coercion, scare tactics, and sensationalism.

Social Responsibility

The concept behind the social responsibility tenet is that organizations have a duty to the good of society at large. This means that organizations cannot ethically be promoting causes, services, products, or events that harm the common good as that would not meet the TARES test.

The TARES model is composed of "interrelated moral safeguards" with principles that are "mutually supporting and validating."[79] As social media professionals attempt to design strategic campaigns, it is crucial that each post, tactic, strategy, and objective is reviewed through an ethical lens in order that the well-being of the relationships in social media and, ultimately, the good of each individual person in the social media community are protected. Ethical decisions should be informed by remembering the core purpose of social media: To engage in conversations with real people who have incredible value just by being human.

KEY CONCEPT SNAPSHOT

1. Before developing social media campaigns, brands need a strategic social media plan that will be the guiding framework for all their campaigns and initiatives in social media.
2. Social media is about people. Every interaction a brand has in social media should be grounded in ethical consideration for the value and worth of people.
3. When developing policies and procedures for social media, organizations should seek to build trust and inspire—not control.
4. Ultimately, each component of a social media campaign is developed from a strong research base and supports the overall vision of the organization's social media plan.

NOTES

1   Broom & Sha, 2013, p. 270.
2   Sorokina, 2014.
3   2014, para. 6.
4   Sorokina, 2014, para. 8.
5   para. 14.
6   Broom & Sha, 2013, p. 270.
7   2015.
8   "Social Search," para. 1.

9   Newberry & Lepage (2020) "How to create a social media strategy in 8 easy steps"
10   Newberry & Lepage (2020) "How to create a social media strategy in 8 easy steps"
11   2010.
12   para. 7.
13   Solis, 2010.
14   2011.
15   para. 2.
16   Schwab, 2015, "Tone."
17   Armstrong, 2011.
18   2015.
19   "language."
20   n.d.
21   para. 2.
22   National Labor Relations Board, n.d.a, "Interfering with Employee Rights," para. 1.
23   National Labor Relations Board, n.d.b, "The NLRB and Social Media," para. 6.
24   National Labor Relations Board, 2015, p. 3.
25   Coca-Cola, n.d., "Social Media Principles," para. 3.
26   "Online social media principles."
27   2010.
28   pp. 10–11.
29   Broom & Sha, 2013, p. 2.
30   Guth & Marsh, 2012, p. 240.
31   Broom & Sha, 2013, p. 273.
32   Wilcox & Cameron, 2009, p. 154.
33   Wilcox & Cameron, 2009, p. 156.
34   Covey, n.d., para. 1.
35   Melcrum, n.d., para. 2.
36   DiStaso & Bortree, 2014.
37   DiStaso & Bortree, 2014, p. xv.
38   McCorkindale, 2014, p. 67.
39   2009.
40   p. 11.
41   Coombs & Holladay, 2014, p. 40.
42   2009.
43   p. 15.
44   DiStaso & Bortree, 2014, p. xvi.
45   Fagothey, 1976, p. 2; Baker & Martinson, 2001, p. 155.
46   1989.
47   p. 97.
48   Baker & Martinson, 2001, p. 155.
49   Jaksa & Pritchard, 1994, p. 107.
50   Rae, 2009, p. 12.
51   1984.
52   Grunig & Grunig, 1992, p. 289.

53 2004.
54 pp. 651–652.
55 DiStaso, 2014, p. 36.
56 Kent & Taylor, 1998, p. 325.
57 DiStaso, 2014, p. 34.
58 1998.
59 p. 322.
60 Bakir & McStay, 2018.
61 Kim, 2019, p. 23.
62 Wang, Y. (2015) p. 7
63 Botan & Taylor, 2004, p. 652.
64 2001.
65 2001.
66 p. 159.
67 1989.
68 p. 26.
69 2009.
70 p. 75.
71 1989.
72 p. 26.
73 Golomb, 1995, p. 204; Baker & Martinson, 2001, p. 162.
74 Baker & Martinson, 2001, p. 162.
75 Baker & Martinson, 2001, p. 163.
76 1994.
77 p. 128.
78 Cahn & Markie, 1998, p. 621.
79 Baker & Martinson, 2001, p. 169.

SUGGESTED READING

Alpert, J. (2012). *The Mobile Marketing Revolution: How Your Brand Can Have a One-to-One Conversation with Everyone.* New York: McGraw-Hill.
Breakenridge, D. (2012). *Social Media and Public Relations: Eight New Practices for the PR Professional.* Upper Saddle River, NJ: FT Press.
DiStaso, M. & Bortree, D. (2014). *Ethical Practice of Social Media in Public Relations.* New York: Routledge.
Smith, M. & Kawasaki, G. (2011). *The New Relationship Marketing: How to Build a Large, Loyal, Profitable Network Using the Social Web.* Hoboken, NJ: John Wiley.

REFERENCES

Armstrong, P. (2011), March 10). "Social media and brands—tone is key." *Memeburn.* Retrieved from: https://memeburn.com/2011/03/social-media-and-brands-tone-is-key/

Baker, S. & Martinson, D.L. (2001). The TARES Test: Five Principles for Ethical Persuasion. *Journal of Mass Media Ethics*, 16(2–3), 148–175.

Bakir, V. & McStay, A. (2018). Fake News and the Economy of Emotions: Problems, Causes, Solutions. *Digital Journalism*, 6, 154–175.

Bok, S. (1989). *Lying: Moral Choice in Public and Private Life*. New York: Vintage.

Botan, C. H. & Taylor, M. (2004). Public Relations: State of the Field. *Journal of Communication*, 54(4), 645–661.

Broom, G. & Sha, B.-L. (2013). *Cutlip and Center's Effective Public Relations*. Boston: Pearson.

Cahn, S. & Markie, P. (1998). *Ethics, History, Theory, and Contemporary Issues*. New York: Oxford University Press.

Coca-Cola. (2009, December 15), "Online social media principles." Retrieved from: https://www.viralblog.com/wp-content/uploads/2010/01/TCCC-Online-Social-Media-Principles-12-2009.pdf

Coombs, W. T. & Holladay, S. J. (2014). *It's Not Just PR: Public Relations in Society*. Malden, MA: Blackwell.

Covey, W. (n.d.). "Introduction to message mapping for effective communication." *Trew Marketing*. Retrieved from: www.trewmarketing.com/smartmarketingblog/best-practices/introduction-to-message-mapping-for-effective-communication/#sthash.0nk0nkts.dpbs

DiStaso, M. (2014). "Bank of America's Facebook engagement challenges its claims of 'high ethical standards.'" In DiStaso, M. & Bortree, D. (Eds.) *Ethical Practice of Social Media in Public Relations*. New York: Routledge, 33–48.

DiStaso, M. & Bortree, D. (2014). *Ethical Practice of Social Media in Public Relations*. New York: Routledge.

Fagothey, A. (1976). *Right and Reason: Ethics in Theory and Practice*. St. Louis, MO: Mosby.

Golomb, J. (1995). *In Search of Authenticity: From Kierkegaard to Camus*. London: Routledge & Kegan Paul.

Grunig, J. E. & Grunig, L. A. (1992). "Models of Effective Communication" In Grunig, J. E. (Ed.) *Excellence in Public Relations and Communication Management: Contributions to Effective Organizations*. Hillsdale, NJ: Lawrence Erlbaum, 285–325.

Grunig, J. E. & Hunt, T. (1984). *Managing Public Relations*. New York: Holt, Rinehart & Winston.

Guth, D. & Marsh, C. (2012). *Public Relations: A Values-Driven Approach*. Boston: Allyn & Bacon.

Jaksa, J. A. & Pritchard, M. S. (1994). *Communication Ethics: Methods of Analysis*. Belmont, CA: Wadsworth.

Kent, M. L. & Taylor, M. (1998). Building Dialogic Relationship through the World Wide Web. *Public Relations Review*, 24(3), 321–334.

Kim, C. M. (2019). Virtues in Public Relations Education. *Teaching Journalism & Mass Communication*, 9(2), 22–33.

Kodak. (2010). "Social media tips." *Kodak.com*. Retrieved from: www.kodak.com/US/images/en/corp/aboutKodak/onlineToday/Social_Media_10_7aSP.pdf

Mayo Clinic. (n.d.). "About sharing Mayo Clinic." *Mayo Clinic*. Retrieved from: http://sharing.mayoclinic.org/about-sharing-mayo-clinic/

McCorkindale, T. (2014). "Private conversations on public forums: How organizations are strategically monitoring conversations and engaging stakeholders on social media sites." In DiStaso, M. & Bortree, D. (Eds.) *Ethical Practice of Social Media in Public Relations*. New York: Routledge, 65–81.

Melcrum. (n.d.). "Developing a message map." *Melcrum.com*. Retrieved from: www.melcrum.com/research/engage-employees-strategy-and-change/developing-message-map

National Labor Relations Board. (2015, April 16). *Laundry's Inc. and Its Wholly Owned Subsidiary Bubba Gump Shrimp Co. Restaurants, Inc. and Sophia Flores (Case 32-CA-118213.)* Washington, DC: US.

National Labor Relations Board. (n.d.a). "Interfering with employee rights (Section 7 & 8(a)(1))." NLRB.Gov. Retrieved from: www.nlrb.gov/rights-we-protect/whats-law/employers/interfering-employee-rights-section-7-8a1

National Labor Relations Board. (n.d.b). "The NLRB and social media." NLRB.Gov. Retrieved from: www.nlrb.gov/news-outreach/fact-sheets/nlrb-and-social-media

Newberry, C. & Lepage, E. (2020, May 27). "How to create a social media strategy in 8 easy steps (free template). *Hootsuite*. Retrieved from: https://blog.hootsuite.com/how-to-create-a-social-media-marketing-plan/

Patel, N. (2015, March 20). "Everything you need to know about the Google–Twitter partnership," *Search Engine Land*. Retrieved from: http://searchengineland.com/everything-need-know-google-twitter-partnership-216892

Rae, S. (2009). *Moral Choices: An Introduction to Ethics*. Grand Rapids, MI: Zondervan.

Rawlins, B. (2009). Give the Emperor a Mirror: Toward Developing a Stakeholder Measurement of Organizational Transparency. *Journal of Public Relations Research*, 21(1), 71–99.

Schwab, S. (2015, July 27). "Finding your brand voice." *Cracker Jack Marketing*. Retrieved from: www.crackerjackmarketing.com/blog/finding-your-brand-voice

Solis, B. (2010, June 14). "The social media style guide: 8 steps to creating a brand persona." *Brian Solis*. Retrieved from: www.briansolis.com/2010/06/the-social-media-style-guide-8-steps-to-creating-a-brand-persona-2/

Sorokina, O. (2014). "Save time on social media: One social media profile, one mission." *Hootsuite*. Retrieved from: http://blog.hootsuite.com/the-purpose-of-each-social-media-profile/

Stoker, K. & Walton, S. (2009). *Corporate Compassion in a Time of Downsizing: The Role of Public Relations in Cultivating and Maintain Corporate Alumni Social Networks*. Institute for Public Relations. Retrieved from: www.instituteforpr.org/topics/corporate-compassion

Wang, Y. (2015). Incorporating social media in public relations: A synthesis of social media-related public relations research. *Public Relations Journal*, 9(3), 2, 1-14.

Wilcox, D. & Cameron, G. (2009). *Public Relations: Strategies and Tactics*. Boston: Person/Allyn & Bacon.

CHAPTER 4

Step 2: Strategic Design Part B

Designing Creative Engagement in Brand Communities

> Meaningful engagement is a delicate art of intertwining winsome words with captivating visuals into the robust science of dynamic timing and communication theory in order to ignite significant connection and relationships within social media.

In order to ignite conversations and build relationships within a brand community, social media professionals need not only to understand the process to create a data-driven campaign design, but also to apply creative strategies to the campaign. The question that needs to be asked by an organization is how it will be able to engage its social media communities in a creative way. With the ever-growing prevalence of brands on social media, innovative campaigns that stand out from the rest are critical. This chapter explores some best practices and opportunities for creative engagement in social media.

As previously mentioned, tactics are the activities or specific initiatives that are used in order to reach an end goal. Wilcox and Cameron[1] explain tactics as "the specific activities that put each strategy into operation and help to achieve the stated objective. In the PR field, the implementation of various tactics is the most visible part of any plan."[2] Broom and Sha[3] further clarify the role of tactics by explaining that they "refer to the actual events, media and methods used to implement a strategy."[4] Tactics, then, would be identified as the actions and activities of organizations or brands that focus on achieving the overall goals, objectives, and strategies of the social media campaign.

To help frame the process of developing creative engagement pieces, this chapter will first highlight some hallmark approaches in social media and tactics that have been used to garner engagement in brand communities. These are helpful frameworks to contextualize a variety of campaigns that have either been successful or really failed to engage their audiences in authentic ways. However, simply understanding what brands have done previously is not enough to provide a complete paradigm that organizations can use to develop creative pieces for a strategic campaign. Instead of spending a great deal of time discussing *what* has been done before, the real question should be *why* creative engagement works. What is it about certain tactics that seems to ignite conversations, grow relationships, and enhance brand communities? To understand this, the chapter will also examine the role of brand credibility in developing and implementing campaigns. Credibility is crucial in sustaining and growing relationships with key stakeholders. Understanding the intersection of credibility with creative engagement, therefore, is critical. Finally, the chapter will conclude by looking at how brands can select the best kinds of strategies and tactics for their unique brand communities. Social media professionals who understand that creative tactics are not about simply repeating brilliant ideas others have had, but about strategically enhancing the organization's ability to engage in vibrant relationships will be able to truly leverage the innovative potential of social media in a campaign.

APPROACHES TO EFFECTIVE ENGAGEMENT IN SOCIAL MEDIA

A helpful strategy in understanding effective social media is to look at leaders in the sector of your organization and campaigns that have been identified for their effective engagement of brand communities. A best-practice to consider is to regularly review "top social media campaigns" for a particular time period (such as 2019, or first quarter of 2021, etc.). You will likely find that particular channels (such as Tik-Tok) will have different leading campaigns than competitors (such as Instagram). In order to provide a strategic perspective for brands that are looking to engage *across* platforms, social media leaders should not only understand the particular brands or campaigns that are effective, but should also understand the *trends* that have given rise to certain campaigns being effective.

Corporate Social Responsibility and Taking a Stand

The public increasingly believes in "obligations that organizations have to society to contribute to good and well-being, not just bottom-line profits."[5] In light of this, the idea of corporate social responsibility (CSR) has grown in prominence. This is true not just in for-profit organizations, where the idea of *corporate* social responsibility was created, but also in non-profits who have adopted the idea of social responsibility as a core component of their initiatives. At the same time, the way organizations contribute to social responsibility has shifted. Whereas historic models of CSR include things such as volunteering and donating of goods, the public now is also looking for brands to contribute their voice and influence to society. The Edelman Trust Barometer is an annual study that examines the factors and impact of trust around the globe on major institutions such as the media, businesses, non-profits, and governments. A trend that has increasingly been noted over recent years is the expectation that organizations, and particularly their leaders, will speak up on issues, create change, and guide their brands into a better future.

> CEOs are expected to lead from the front. Ninety-two percent of employees say CEOs should speak out on issues of the day, including retraining, the ethical use of technology and income inequality. Three-quarters of the general population believe CEOs should take the lead on change instead of waiting for government to impose it.[6]

Brands that engage with the idea of CSR and leading change in society using a campaign on social media have the opportunity to create a strong connection with their brand communities. After all, CSR is about contributing to good and society—and so, when done well, this is a powerful way for brands to illustrate their character, integrity, and value as an organization in our global world. For example, in 2017, during the Syrian refugee crisis, there was increasing racism against people from the non-white minority. In response, during the Super Bowl, Airbnb released a campaign with the hashtag #WeAccept which had a 30-second video address the value and role of diversity in society.[7] This is an excellent example of a time when a brand took a stand on societal issues and also issued a commitment to society (CSR) through tangible action:

> Airbnb's stance, combined with the quality of its message and timing resulted in #WeAccept becoming the most tweeted hashtag during Super Bowl LI, with over 33,000 tweets and 87 million earned impressions. The news was covered in 60 global news outlets, crediting Airbnb for not only making a bold statement, but for creating a strong call to action for its community to join in and help.[8]

Another powerful example of this type of approach comes from P&G's "Love over Bias" campaign that was launched during the 2017 Winter Olympics. This campaign received a Shorty Award in social media for social justice. Ellen DeGeneres also supported this campaign by sharing a clip of the campaign on her show. The campaign showcased how a mother's love can help overcome obstacles in life, such as biases, and then highlighted the stories of Olympians and their individual struggles. Audiences had an incredible reaction to this campaign, with mothers around the globe sharing their own stories of helping their children overcome bias. In addition:

> The Ellen release of the YouTube video gained over 170,000 views, and 3,700 likes, as well as a reported 300 million video views and more than five billion earned media impressions globally. But perhaps the best measure of how well this campaigned tracked, was the social sentiment.[9]

Newsjacking

When a brand leverages a national event or news in order to gain attention for its organization, it is called *newsjacking*. This is a term that was popularized by David Meerman Scott, who wrote a book with this title. To do this effectively, brands need to have a finger on the pulse of the news and what is trending, in addition to understanding how to effectively engage the conversation (there are plenty of examples of brands that attempted to newsjack only to see significant backlash). However, there are numerous examples of brands that have effectively engaged in newsjacking and increased their brand awareness, community conversations, and overall impact in social media. For example, in late 2019, as Christmas commercials were coming out with all the various gift ideas for people, Peloton released an ad where a man gave his wife a Peloton exercise bike. The backlash to this campaign was significant, with people reacting to gender stereotypes that were elevated through the campaign. Seeing the trending news and backlash to the ad, Aviation Gin hired the same actress from the original commercial to film a sequel, where she is no longer working out on a bike but rather on a girls' night out and drinking Aviation Gin. This newsjacking campaign elevated Aviation Gin's brand and resulted in "over 6.2 million YouTube views and 42 thousand retweets on Twitter."[10]

A second excellent example of newsjacking comes from Aeromexico, an airline that was particularly impacted during the Trump administration's plan to build a wall between the United States and Mexico, which gave rise to a national conversation on whether Americans even wanted to visit Mexico. In order to enter the conversation, Aeromexico provided free DNA tests to rural Americans. When initially asked if they would want to visit Mexico, participants were reluctant. However, after finding out their heritage with Mexican ties, participants were interested in traveling and learning more about Mexico. The company released videos using social media with a successful 1.6 billion impressions and 33.7% increase in ticket sales between the US and Mexico.[11]

Influencers: Macro and Micro

Using social media influencers (SMIs) as a key strategy in campaigns is a significant element of today's social media campaign planning. Influencers tend to be picked based on whether they have a large reach or following (such as celebrities) or they fill a particular niche that the brand aligns with and finds valuable (Schomer, 2019). Influencers can be on any social media platform, as they are simply individuals who are compensated by brands to share messages on their personal social media platforms. Instagram, however, is currently one of the most popular platforms, with nearly four out of every five brands choosing Instagram influencers for SMI campaigns.[12] It could be argued that SMI investments are a rising form of preferred advertising, allowing for a more customizable engagement of audiences based on connections with public figures or niche interests. A review of data between 2014 and 2019 shows that organizations were investing more in influencer marketing while traditional print (sometime called legacy) advertising decreased.[13]

When many people hear the term "influencer" what they usually are thinking of is a *mega* or *macro* influencer. As the world of SMI has grown, professionals working to leverage influencer relationships have created different categories of influencers. For example, some suggest the following: Mega influencers have more than 1 million followers; macro influencers have 200,000–900,000; midi influencers have 50,000–200,000; micro influencers have 10,000–50,000; and nano influencers have 800–10,000.[14] The reality is that a quick review of agencies and classifications of influencers will reveal deviations in the actual follower numbers (for example, some classify micro influencers as 1,000–10,000 where the above list has a recommendation of 10,000–50,000). In general, these are simply metrics that help clarify the reach and engagement of influencers. Although mega and macro influencers have a much larger reach, owing to their higher following, recent studies indicate that people actually engage and interact at a much higher rate with micro and nano influencers.[15]

Reports indicate that top Instagram influencers can earn nearly $1 million per post. On YouTube, a rising group of influencers are kid influencers, or children who do things like open toys, visit parks, and do other child-friendly activities online. Many of these children are now millionaires. LinkedIn boasts of nearly 90 million senior-level influencers, providing a niche type of influencer market that focuses on educational backgrounds and professional expertise (Influencer Marketing Hub, 2020).[16]

Although there are many successful SMI campaigns that have run, a growing concern has been about disclosure and trust. In the early days of SMIs, there were no regulations about disclosure of partnerships between brands and influencers. However, as the practice became pervasive, regulations began to be developed. In 2019, the Federal Trade Commission (FTC) issued explanations on partnerships that explained people needed to disclose:

> when you have any financial, employment, personal, or family relationship with a brand. Financial relationships aren't limited to money. Disclose the relationship if you got anything of value to mention a product. If a brand gives you free or discounted products or other perks and then you mention one of its products, make a disclosure even if you weren't asked to mention *that* product.[17]

In addition, the FTC explained that those who are compensated need to make it hard to miss, which is why influencers now use hashtags such as #Ad and #sponsored. This change has shifted the impact of influencers, as the public sees the interaction more as a direct advertisement rather than an interaction via social media. But studies indicate that people, particularly the under-30 demographic, still respond significantly to influencer marketing on social media.

Dark Social and Messaging

It would be nearly impossible to fully address effective engagement by brands without a conversation about privacy. There are numerous examples of ways that users' personal data and/or privacy have been breached thanks to profiles on social media, but one of the most prominent examples is from the scandal involving Facebook and Cambridge Analytica (CA). This high-profile situation where Facebook user data were scraped from profiles and shared without consent in order to improve targeting of political advertisements significantly impacted the confidence people had in the security of their personal data held by social media companies.[18] Although the situation occurred in 2016, it became popularly known in the following years with various news outlets covering the scandal and a documentary movie in 2019 which examined the situation. Prior to the CA situation gaining attention, people already had privacy concerns relating to social media. For example, in 2014, a survey found that 80% of users in America had concerns about organizations gathering their data on social media, and 64% of people believed that the government should be regulating this more.[19] Over the last several years, policies and legal processes have examined this issue. And, while all that has happened, social media strategists have seen a change in user behavior on social media—a move toward using dark social.

The term *dark social* was introduced by Alexis Madrigal in 2012 when he wrote an article for *The Atlantic* called "Dark Social: We Have the Whole History of the Web Wrong." The term can be defined as "when people share content through private channels such as instant messaging programs, messaging apps, and email."[20] The reason this is referred to as "dark" is that it is not in the public profile or main streams of content and thus it is hard to track using business analytics. For analytic programs, the data are "dark" since they cannot be directly seen or monitored, as public information is for many users. Typically, organizations use analytics to discover which channels (such as social channels) are driving the actions and behaviors of people. For example, did the Instagram campaign lead to sales? Did the YouTube campaign result in more volunteers? Did TikTok help get the petition signed? However, when the data are "dark," it is challenging to truly attribute this kind of information. Put simply, in analyses of data reports for this kind of information: "Dark social is essentially the traffic that gets lumped into direct traffic in your analytics platform but actually comes from untrackable referrals."[21] But the fascinating part of this is that, with the rise in people being concerned about their privacy and moving to sharing information in more private, one-to-one actions via functions such as Messenger, brands noticed another trend. People now prefer the private, one-to-one interaction with brands as a communication method. In fact, 64% of people would rather message a brand than call or email, which has led to more than 20 billion messages going between businesses and people via Facebook's Messenger each month (which only represents one social media message platform).[22] In early 2019, in the wake of the CA scandal, Mark Zuckerberg released what he termed "A Privacy-Focused Vision for Social Networking." In this statement, he acknowledged that private messages, stories, and small groups are the fastest growing sector of online communication methods. He also noted:

> People increasingly also want to connect privately in the digital equivalent of the living room. As I think about the future of the internet, I believe a privacy-focused communications platform will become even more important than today's open platforms. Privacy gives people the freedom to be themselves and connect more naturally, which is why we build social networks.[23]

Thus, the rise in privacy concerns, the shift to smaller and more personalized communication, and the increase in desire to connect via private messages with brands mean this: Brands now have at least three layers of communication to manage with each campaign. First, the public, general posts and content that are created. Second, the individual interaction with users in public-facing spaces on social media (such as when someone comments, shares, etc.). And third, brands need to engage in private, message-based social media with as much commitment and intentionality as when their interaction is publicly shared for the world to observe. But really, this is the heart of what social media has always been. It was designed and fostered through one-to-one connections. The rise of dark social and private messaging is not an obstacle, but an opportunity. It is one more place where brands can show that they are committed to dialogue, to people, and to authentic relationships.

These are just four emerging trends (at least, "emerging" at the writing of this second edition). But the reality is, new trends and approaches will consistently arise in social media both as platforms change functionality and as people change perspectives about how, when, and why brands should interact online. Effective leaders really should be tracking more than just winning campaigns on social platforms—rather, they should be analyzing the reason for success and looking for connecting data that provide insight into the values, opinions, beliefs, and behaviors that drive brand communities to engage, connect, and champion brands in social spaces.

ELEMENTS OF MEANINGFUL COMMUNICATION

Meaningful communication is a critical element to keep in mind throughout a campaign. After all, if the social media efforts do not effectively communicate and connect with a brand community, it does not really matter how creative or edgy it was supposed to be—it did not fulfill the objective. Social media campaigns need to be designed with people and relationships in mind. No matter what platform or campaign, there are certain common elements that are necessary in the development of creative campaign design pieces. One of the foremost skills that it is important to remember is *writing*.

Writing for Social Media

Although this book is not about writing for social media, and there are already a number of books dedicated to this vast topic, it is important to give it some focus owing to its value in a campaign. With the fast-paced environment of social media and the ever-shrinking length of written components, the need for strong writing is sometimes overlooked. This may be because there is an illusion that the ability to craft a well-written piece is not as crucial. Nothing, however, could be further from the truth! Every platform may have certain ways to write that break all grammar rules (#TBT, for example), but basic things such as a spell-check and grammar review are still important. And, beyond these basic checks, it is important to consider *what* to write and *how* to write it.

There are several approaches that can be helpful to brands determining what type of content to post. For example, Matt Prince,[24] the PR and newsroom manager at Taco Bell suggests the IFE IFE rule. Content should at minimum have two of the following qualities: interesting, funny, entertaining, intellectual, flattering, or embarrassing. (A point of clarification: Matt Prince identified embarrassing as the humanizing type of content people can relate to and laugh with, not the kind of content that leads to loss of credibility or trust.)

Another approach that can be helpful is from Mark Schaefer,[25] who uses RITE: relevant, interesting, timely, and entertaining. It all comes down to engaging communication. Brands must understand what type of content resonates with their audience and review any posts through those filters. If the brand is posting boring, uninteresting, or irrelevant content, the community will stop interacting, and the power of social media will be lost to the organization. It is all about being the kind of brand people *want* to interact with, respond to, and engage with. Writing for social media is absolutely an art that can be learned when keeping the purpose of social media in mind: relationships. Above all else, writing in social media compels brands to develop content designed for *people*—not for *publicity*.

The second element to effective communication is ensuring that the credibility, or trustworthiness and expertise, of the brand is strong in the publics' perception.

Writing for Social Media

IFE IFE Policy	RITE Review
• Interesting	• Relevant
• Funny	• Interesting
• Entertaining	• Timely
• Intellectual	• Entertaining
• Flattering	
• Embarrasing	

Figure 4.1 Approaches to Social Media Writing

Credible Engagement

Because social media is all about relationships and common interests, the credibility of a brand plays a significant role in social media engagement. *Social credibility* is essentially the publics' perception of a brand's expertise and trustworthiness illustrated by being authentic, transparent, and truthful in communication. Mark Schaefer[26] describes credibility as being a conduit through which social influence happens. When brands are credible in the eyes of the public, they are viewed as trustworthy experts, or authorities, in their industry. As this occurs, organizations are able to develop meaningful influence among their key publics and develop relationships within brand communities that are long term. But the real question is, what leads to this kind of authority? How is a brand able to develop trust? If it is such a crucial part of the success of relationships between publics and brands, it needs to be a prominent area of focus for social media. This all goes back to credibility.

History of Media Credibility

The concept of credibility has a long history in communication, marketing, and PR. One area of interest for scholars has been source credibility, which looks at specific individuals or organizations (the source) that are delivering the information and the publics' perception of the credibility of the individual or brand.[27] Another dimension of credibility studied is based not on the source, but on the medium itself through which the communication occurs. In other words, medium credibility studies examine specific platforms, such as television, newspapers, or the internet, to understand the publics' perception of credibility.[28]

Credibility, as a concept, is composed of multiple dimensions that are perceived and evaluated by the public when interacting. Essentially, these dimensions are factors that are considered to be influential and important in developing the perception of credibility. Some dimensions that have historically been considered to constitute credibility in both source and medium studies include trustworthiness, expertise, accuracy, completeness, fairness, believability, and community affiliation.

In addition to source and medium credibility and the dimensions contained within those concepts, scholars have also specifically looked at organizational credibility, particularly in corporate brands, and found that trustworthiness and expertise are especially important.[29] In examining how to develop effective campaigns in social media *for* organizations, this is particularly important to understand. Trustworthiness and expertise have long been the two hallmark pillars considered essential to credibility—applying them to the idea of organizational credibility in social media holds implications for the kinds of tactics and strategies that professionals select for campaigns. Simply put, in social media, which has a distinct focus on building relationships and two-way communication between a brand and its publics, credibility is critically tied to the effectiveness of relationship-building activities.[30]

EXPERT INSIGHT

Karen Sutherland

What do you think is one hallmark competency social media professionals need to succeed?

Adaptability. With social media, the only constant is change, so a social media professional must stay on top of changes to the platforms, business environment, and client and consumer needs.

What are some tips to write well for social media? It can seem challenging to create relational text while maintaining brand standards.

Knowing your audience is the absolute key to writing well on social media. It is essential to understand the stories and the language that will resonate deeply with the target audience to prompt the preferred action you are attempting to achieve. The best way to manage this is by thoroughly researching exactly who it is that you are trying to connect with and speaking only to them. When you try to write for everyone, you will not connect with anyone. Once you understand what works, you can craft copy that is optimized for the characteristics of each platform and incorporates key messages.

How can a brand determine which types of social media tactics would resonate most with their audience?

Again, audience research is key. This also involves reviewing social media performance data to understand what tactics have worked in the past so they can be further leveraged. Furthermore, research into current trends and case studies can help with this selection process too. It is also important to monitor how tactics are performing once they are live so that they can be fine-tuned to meet strategic goals if at first they are not performing as planned.

It can seem impossible to be an innovator in social media creativity with so many stellar campaigns out there. Do you have a strategy to help keep authentic creativity flowing instead of falling into a pattern of repeating others' successes?

The best campaigns tell a heartfelt story and make the audience feel connected to the people telling their story. Always coming back to quality storytelling is the key to keep creativity flowing. Making every campaign about people and their unique experiences is an extremely effective way to achieve this. The rest is only window-dressing.

How can brands create a social community where the people *within* the community are engaging with each other as well as the brand?

Communities usually evolve out of a common need. Rather than a brand trying to create a community about their products, it is much more effective to facilitate a space where a community can grow organically round the needs of its participants. For example, Nike discovered that, in Australia, its shoes were not the first choice of female runners. Rather than trying to create a community to try to sell its products, its research found that a common issue experienced by female runners was the fear of running alone at night. Nike then launched the *Nike—She Runs the Night* campaign and facilitated an online community of female runners who could run together and feel safe. This is the perfect example of a brand community evolving out of the needs of its participants.

What's your perspective on using contests within social media as part of a campaign?

They can be very effective when a brand is starting to build its presence as long as the people entering are from the brand's target audience. If not, the brand can end up with a heap of followers who are not prospective customers, and this will reduce the reach of content making it to the newsfeeds of its target audience.

What are the strategies to leverage influencers and how might those differ between macro and micro influencers?

Relevance, appropriateness, engagement, and budget are the key factors when working with influencers. It is much more effective to select an influencer who has a smaller following but a highly engaged audience than someone with millions of followers who rarely engage.

It is also essential to select an influencer based on their fit with the brand or product and check that they are appropriate for the target audience that a brand is trying to reach. The main reason for using influencers is to achieve increased exposure and endorsement of a brand or product with the audience most likely to be customers. Therefore, it is important for brands to do thorough research before building relationships with an influencer to make sure that they are the most appropriate choice.

How can a brand determine if getting on the newest and latest social media channel would be important for their strategies?

The most important thing is to be where a brand's target audience is. It can be a waste of time and resources to jump on a new platform if the people most likely to buy a brand's products (now or in the future) are not there. It is better to have a strong presence on two platforms that are used by most of the target audience than for a brand to spread itself too thin by trying to have a presence in too many places.

Connect with Karen: drkarensutherland.com; LinkedIn:/karenesutherland/; Facebook:/drkarensutherland; Twitter: @kesutherland777; Instagram: @kesutherland777; TikTok: @karen-sutherland; YouTube: Dr. Karen Sutherland

Dr Karen Sutherland is a social media and public relations educator, author researcher, and consultant with more than 20 years industry experience in marketing, public relations, and communication roles. Karen is the Program Coordinator and creator of the Bachelor of Communication (Social Media) degree at the University of the Sunshine Coast, Australia

New Media and Credibility

As can be seen from the above discussion, historically credibility was considered in a single context, such as being a source, medium, or organization. But, with the advent of new media, which seem to combine sources and platforms into a unique presentation of information to the public, Moriarty[31] suggested credibility should be viewed as a concept of both the source *and* medium. This is especially true in today's digital media environment, and particularly in the case of social media. In other words, brands are not *just* an organization or brand communicating on social media platforms—they are also viewed as possessing a *personality*[32] or being a source of the communication. In the world of social media, source credibility dimensions, such as trustworthiness, affinity, and authenticity, merge with medium dimensions such as fairness, believability, and accuracy. All these dimensions play a role in the publics' perception of a brand's credibility in social media, which ultimately holds the power to make or break key stakeholders' relationships with the brand.

It is of pivotal importance, therefore, that professionals use social media to communicate in ways that enhance and support the publics' perceptions of an organization's credibility in order to maintain and build relationships with audiences. Studies have found that there are, indeed, specific approaches that can increase the quality of relationships and credibility between publics and brands, particularly in the fluid environment of social media.[33]

Credible Approaches to Interaction

An organization's engagement approach, or methods used in social media, influences its perceived credibility and ultimately its ability to build trust and relationships. There are three main methods that brands can use to help bolster the publics' perception of their credibility: ones that highlight a brand's persona, ones that focus on conversation building, and ones that illustrate shared values. When used effectively, these three categories tend to build the credibility of an organization in the minds of brand communities.

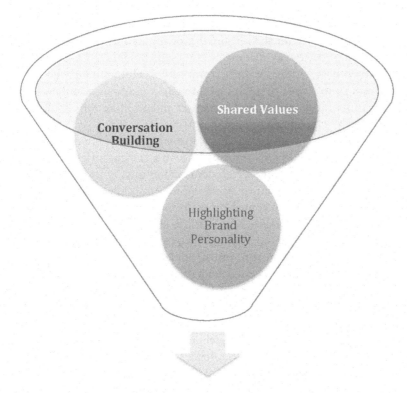

Building Credibilty

Figure 4.2 Methods for Building Brand Credibility

Highlighting Brand Personality

The first category of engagement includes specific actions or tactics that are designed to highlight a brand's personality. As discussed in the previous chapter, a brand's persona is particularly important in the world of social media. The concept of a brand's personality is often thought of as the "set of human characteristics associated with a brand."[34] Brands that approach social communication using this method of engagement tend to focus on enhancing the perception of their trustworthiness, expertise, and organizational reputation. These areas have a direct correlation to the personality of a brand, or the "set of human characteristics," as they are often associated with personhood or relationship.

The humanizing of the organization through this method is specifically designed to showcase a brand's personality and display the ways in which an organization is trustworthy to maintain relationships with people in the brand community. It can also demonstrate that the brand is an expert in a topic within the industry of the organization. All in all, the goal is to build the personality or reputation of the brand with publics in a positive way that encourages stakeholders to continue being active members of the brand community.[35] Humanizing the brand, showcasing the brand persona and personality, allows members of the brand community to form a connection and feel like they truly know the brand. It helps solidify the relationships.

A great example of showcasing personality and humanizing a brand to help build credible relationships in brand communities comes from Oreo. In 2013, Oreo made social media brand history by capitalizing on the blackout during the Super Bowl. Posting a simple image of an Oreo with the words "You can still dunk in the dark," the brand received more than 15,000 retweets in 14 hours, along with exceptional press coverage.[36] Since then, the brand has continued showcasing its fun personality while leveraging the power of social media across platforms. Despite the time that has passed since this campaign ran, it is still referenced as a model of quick responses and personalization for social media engagement. On Instagram, for example, creative photos are uploaded that highlight recipes and creative images of Oreos throughout various parts of someone's day. From celebrating events such as Elvis Presley Week by posting an Oreo in the shape of the head of Elvis to fun banter with brands such as Kit Kat and Taco Bell, the brand's persona and character can be felt in the images, tone, and media on any social media platform. It is warm, fun, and relaxed. This consistent approach to the brand's persona has built credibility in the brand community, making it one that is incredibly interactive.

While highlighting a brand's persona, it is also important to keep in mind that credibility is not a permanent state of being for organizations, but is rather reliant on the *perceptions* of the public with which they interact.[37] Perception truly dictates reality for brand relationships. That is why consistency is so important—perceptions can change immediately if a brand interacts in a way that seems counter to the usual brand persona or character. In light of this, it is important to consider how a brand community will perceive certain actions or behaviors in social media. Each time a brand interacts on social media, it adds to the perception of the brand's personality or character. Every post, image, video, and comment contributes to what the public believes the brand is like. As illustrated by Oreo, using social media profiles to intentionally highlight the brand persona is one approach that helps organizations connect their brand persona with the publics' perception of the organization. Appearance on social media platforms allows organizations to add their unique flavor to the social media environment in a professional and credible way, while also tying into existing ideas that publics have regarding what the brand should look like based on the reputation and previous interactions they have had with the brand. Just like an individual's profile presence reveals their personality, interests, and character traits, a brand's official profile pages serve the same purpose. Be sure that the branding is consistent, and that the brand persona and personality shine through in every area of the social media profiles.

Appearance or character, however, is not the only component that needs to be considered in social media credibility. Poster[38] suggests that social media activity is more like face-to-face interaction than mass media such as television or print publication, since social media allows for instant feedback and personal interaction. Although this is true, social media also still has dimensions and characteristics similar to other media that are not present in person-to-person interactions. It is both a *source* and a *medium*. This unique blend in social media, therefore, requires consideration of not only the source, which would be the brand's persona and the organization itself, but also the medium, which would be the consumption of information through an actual social media platform. This aligns with many scholars' claims, such as Moriarty's,[39] who argues that credibility is a multifaceted concept that cannot simply be confined to *either* a source *or* a medium. It is important, therefore, to understand what dimensions influence perceptions of credibility not only in sources, but also in the way people perceive information through mediated communication, such as social media. This is why the second area for enhancing credibility in social media, conversation building, is so crucial. It connects the consideration of credibility not only to the source (appearance and character) but also to the medium through which communication within a social media campaign is occurring.

Conversation Building

This genre of engagement has the focus of contributing to, interacting with, and responding to communication from publics through social media in ways that build conversations. Although writing is a crucial part of meaningful communication, the *approach* to the message is also very important, particularly as it influences the perception of a brand's credibility. Four key areas to consider are engagement speed, brand accessibility, transparency, and individualized communication.

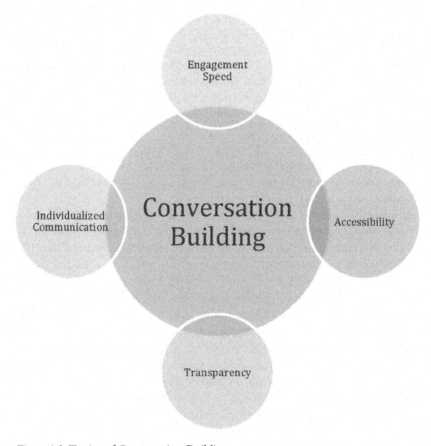

Figure 4.3 Tactics of Conversation Building

Engagement speed: The first approach to conversation building that has a significant influence on a brand's credibility is the speed at which it interacts and engages. Studies have identified that engagement speed is a particularly important element of brand credibility in social media owing to the very nature of the platforms. Because social media is a place where brand communities anticipate dialogue and engagement, the value of interaction has grown exceptionally in the eyes of the public. For example, a recent Edelman study[40] found that 93% of the public wanted dialogue as a key component in the relationships they had with brands. This desire is indicative of the fact that many organizations now have the capacity to offer interactive communication with their publics through social media and the publics *expect* that organizations are engaging in dialogue with brand communities. When this engagement is lacking, slow, or diminished, publics may assume that the brand is either uninterested in the larger community or hiding something. This falls in line with what Scott and Scott[41] address when they focus on some changes based on the public expectation of organizational accessibility and interactivity.

The expectation of relational and interactive components of brand communication is partly why mobile marketing has been so successful—it has formed an interactive, responsive, two-way communication between brands and publics.[42] The pace of social media and mobile and digital technology have caused publics to expect brands to be swift in responding to comments, questions, or complaints and active in communicating information, and for them to invite publics into their decision-making process.[43] Brands' rapid responses and updates serve as indicators to the public that the platform is the official organizational presence on the social media sites, that information found on the social site is accurate, and that the brand community is monitored and engaged with actively by the organization.[44]

Accessibility and prosumers: The second method of conversation building that directly impacts a brand's credibility is the accessibility to decision-making that organizations provide for the public. Rather than functioning in the paradigm of historical approaches to marketing and PR, Smith[45] suggests that technology has revolutionized the way organizations need to function in today's technologically savvy, digital-native world. Essentially, brands should move into the social business paradigm previously discussed. Smith's findings indicate that greater engagement with publics, more accessibility to information and decision-making, and responding to interaction in the digital world are all pivotal to the image and, ultimately, credibility of brands. Today's public expects organizations to incorporate their feedback and allow participation in organizational decisions. Especially in the age of social media, the expectation of having an active voice in organizational decisions is growing among publics.[46] It is apparent that publics are not interested in only hearing from a brand or simply being a consumer, but rather want to help produce. As prosumers, they want to have a direct say in the focus, objectives, and future of organizations or brands.

Transparency: The third method of conversation building, which influences a brand's credibility, is transparency in communication. Expectations of transparency have been identified as core components of the perception of the credibility of brands.[47] *Transparency* in the world of social media relates to brands providing timely, accurate, complete, and fair information on a variety of organizational aspects, including fundraising structures and processes; updates on investigations and causes during crises; and details on leadership transitions, employee activity, and organizational initiatives. People expect that a brand will disclose information about its organization in authentic, truthful, accurate, and complete ways, and there are plenty of examples that illustrate the danger brands face when deceiving the public on social media. One "textbook" example of this comes from 2009 when Honda originally set up a Facebook page to highlight a new vehicle that was being launched. Eddie Okubo posted to the page talking about how much he liked the new vehicle. What was quickly discovered, however, was that Eddie was Honda's manager of product planning. Since he did not disclose that he worked for Honda, but rather posted in the same way that any other member of the brand community might, there was a public backlash regarding the transparency of the endorsement, and Honda's social media interaction was called into question. Although Honda did end up removing Eddie's post, citing that the company had an employee policy to disclose connections to Honda when posting on social media regarding Honda products, it was a little too late. Honda's credibility in the eyes of the social media community was already damaged.[48]

Individualized communication: The fourth method of conversation building that strongly influences credibility in social media is individualized communication. A reality of the dynamic nature of digital communication between brands and publics is that they cannot be mechanized, or created and sent without additional interaction. Rather, social media requires interactions that are similar to a face-to-face conversation— dynamic, responsive, and unscripted.[49] Not surprisingly, studies find that being personable on social media increases the quality of relationships and credibility between publics and organizations.[50] In line with this, Smith and Kawasaki[51] stress that relationships, engagement, and dialogue are essential to publics' perceptions of organizations through social media. From customizing responses to individual questions and comments to highlighting prominent individuals within key publics, organizations can utilize personal interaction, or conversation building, in order to increase relationships and build credibility with publics.[52] Although individualized interaction seems like a given, particularly on a platform designed for relationships and communication, there are many brands that have faced challenges to their credibility owing to mechanized communication. An unfortunate illustration that is often used as an example of what not to do on social media comes from Domino's Pizza when a customer posted on Facebook about how much she enjoyed the pizza she had received. The brand's response caused quite a reaction: "So sorry about that! Please share some additional information with us at bit.ly/dpz_care and please mention reference# 1409193 so we can have this addressed."[53] The reason for the reply was debated, but one thing was clear: The meaning of communication and the authenticity of the relationship were called into question with a response that seemed pre-programmed and unrelated to the actual interaction.

Although the damage caused to a brand by mechanized communication is significant, the power to build credibility and relationships with *individualized* messages is just as strong. A classic example of this comes from Old Spice when it launched a campaign that capitalized on the very nature of customized engagement. Old Spice Guy Isaiah Mustafa created more than 120 personalized video responses to brand community questions from Twitter, blogs, and other digital platforms in a single day. Many responses were to social influencers, enhancing the reach of the campaign, but responses were also sent to general brand community members. The enthusiastic response of the campaign and the eagerness by many in the community to receive their own personal video response led to the campaign's wildly successful impact.[54]

Having addressed the role of brand personality and communication building, the final consideration for building credibility is how brands and social media users share similar values. Often, these values or mutual interests are among the strongest ties that connect organizations with their brand community.

Shared Community Values

Illustrating how the brand community and organization have mutual interests, concern for the community, and similar values is a powerful way to build credibility. When using this method, brands must be able to authentically identify with the personal values held by key publics. These values are concepts or convictions that publics consider important.

Remember the social principle from the first chapter? Social media is about those shared values or mutual interests. They are what form the cohesive glue for tribes. Altruistic showcasing, therefore, is how the organization tangibly engages with the personal values of its publics.

In light of this, it should be no surprise that organizations that are involved in giving back to the community and actively participating in the brand community are perceived as more credible. This idea is sometimes called corporate citizenship, CSR, or social good. Each of these terms involves a unique approach to the method in which the brand contributes to the good of the community beyond the specific organizational objective or bottom line, but they all can be categorized under the concept of altruism. One study found that 90% of Americans are more likely to trust and remain loyal to brands that are trying to make a positive difference by supporting causes.[55] People want to know that the brands they care about, the organizations they support, and the social communities they are active in are committed to the same values. There are so many strong examples of brands that have led the way in illustrating shared values with the community. One common approach is to partner the brand with a cause. For example, in 2014, Toys"R"Us partnered with Shaquille O'Neal and the Toys for Tots Foundation to help provide toys to kids in need during the holiday season. When customers donated an item and took a selfie, using the hashtag #PlayItForward, Toys"R"Us would donate an additional toy to the cause. The campaign ended up raising more than $5 million.[56] But brands don't always have to partner with well-known causes and celebrities. For example, Ford gained attention by supporting a little-known cause called Invisible People, an initiative set up by Mark Horvath to help with homelessness in America. By providing him with a Ford Flex and a company-promoted social site, "Ford made homelessness a primary issue on the nostalgic American road."[57] Scott Montey, former social media lead for Ford, explained the brand's support by saying, "Ford's support of the Invisible People project was never one of lead generation; it was mainly because we believed in Mark's mission and because it aligned with our own strategic initiatives." He added, "Since the very earliest days of the company, we've always believed in giving back to the communities in which we do business—it's just in our corporate DNA."[58]

This method of building credibility and fostering relationships in social media is widely held to be one of the most powerful because it ties directly into the passions and convictions that the brand communities share. Research confirms that people trust brands that share the same values as they hold.[59] This is a concept very similar to the dimension of personal affinity that was discovered during the early years of credibility study research, which identified that people are more likely to believe in the credibility of someone they like and are attracted to than someone who may be just as qualified but is less personable. Organizations use this method to build connection and affinity in brand communities, intentionally highlighting the areas of mutual interest, values, and concern for the community through social media channels.

It is very important, however, that this method is only applied in ways that genuinely align with the values of the brand community and organization. When it seems like this method is being used by brands for personal gain not only is the backlash quite severe, but there is also permanent damage to the relationships in the brand community. Matt Petronzio, the social good editor at Mashable, points out the danger of just tacking on causes to campaigns in an effort to look good: "your company needs to be genuine. Don't underestimate your consumers' intelligence by simply jumping on this bandwagon. 'Causewashing' is a serious issue, and odds are your consumers will smell it a mile away."[60] Causewashing is a term used to describe brands that attempt to appear philanthropic or to care about social good, when in reality the brand is not as authentically altruistic as it is presenting itself to be.

A prime example of the danger of appearing inauthentic in expressing shared values or community concern comes from Kmart. In 2012, the United States was shocked when 26 people, many of whom were children, were killed by a gunman at Sandy Hook Elementary School in Newton, Connecticut. Many brands took to social media to share their support and concern. Kmart, however, made a terrible misstep on Twitter when it posted, "Our thoughts and prayers are with the victims of this terrible tragedy. #PrayforNewton #CTShooting #Fab15Toys."[61] The last hashtag, #Fab15Toys, was one the brand was using as part of a campaign. The backlash from the public, claiming that the brand was using concern for those impacted by the tragedy for self-promotion and inauthentic engagement, came quickly. One Twitter user tweeted, "An example of heinous social marketing behavior from Kmart."[62] Although Kmart responded that it only used the hashtag so that participants in a Twitter chat, which it ended once news of the tragedy broke, would see the support of the brand for the tragedy and not to make profit, the damage was already done. The brand community felt that, rather than sharing values and being a good corporate citizen, the organization was actually self-focused and deceptive.[63]

Having addressed writing for social media and credible engagement methods, the third and final area to consider when designing meaningful communication is an analysis of brand positioning and creative strategies.

Brand Positioning and Creative Strategies

Keeping in mind the many ways that interaction enhances or diminishes credibility with key audiences, social strategists should strive to develop campaigns that can enhance credibility while wielding exceptional creativity and dynamic engagement with brand communities. This is definitely easier said than done.

Designing creative *and* effective tactics involves understanding the essence of the brand and positioning the organization appropriately within the brand community in order to optimize relationships. It is important to design campaigns with methods that support the overall campaign goal (discussed in the previous chapter), align with the brand's persona, and foster the publics' perception of credibility. To understand how to create tactics that accomplish this, three general approaches will be addressed: tactical methods to position the brand based on certain persona traits, tactical methods to ignite interaction in social media brand communities between users themselves, and tactics that capitalize on strategic functions of social media platforms to develop relationships.

Positioning Based on Brand Persona

As discussed above, part of the consideration when building credibility is to position the *source* or the brand's personality as one that is trusted and an expert in the industry. The brand persona plays a critical part in knowing how to select and apply certain types of tactics within social media.

Tactics Focusing on Trustworthiness

Some scholars have argued trustworthiness to be the cornerstone for all long-term relationships. Basically, it is the most important dimension to maintaining relationships with key stakeholders. It is the lifeblood of the organization. Once a brand loses trust, it can be incredibly challenging, if not impossible, to rebuild it. Because trustworthiness is so essential, strategists should regularly consider how the engagement they design in campaigns contributes to or builds an organization's trustworthiness in the eyes of the brand community. *Trustworthiness* in social media means the organization using social media is perceived as honest and reliable and possesses integrity.[64] Brent Gleeson,[65] a leadership and entrepreneur marketing journalist, points out, "Trust is the most crucial element of social media, but it's where brands continue to fall short right out of the gate."[66] To develop trust, brands must recognize that they need to consistently care for, contribute to, and build the relationships in their social media communities. Key stakeholders are looking for transparency, authenticity, and honesty in organizations that also share their values and want to truly engage in two-way dialogue with them as *prosumers*. Strategists can regularly contribute to building the trust in the brand through social media by genuinely communicating with and being dedicated to the relationships in the community.

Southwest Airlines had an opportunity to illustrate its commitment to the community when its brand came under fire on Twitter. Filmmaker Kevin Smith sent a tweet to his 1.6 million followers explaining his frustration with being removed from a flight for being overweight. Naturally, Southwest immediately experienced the fury of the Twitter world as people chastised the insensitive nature of the experience and criticized the brand.[67] In the midst of this crisis, Southwest remained true to its brand's persona as a caring and relatable organization, directly reaching out to Smith, apologizing, and updating the social media community with full details on a public blog post once the situation had been addressed. Although the situation was less than ideal for the brand, the response and care for individuals, time invested to personally reply to tweets, as well as public transparency in the recap of the situation led to the perception within the brand community that Southwest did truly value people, even if there was frustration with this situation.

Building trust is not something that happens overnight in brand communities. It requires time. It necessitates consistency. And it is never secure. Brands always have the potential to damage trust when they dehumanize interaction. Social media, as has been reiterated so many times before, is about people and relationships. To build trust, brands must have this as a primary commitment. Social media campaigns designed with people in mind and focusing on enhancing relationships through authenticity, creativity, and engagement illustrate to the brand community that the organization is trustworthy.

Tactics Focusing on Brand Expertise

In addition to the brand's persona being positioned as trustworthy, it is also important that the brand appear credible as an expert, competent in the field, and informed as an organization. For a brand to be perceived as having *expertise*, it needs to possess experience or knowledge relating to the industry and have the ability to provide unbiased and accurate information around topics of interest.[68] One way brands can do this is by providing thought leadership.

When brands use tactics that focus on thought leadership, they ultimately end up building the publics' perceptions of their authority as a trailblazer in the industry. Many brands benefit from using this approach in a social media campaign, as providing thought leadership in social media is one way to also tie into a primary habit of social media users: finding and sharing news. There are a number of ways that an organization may choose to build expertise through thought leadership. For example, using infographics in social media is a powerful way to distill a large amount of otherwise text-heavy information into a friendly, easily understandable, sharable format. People enjoy not only learning from infographics, but also sharing them with others. There are many free tools that brands can use to create an infographic, such as Piktochart, or paid subscriptions offer more robust selections. Another approach might be providing white papers from the organization around various topics. If the brand is a tech organization, for example, it can consider providing a how-to guide for people on various activities they need to perform with new technology and tools. If the brand is a humanitarian organization, creating a white paper with the background and current standing of some top issues in which the organization is advocating for change is a way that it can provide information for which its publics are looking. The goal of thought leadership is not to position the brand as elitist and superior to those in the brand community. Rather, the focus is to provide information that the brand community cares about but may not have known about previously and to empower members to then share that information with their friends, which will help give them social credibility as information providers too. It is of value to them to receive and also of value to them to *share*. This helps the brand by spreading awareness of topics, building trust as an authority, and ultimately being considered to be a brand that makes valuable contributions to the community.

With the background of how the public perceives credibility and its connection to trustworthiness and expertise, it is easier to understand the theoretical support for developing thriving relationships in social media through two-way dialogue. When an organization only uses social media as a promotional conduit, repeatedly pushing information and product ads to users through the brand's profile, the credibility of the organization is not highlighted. Instead of looking like an authentic brand with expert insight, the organization will, at best, appear to have a fundamental misunderstanding about the nature and purpose of social media or, at worst, reflect the organization's view that the public is merely a means to an end. Social media professionals should, therefore,

Brand Positioning & Creative Tactics

Brand Persona	Ignite Connection	Platform Functionality
• Trustworthiness • Expertise	• Brand Community Relationships • Prosumer Engagement	• Advertising • Contests

Figure 4.4 Brand Positioning and Creative Tactics

view the engagement opportunities using social media as a way to position the organization as a trustworthy brand with robust expertise within the industry.

Creative Tactics to Ignite Brand Communities

In addition to positioning the brand's persona using creative tactics, social media strategists should also purposefully develop connections and conversations with the individual members of the brand community as part of a campaign's strategic design.

Brand Community Relationships

Social media, essentially, is all about the brand community relationships. It is the shared conversations around mutual interests and values. Effective campaign design recognizes that tactics should be created to develop relationships not only between the brand and the members of the social media community, but also between the individual members of the social media community. Some brands highlight the community by giving shout-outs to particularly active users during a given week, or reposting Instagram photos to the brand's account, or sharing videos created by the community while tagging the original authors. When a brand highlights the online community, it is an intentional effort by the brand to illustrate what others within the social community are doing on a regular basis. When creative engagement focuses on this highlighting of the community, it actually helps foster relationships *between* individual members of the brand community, as it connects and introduces people who may otherwise never have interacted. The joint interest is the brand, and the mutual connection is the content posted by the brand that highlighted an individual within the community. This developing of inter-community relationships helps the organization build stronger brand communities and can, therefore, be one of the most powerful ways to use social media.

As result of using methods that highlight others, brands end up encouraging brand community members to engage with each other more, as well as with the brand. Oftentimes, this engagement will end up including comments about the brand, using campaign hashtags, or generally contributing to the SOV that a brand has in the social media world. This type of interaction in brand communities is highly significant, as studies have found that perceptions of organizations acquired through social media are influenced not only by the brand's activity, but also by the conversations that are happening *among the publics* regarding the brand. This means that publics often are as much influenced by peer-to-peer interaction as by brand-to-individual interaction, if not more.

What does this all mean? Essentially, when a brand's community members share positive posts, tweets, and mentions, it will go far further in building the organization's credibility and the trust in the brand held by the social media community than any posts that the brand publishes on its own platform. These user-generated posts also help create a culture for the brand community, expanding the values, shared passion for a brand, and mutual appreciation of similar interests. A great example of this is Tough Mudder, which often creates graphics that social media users opt to use on their personal sites, share on the walls of friends, or mention other connections with in order to connect with the theme of fitness. These graphics carry messages that have the tone and approach of the brand community, rather than seeming to have the brand's official voice or message.

Knowing that members of key publics have a strong influence on each other is not something new to the PR and marketing industry. Historically, organizations knew credibility and exposure would increase as positive word of mouth spread among key publics. That is why there has been so much focus on grass-roots campaigns, getting people to "tell a friend" and finding man-on-the-street endorsements for various organizations. In the social media world, this same principle applies. It is called electronic word of mouth (E-WOM) and through social media has taken an impressive role in shaping brand credibility. In fact, it is often suggested that, in order to be highly effective, professionals should ignite conversations on social media so that others (review boards, friends, and brand community members) share the message of the organization, as opposed to the organization saying it itself. Additionally, because social media has the potential to go viral and extend to more individuals than is the case with word-of-mouth campaigns conducted in the offline world, social media E-WOM is even more significant for organizations. Because the information is coming from a peer and not the organization, it appears to be less biased, more authentic and reliable.[69] All of these dimensions are long-standing elements of credibility and provide the foundation for *why* so many brands try to get E-WOM tactics as a central part of campaign design.

A social media example that has made history using E-WOM is the ALS (amyotrophic lateral sclerosis) Ice Bucket Challenge (this is an example of how social media has also shifted into a fundraising platform driven by users on behalf of causes, organizations, or products). This social media fundraising campaign went viral in 2014 and ultimately raised more than $2.3 million for the ALS Association.[70] This E-WOM campaign is credited with being initiated by Pete Frates, a Boston College baseball player who was diagnosed with ALS in 2007, at the age of 27.[71] In the campaign, people posted a video of themselves being drenched by a bucket full of ice-cold water. In the post, they would use the hashtag #IceBucketChallenge and then tag friends, challenging them to either donate to ALS, pour a bucket of ice over their own heads, or both, within a 24-hour period. Truly showing the power of E-WOM in social media, this campaign reached all kinds of people, from famous celebrities such as Bill Gates, Oprah, and Taylor Swift to more than 17 million people who uploaded videos to Facebook of themselves taking the challenge.[72] These videos ended up being watched by 440 million people, a total of 10 billion times.[73] This is the power of social media communities, connected together and talking about mutual interests.

Developing Prosumer Engagement in Brand Communities

As previously discussed, individuals in online communities want to be prosumers, not consumers. Therefore, creative campaign design should also consider how the brand can be personable, inviting conversation, and foster opportunities for the brand community members to directly participate in creating content or making decisions. If brands are personable and invite collaboration, they are essentially allowing the "audience to contribute to the generation of ideas."[74] Sometimes, the generation of ideas may relate to core elements of the brand, and other times the generation of ideas may involve creating content that is useful and inspiring to *others* in the brand community. Contributions and collaboration, in this sense, may involve an organization's willingness to provide an opportunity for publics to have a say in the direction and focus of the organization by being included in the planning, launching, and evaluation of the organization's activities, products, initiatives, and goals through social media. It is important to note: This cannot be an inauthentic commitment to collaboration or inclusion—the organization has to be transparent in the level of involvement and role that consumers will genuinely have as a result of interaction through social media.

A strong example of prosumers being invited to have a say was seen in Hasbro's "Save Your Token" campaign, focusing on the popular board game Monopoly. The social media community had the opportunity to vote for which classic token should be removed from the board game and which new token should be added to an updated version of the game. With more than 10 million people clicking the like button on the Facebook voting page, users chose to remove the iron from the classic game and replace it with a cat.[75] The real value of this campaign was the fact that the social media community actively had a role in shaping the future of a brand that they loved.

Sometimes, rather than direct collaboration on the brand's content or direction, the collaboration involves creating ideas for others within the brand community. Again, strategists should always keep in mind that they are developing relationships *with* members of the brand community and *among* members of the brand community. A great example of this type of approach comes from Target's Christmas campaign that utilized the hashtag #MyKindOfHoliday. What stands out about this campaign is that the hashtag was not strictly about the organization or brand, but rather about a concept that the brand community could interact with and dialogue around, thereby inviting participation and interaction. This allowed users to be prosumers as they shared unique ways they approached the holidays, made meals, created gifts, and celebrated the season.

Hashtag Creation

In campaigns that are designed to foster conversations within the social media world, the development of hashtags is crucial. Although some people may suggest "coming up with a hashtag" for a campaign and view that as an idea in and of itself, the real art behind hashtag creation is recognizing that its power rests in the ability to enable a brand community to be participatory contributors or prosumers. Hashtags should be designed to elicit the brand community's ideas and perspectives, driving conversations and igniting ideas. Brands should always carefully research hashtag ideas to see what other brands are using the hashtag and what kind of conversation is taking place. The beauty of building conversations in social media through creative hashtags is that this is far more powerful than simply starting conversations that are contained in a single brand's community. It is actually a method to expand conversations *beyond* the confines of a set brand community and into the connections of others as users engage with the hashtag and contribute to the conversation, reaching their friends and networks. This kind of interaction demonstrates that the organization values individuals in the community and welcomes input. That is why this type of strategic design of hashtags is more than simply a method to ignite online engagement: It generates confidence in the organization's credibility by showing that the brand genuinely cares about its publics beyond merely persuading or coercing them into certain behaviors. It shows respect for the ideas and thoughts of the brand community.

Creative Tactics with Platform Functionality

After considering brand positioning and collaboration in the brand community when designing creative engagement, the final method of tactic design that social media strategists should consider involves analyzing the functions or capabilities of social media platforms and determining which would be most effective in the design of a campaign.

Advertising Engagement

Key components of many campaigns that brands opt to use are paid strategies and tactics using social advertising. As of 2013, online advertising became the second largest ad medium, passing the long-standing medium of newspapers.[76] Spending in the US on advertising in social media was estimated to hit $43 billion by the end of 2020.[77] Each platform tends to eventually have paid content integrated. For example, a social media platform will typically launch without a business integration component (for example, in the early days of Facebook, there were no "pages" for businesses; it was all just personal profiles). As the platforms develop, they launch business integration elements that allow brands to create a unique space on the platform. This often comes with the ability to track analytics at a deeper level and to pay for a brand's content to reach more people on the platform. For example, in 2016, when Instagram made the move to reshape brand profiles, it announced new business profile options (which it determined after working with existing brands on the platform), and it also highlighted that businesses would get access to in-depth audience analytics and the capability to shift an Instagram post directly into a paid ad for greater reach.[78] This final part, the capability to seamlessly integrate an organic post with a paid placement indicates the reality for brands on social media: Both organic and paid engagement is needed in order to successfully navigate the social environments. Similarly, in mid-2020, TikTok announced "TikTok for Business," moving the platform into a similar model where brands could leverage paid placements alongside organic campaigns. One of the most valuable components of social media advertising is its ability to help reach beyond a current social media community. This is a key value, which is why, when TikTok launched its business model, it presented it as follows: "TikTok for Business is where you can unleash your brand's creative side. A fully immersive no judgement world where there's an audience for every voice."[79] Brands, more than ever, are trying to leverage platforms not simply to reach their current stakeholders, but to engage *new* stakeholders. The reality is, more often than not, the integration of paid elements is crucial, since the reach brands achieve organically can be limited owing to social algorithms and community interaction. In their efforts to expand audience reach, raise awareness, engage more people, and have posts placed in locations that key audiences will see, brands benefit from paid tactics.

Thanks to the hard work done during the listening stage, brands should have a clear audience profile. Using social media advertising, brands are able to pick the specific demographics of the audience they would like to engage with social advertisements. This is a strong way to bring more people into a community who would otherwise likely not see the content. Organizations may target people with specific job titles via LinkedIn or certain types of entertainment preferences on Facebook. Brands are able to target ads in a number of ways, depending on the platform.

When beginning advertising on social media, be sure to keep focused on the ultimate reason for the campaign. Having the goal in mind will guide what kinds of advertisements a brand should create. For example, if the goal is to drive people to a specific page on a website, with the hopes of generating leads for the sales team, review which posts have been most effective with the brand's organic (non-paid) social media tactics. Social media advertising still holds many of the same principles as organic posts—it should be engaging, humanized, and relational.

People on social media respond to relationships. Brands may consider using higher-performing posts in a paid function, as they already know the posts seem to resonate with target demographics. In fact, this is often a best practice when beginning social media advertising. Find the content that has had the highest performance on the platform on which a brand wants to advertise and use that to create engagement within the advertising tactic.

A general checklist for whether a platform will be helpful is:

1. Does the purpose statement of the platform match the goal in the advertising call to action?
2. Does the platform's capabilities for demographic targeting allow the brand to strategically reach key audiences on the platform?
3. Will the advertising functions available on the platform contribute to the ability to reach the campaign goal and objectives?

If the answer to all three questions is yes, it is worthwhile to consider advertising on the platform.

Organizations will want to test several ads to determine which yields the highest return on investment (ROI) for paid efforts. Be sure to regularly check in with the campaign to see what is being viewed, what is being clicked on, and whether those clicks are leading to conversions. Perform a lot of tests in social advertising—do not be afraid to use small budget amounts to learn which ads work best and at what times. The goal is to strategically drive activity that progresses the campaign toward success. That means a lot of measurement, adjustment, and monitoring will need to occur. Also, be sure to compile several ads so that the brand can rotate them regularly. People may tune social advertising out because it is boring or they have seen it too often. The key is fresh content: Rotate ads, regularly refresh paid placements, and always keep content new and interesting. Finally, always keep mobile viewing in mind. Brands creating advertising for social media must realize that they are creating it for both desktop social media and mobile platforms. With more and more users accessing social media via mobile devices, it is extremely strategic to design ads specifically for mobile access.

Contest Strategies

One idea that many brands use in social media is contests. Although many contests are often run across platforms, it is important that a brand understands the exact rules for each social media platform before beginning a contest or sweepstake. For example, on Facebook, organizations cannot have people share information on their personal timelines in order to enter a contest. Instagram prohibits brands from encouraging users to tag themselves in photos that they are not actually in as a way of participating in contests. Each platform has unique requirements for participating and running contests, which will be outlined in the platform's contest policy document. Before running a contest, be sure that it supports the goal of the campaign; stays true to the purpose of the platform's vision statement; and aligns with the platform's regulations regarding contests and promotions.

IDENTIFYING APPROPRIATE STRATEGIES AND TACTICS

One of the most challenging things in social media is to identify the best tactics for an organization. Thankfully, it becomes much easier when developing strategies and tactics from the research and campaign design, rather than in a vacuum. Sometimes, organizations are eager to try a specific tactic because "it worked for others." That is never a good enough reason to decide to launch a social media tactic. Each strategy and tactic should directly relate to the objectives of the campaign and the unique audience with which the brand is engaging. Be sure to understand the audience's values, behaviors, and reasons for being in the social community before developing tactics to engage with them.

Additionally, each tactic that is created has to be true to the brand persona. Some brands have very edgy tactics. Those likely work well with their organization and resonate with their audiences. However, if a brand persona is sophisticated and elegant, an edgy tactic is likely not an approach that would be beneficial in engaging the brand community. That is why it is critical to always review the social brand voice. Consider the persona, tone, and purpose of communication. Only after appropriately aligning the audience's values with the brand's voice is it possible to select creative and engaging strategies and tactics.

When developing each tactic, be sure to refer to the vision statement for each platform. This will ensure that each strategy and tactic aligns with the overall vision for the platform. Remember, no strategy or tactic should be created apart from a rigorous review of the social media design for the campaign. It should be informed by research and background, giving the potential for exponentially increasing value in the social community.

Each campaign that is designed will have unique needs. And every social media brand community should be paid specialized attention as it is comprised of a distinctive group of members who each have different personal values and traits. No two brand communities are alike. Additionally, the brand will be communicating across multiple platforms, each with their own capabilities and purpose. It is critical, therefore, for social media strategists to refine each strategy and tactic so that it reflects the tapestry of diversity of each unique social media platform and audience, supporting the campaign's individual goal rather than simply modeling what every other brand is doing in social media.

SOCIAL MEDIA GOLDEN RULES

In conclusion, when a brand designs strategies and tactics for a social media campaign, it should keep in mind the golden rules of social media, as illustrated in Figure 4.5.

1. Engage with others as you would want to be engaged with: Social media is about the community and mutual interest. It is not a place to simply promote and publicize without interacting. Mirror the type of engagement you would want to see from your community. Be authentic, real, and genuine. This will develop the brand's credibility, making it trustworthy and an authority in the industry.
2. Build a community, not a broadcast platform: The goal of social media is to contribute to the social tribe that has connected around the brand. In order to build the community, provide interesting and relevant content for the community. You should always filter the content through the lens of what is valuable to the online community, what resonates with them, and what they would find engaging.
3. Leverage the platform culture: Each platform is unique. There are different functions, social netiquette, and expectations of communities. Never simply plaster the same tactic or strategy across all platforms. Rather, strategically leverage each platform to uniquely engage the culture that is present.

Figure 4.5 Social Media Golden Rules

KEY CONCEPT SNAPSHOT

1. Social media engagement is most powerful when it focuses on *relationships*, developing written and visual content around the values of the online brand community.
2. The methods, or tactics, that an organization uses on social media directly influence the publics' perceptions of the brand's credibility, authority, trustworthiness, and relevance.
3. Organizations should consider what qualities or traits they are focusing on illustrating via social media in order to develop the appropriate creative strategies that reach campaign objectives.
4. Creative communication tactics should be designed with expert insight into the brand, the community values, and the platform capabilities.

NOTES

1   2009.
2   p. 156.
3   2013.
4   p. 273.
5   Kim, 2019, p. 254.
6   Edelman, 2019, para. 7.
7   Jarvis, 2019.
8   Walter, 2018, para. 7.
9   Zavy, 2019, para. 13.
10 Bump, 2020, para. 15.
11 Bump, 2020 "AeroMexico", para. 10.
12 Schomer, 2019.
13 Influencer Marketing Hub, 2020.
14 Hosie, 2019.
15 Hosie, 2019; Ismail, 2018.
16 Influencer Marketing Hub, 2020.
17 Federal Trade Commission, n.d., "When to Disclose," paras. 1-3.
18 Granville, 2018.
19 Rainie, 2018, para. 9.
20 Parker, 2017, "What is Dark Social?"
21 Simpson, 2016.
22 Sehl, 2020, para. 1-2.
23 Zuckerberg, 2019, para. 1.
24 2014.
25 2012.
26 2012.
27 Gaziano & McGrath, 1986; Hovland & Weiss, 1951.
28 Gaziano & McGrath, 1986.

29   Newell & Goldsmith, 2001.
30   Wilcox & Cameron, 2009, pp. 73-96.
31   1996.
32   Aaker, 1997.
33   Aaker, 1997.
34   Aaker, 1997, p. 347.
35   Kietzmann, Hermkens, McCarthy, & Silverstre, 2011.
36   Harris, 2013.
37   Berlo, Lemert, & Mertz, 1969.
38   1995.
39   1996.
40   Edelman, 2013a.
41   Scott and Scott, 2019.
42   Alpert, 2012.
43   Edelman, 2013a; Edelman, 2013b.
44   Treadaway & Smith, 2010.
45   2010.
46   Edelman, 2013a.
47   Coyle, Smith, & Platt, 2012.
48   Kingma, 2013; O'Neill, 2009.
49   Parent, Plangger, & Bal, 2011; Kerpen, 2011.
50   Aaker, 1997; Smith, Fischer, & Yongjian, 2012; Smith, 2013; Schau, Muniz, & Arnould, 2009.
51   2011.
52   Briones, Kuch, Liu, & Jin, 2011; Brown, Broderick, & Lee, 2007.
53   Walsh, 2013, para. 4.
54   Ehrlich, 2010; Hepburn, 2010.
55   Cone Communications, 2013, p. 8.
56   Cassinelli, 2014.
57   Livingston, 2010, "Ford Helps" para. 1.
58   as quoted in Livingston, 2010, "Ford Helps" para. 4.
59   Aggarwal, 2004; Ambler, 1997.
60   Petronzio, 2015, para. 5.
61   Keller, 2012, para. 3.
62   Blanchard, 2012.
63   Keller, 2012.
64   Morgan & Hunt, 1994, p. 23.
65   2012.
66   para. 4.
67   Cashmore, 2010.
68   Hilligoss & Rieh, 2008; Fogg, 2003.
69   Brown, Broderick, & Lee, 2007.
70   Worland, 2014.
71   Freberg, 2014.
72   Allen, 2014; ALS Association, n.d.
73   ALS Association, n.d.
74   Foss & Griffin, 1995, p. 16.

75   Payne & Pearson, 2013.
76   Johnson, 2013, "The internet is now the world's second-largest ad medium."
77   Cooper, 2020, "General Social Media Advertising Statistics, #1."
78   Perez, 2016.
79   TikTok, 2020.

SUGGESTED READING

Aaker, J. L. & Smith, A. (2010). *The Dragonfly Effect: Quick, Effective, and Powerful Ways to Use Social Media to Drive Social Change.* San Francisco: Jossey-Bass.

Gil, C. (2019). *The End of Marketing: Humanizing Your Brand in the Age of Social Media and AI.* London: Kogan Page.

Godin, S. (2008). *Tribes: We Need You to Lead Us.* New York: Portfolio.

Scott, D. M. & Scott, R. (2019). *Fanocracy: Turning Fans into Customers and Customers into Fans.* New York: Portfolio/Penguin.

REFERENCES

Aaker, J. L. (1997). Dimensions of Brand Personality. *Journal of Marketing,* 34(3), 347–356.

Aggarwal, P. (2004). The Effects of Brand Relationship Norms on Consumer Attitudes and Behavior. *Journal of Consumer Research,* 31(1), 87–101.

Allen, K. (2014, August 27). "How the ALS ice bucket challenge could change PR for nonprofits." *PR Daily.* Retrieved from: www.prdaily.com/Main/Articles/How_the_ALS_Ice_Bucket_Challenge_could_change_PR_f_17156.aspx

Alpert, J. (2012). *The Mobile Marketing Revolution: How Your Brand Can Have a One-to-One Conversation with Everyone.* New York: McGraw-Hill.

ALS Association. (n.d.). *ALS ice bucket challenge FAQ.* Retrieved from: www.alsa.org/about-us/ice-bucket-challenge-faq.html

Ambler, T. (1997). How Much of Brand Equity Is Explained by Trust? *Management Decision,* 35(4), 283–292.

Berlo, D. K., Lemert, J. B., & Mertz, R. J. (1969). Dimensions for Evaluating the Acceptability of Message Sources. *Public Opinion Quarterly,* 33(4), 563–576.

Blanchard, O. (2012, December 14). "@ryanschade An example of heinous social marketing behavior from Kmart http://on.fb.me/U0RvmA ht: @cbarger cc: @armano #fab15toys" (Tweet). Retrieved from: https://twitter.com/thebrandbuilder/status/279705756369047552

Briones, R. L., Kuch, B., Liu, B. F., & Jin, Y. (2011). Keeping Up with the Digital Age: How the American Red Cross Uses Social Media to Build Relationships. *Public Relations Review,* 37(1), 37–43.

Broom, G. & Sha, B. L. (2013). *Cutlip and Center's Effective Public Relations.* Boston: Pearson.

Brown, J., Broderick, A. J., & Lee, N. (2007). Word of Mouth Communication within Online Communities: Conceptualizing the Online Social Network. *Journal of Interactive Marketing,* 21(3), 1–19.

Bump, P. (2020, February 27). "5 examples of brands newsjacking in 2019." *Hubspot.com.* Retrieved from: https://blog.hubspot.com/marketing/newsjacking-examples

Cashmore, P. (2010, February 14). "Southwest tweets, blogs apology to Kevin Smith." *Mashable.* Retrieved from: http://mashable.com/2010/02/14/southwest-kevin-smith/

Cassinelli, A. (2014, December 31). "14 best social media campaigns of 2014." *Postano.* Retrieved from: www.postano.com/blog/14-best-social-media-campaigns-of-2014

Cone Communications. (2013). *Social Impact Study.* Retrieved from: www.conecomm.com/stuff/contentmgr/files/0/e3d2eec1e15e858867a 5c2b1a22c4cfb/files/2013_cone_comm_social_impact_study.pdf

Cooper, P. (April 23, 2020). "43 social media advertising statistics that matter to marketers in 2020." *Hootsuite.* Retrieved from: https://blog.hootsuite.com/social-media-advertising-stats/

Coyle, J. R., Smith T., & Platt, G. (2012). I'm Here to Help: How Companies Microblog Responses to Consumer Problems Influence Brand Perceptions. *Journal of Research in Interactive Marketing,* 6(1), 27–41.

Edelman (2013a). *Brandshare.* Retrieved from: www.edelman.com/insights/intellectual-property/brandshare/

Edelman (2013b). *2013 Edelman Trust Barometer.* Retrieved from: www.edelman.com/insights/intellectual-property/trust-2013/

Edelman (2019). *2020 Edelman Trust Barometer Reveals Growing Sense of Inequality is Undermining Trust in Institutions.* Retrieved from: www.edelman.com/news-awards/2020-edelman-trust-barometer

Ehrlich, B. (2010, July 13). "Old Spice Guy now making custom videos for fans via social media." *Mashable.* Retrieved from: http://mashable.com/2010/07/13/old-spice-gu/

Federal Trade Commission. (n.d.). *Disclosures 101 for Social Media Influencers.* Retrieved from: www.ftc.gov/tips-advice/business-center/guidance/disclosures-101-social-media-influencers

Fogg, B. J. (2003). *Persuasive Technology: Using Computers to Change what We Think and Do.* Boston: Morgan Kaufmann.

Foss, S. & Griffin, C. (1995). Beyond Persuasion: A Proposal for an Invitational Rhetoric. *Communication Monographs,* 62(1), 2–18.

Freberg, K. (2014, August 22). "Power of storytelling & viral fundraising: Exploring the ALS #IceBucketChallenge case." *KarenFreberg.com.* Retrieved from: http://karenfreberg.com/blog/power-of-storytelling-viral-fundrasing-exploring-the-als-icebucketchallenge-case/

Gaziano, C. & McGrath, K. (1986). Measuring the Concept of Credibility. *Journalism Quarterly,* 63(3), 451–462.

Gleeson, B. (2012, October 31). "6 ways brands build trust through social media." *Forbes.* Retrieved from: www.forbes.com/sites/brentgleeson/2012/10/31/6-ways-brands-build-trust-through-social-media/

Granville, K. (2018, March 19). "Facebook and Cambridge Analytica: What you need to know as fallout widens." *New York Times.* www.nytimes.com/2018/03/19/technology/facebook-cambridge-analytica-explained.html

Harris, R. (2013, July 29). "Eight great examples of agile marketing from Oreo." *Econsultancy.* Retrieved from: https://econsultancy.com/eight-great-examples-of-agile-marketing-from-oreo/

Hepburn, A. (2010, July 14). "Old Spice sends personal twitter video replies." *Digital Buzz Blog.* Retrieved from: www.digitalbuzzblog.com/old-spice-twitter-social-video-replies/

Hilligoss, B. & Rieh, S. Y. (2008). Developing a Unifying Framework of Credibility Assessment: Construct, Heuristics, and Interaction in Context. *Information Processing and Management,* 44(4), 1467–1484.

Hosie, R. (2019, April 9). "Why brands are turning away from big Instagram influencers to work with people who have small followings instead." *Business Insider.* Retrieved from: www.businessinsider.com/brands-turning-to-micro-influencers-instead-of-instagram-stars-2019-4

Hovland, C. & Weiss, W. (1951). The Influence of Source Credibility on Communication Effectiveness. *Public Opinion Quarterly,* 15(4), 635–650.

Influencer Marketing Hub. (2020, June 15). *80 Influencer Marketing Statistics for 2020.* Retrieved from: https://influencermarketinghub.com/influencer-marketing-statistics/

Ismail, K. (2018, December 10). "Social media influencers: Mega, macro, micro, or nano." *CMS Wire.* Retrieved from: cmswire.com/digital-marketing/social-media-influencers-mega-macro-micro-or-nano/

Jarvis, L. (2019, July 20). "The best & worst social responsibility campaigns." *Remesh.com.* Retrieved from: https://blog.remesh.ai/corporate-social-responsibility-campaigns-new-customers

Johnson, B. (2013, December 8). "10 things you should know about the global ad market." *Adage.com.* Retrieved from: http://adage.com/article/global-news/10-things-global-ad-market/245572/?utm_source=Webbiquity.com

Keller, J. (2012, December 14). "Kmart's Connecticut-shooting Twitter fail." *Bloomberg Business.* Retrieved from: www.bloomberg.com/bw/articles/2012-12-14/kmarts-connecticut-shooting-twitter-fail

Kerpen, D. (2011). *Likeable Social Media: How to Delight Your Customers, Create an Irresistible Brand, and Be Generally Amazing on Facebook.* New York: McGraw-Hill.

Kietzmann, J. H., Hermkens, K., McCarthy, I. P., & Silvestre, B. S. (2011). Social Media? Get Serious! Understanding the Functional Building Blocks of Social Media. *Business Horizons,* 54(3), 241–251.

Kim, C. M. (Ed.). (2019). *Public Relations: Competencies and Practice.* Routledge.

Kingma, G. (2013, November 21). "Why transparency is important on social media." *Canadian Marketing Association.* Retrieved from: www.the-cma.org/about/blog/why-transparency-is-important-on-social-media

Livingston, G. (2010, February 18). "5 winning corporate social good campaigns." *Mashable.* Retrieved from: http://mashable.com/2010/02/18/corporate-social-good-campaigns/

Madrigal, A. (2012, October 12). "Dark social: We have the whole history of the web wrong." *The Atlantic.* Retrieved from: www.theatlantic.com/technology/archive/2012/10/dark-social-we-have-the-whole-history-of-the-web-wrong/263523/

Morgan, R. M. & Hunt, S. D. (1994). The Commitment Trust Theory of Relationship Marketing. *Journal of Marketing,* 58, 20–38.

Moriarty, S. E. (1996). The circle of synergy: Theoretical perspectives of and an evolving IMC agenda. In Thorson, E. and Moore, J. (Eds.) *Integrated Communications: Synergy of Persuasive Voices*. Mahwah, NJ: Lawrence Erlbaum, 333–354.

Newell, S. J. & Goldsmith, R. E. (2001). The Development of a Scale to Measure Perceived Corporate Credibility. *Journal of Business Research*, 52(3), 235–247.

O'Neill, N. (2009, September 4). "When Facebook fans turn ugly examining the Honda Crosstour page." *Adweek Social Times*. Retrieved from: www.adweek.com/socialtimes/when-facebook-fans-turn-ugly-examining-the-honda-accord-crosstour-page/310733

Parent, M., Plangger, K., & Bal, A. (2011). The New WTP: Willingness to Participate. *Business Horizons*, 54(3), 219–229.

Parker, S. (2017, February 6). "Why your business can't ignore dark social." *Hootsuite*. Retrieved from: https://blog.hootsuite.com/dark-social/#whatis

Payne, E. & Pearson, M. (2013, February 6). "Out with the iron, in with the cat: Monopoly has a new token." *CNN*. Retrieved from: www.cnn.com/2013/02/06/living/monopoly-new-token/

Perez, S. (2016, May 31). "Instagram officially announces its new business tools." *TechCrunch*. Retrieved from: https://techcrunch.com/2016/05/31/instagram-officially-announces-its-new-business-tools/

Petronzio, M. (2015, Jan. 11). "90% of Americans more likely to trust brands that back social causes." *Mashable*. Retrieved from: http://mashable.com/2015/01/11/corporate-social-causes/

Poster, M. (1995). *The Second Media Age*. Cambridge, UK: Cambridge, MA: Polity Press; B. Blackwell.

Prince, M. (2014, January 27). "How to: Get a job without a resume," *MattPrince.Me*. Retrieved from: http://mattprince.me/defining-your-personal-brand/

Rainie, L. (2018, March 27). "Americans' complicated feelings about social media in an era of privacy concerns. *Pew Research Center*. Retrieved from: www.pewresearch.org/fact-tank/2018/03/27/americans-complicated-feelings-about-social-media-in-an-era-of-privacy-concerns/

Schaefer, M. (2012). *Return on Influence: The Revolutionary Power of Klout, Social Scoring, and Influence Marketing*. New York: McGraw-Hill.

Schau, H. J., Muniz, A. M., & Arnould, E. (2009). How Brand Community Practices Create Value. *Journal of Marketing*, 73(5), 30–51.

Schomer, A. (2019, December 17). "Influencer marketing: State of social media influencer market in 2020." *Business Insider* .Retrieved from: www.businessinsider.com/influencer-marketing-report

Scott, D. M. (2011). *Newsjacking: How to Inject Your Ideas into a Breaking News Story and Generate Tons of Media Coverage*. John Wiley

Scott, D. M. & Scott, R. (2019). *Fanocracy: Turning Fans into Customers and Customers into Fans*. New York: Portfolio/Penguin.

Sehl, K. (2020, February 12). "Facebook Messenger: The complete guide for business." *Hootsuite*. Retrieved from: https://blog.hootsuite.com/facebook-messenger/

Simpson, J. (2016, February 16). "The rise of dark social: Everything you need to know." *Econsultancy*. Retrieved from: https://econsultancy.com/the-rise-of-dark-social-everything-you-need-to-know/

Smith, B. G. (2010). Socially Distributing Public Relations: Twitter, Haiti, and Interactivity in Social Media. *Public Relations Review*, 36(4), 329–335.

Smith, C. (2013, July 19). "10 social media statistics that should shape your social strategy." Retrieved from: www.businessinsider.com/strategic-social-media-statistics-2013-7

Smith, M. & Kawasaki, G. (2011). *The New Relationship Marketing: How to Build a Large, Loyal, Profitable Network Using the Social Web.* Hoboken, NJ: John Wiley.

Smith, A. N., Fischer, E., & Yongjian, C. (2012). How Does Brand-Related User-Generated Content Differ across YouTube, Facebook and Twitter? *Journal of Interactive Marketing,* 26(2), 102–113.

TikTok. (2020). *TikTok for Business.* Retrieved from: www.tiktok.com/business/en

Treadaway, C. & Smith, M. (2010). *Facebook Marketing: An Hour a Day.* Indianapolis: Wiley.

Walsh, M. (2013, August 13). "Domino's pizza is so used to apologizing it begs pardon from fan for 'best pizza ever.'" *NY Daily News.* Retrieved from: www.nydailynews.com/news/national/domino-pizza-accidentally-apologizes-fan-article-1.1425564

Walter, E. (2018, November 1). "Bold brand storytelling: Lessons from companies who take a stance." *Forbes.* Retrieved from: https://www.forbes.com/sites/ekaterinawalter/2018/11/01/bold-brand-storytelling-lessons-from-companies-who-take-a-stance/#1b63d22a58b6

Wilcox, D. & Cameron, G. (2009). *Public Relations: Strategies and Tactics.* Boston: Person/Allyn & Bacon.

Worland, J. (2014, August 11). "Here's how much money the ALS ice-water stunt has collected." *Time.* Retrieved from: http://time.com/3101166/als-ice-bucket-challenge-fundraising/

Zavy. (2019, September 6). "3 social campaigns that nailed CSR and made a difference." *Zavy.co.* Retrieved from: www.zavy.co/blog/3-social-campaigns-that-nailed-csr-and-made-a-difference

Zuckerberg, M. (2019, March 6). "A privacy-focused vision for social networking." *Facebook.* Retrieved from: www.facebook.com/notes/mark-zuckerberg/a-privacy-focused-vision-for-social-networking/10156700570096634/

CHAPTER 5

Step 3: Implementation and Monitoring

Joining Conversations and Creating Purposeful Interaction

> Strategic campaigns recognize that brands must engage and build meaningful conversations within social spaces to truly be effective in leveraging the potential of social media platforms.

Having completed the first two steps of developing a social media campaign, formative research in social listening and strategic design in campaign creation, it is now time to implement the campaign. This is the most visible part of any social media effort. Sometimes, in an effort to stay relevant and be engaged, brands jump straight to this stage. They neglect the listening that helps identify what conversations and people are most relevant in their social communities and the strategy to ensure their social efforts support organizational goals. Both of those steps are essential in order to effectively implement a social campaign and develop robust engagement with social media communities. This chapter will explore two general areas: implementing content through the use of a content calendar and monitoring the impact of the campaign using constant engagement with social communities. Prior to looking at these approaches to engagement, it is also important to examine the overall structure that brands are using in order to effectively implement and interact through social media.

SOCIAL CARE

Increasingly, brands are aware that social media is not simply a pre-programmed communication platform but a dynamic relational tool to engage stakeholders. This concept is known as *social care* and is defined as "stakeholder engagement on social media channels that bolsters an organization's credibility and reputation in order to develop loyalty and commitment from the public."[1] This means that it is not simply about publicity, selling a product, or only interacting with customers. Rather, social media is a direct connection to a variety of publics—people who are customers, but also *potential* customers, investors, donors, volunteers, the local community, and many other groups. In light of this, interactions on social media, both positive and negative, have the potential to influence factors such as brand reputation, loyalty, credibility, and trust.

To help create accessibility, responsiveness, and interaction, brands have begun launching social care teams. These are often composed of representatives from a variety of organizational departments such as marketing, HR, legal, communication, PR, and so on. This allows the team to effectively respond to a variety of stakeholder communication pieces effectively. Keith Quesenberry points out that, "Distributing social responsibilities to relevant people across the organization can be efficient, be effective, and help make one-on-one customer engagement scalable.[2] These kinds of teams meet the new expectations that Kim and Freberg[3] recognized when they said,

> Ultimately, social care seems to be a communication method that is established with the presumption that key publics desire and expect to have the ability to personally interact with brands, receiving customized responses and care from a variety of touch-points within the organization.[4]

While this chapter will continue to explore the particular applications, tools, and practices needed to effectively monitor and interact during the life cycle of a particular campaign, it is critical to remember that brands have *ongoing* conversations with the public. Thus, using the recommended ethical decision-making model for social care communication can also be a useful metric for monitoring ethical communication practices in any specific campaign's implementation cycle as well. The acronym SOCIAL[5] asks social media communicators to consider whether the particular communication is:

- *Specific* to the individual the communication is intended for rather than a mass-communication response that appears to be individual;
- *Open*, meaning that the information is transparent and honest for both the individual as well as the public who may read the information if it is posted as a public reply;

- *Collaborative* among departments in the brand so that the individual receives information that is needed from any or multiple departments through the social media communication rather than a social media reply that requires the individual to then email/call multiple other departments in the brand, which is why the cross-functional team is so critical;
- *Immediate* for the individual, which requires a rapid response and dedicated team that is actively listening and interacting with a variety of social media communication pieces (not just emergencies, crises, or the "loudest" individuals);
- *Authentic* so that it is designed for a relationship, which focuses on the values of being respectful and transparent in public-centric communication; and finally
- *Loyalty*, which focuses on the ultimate outcome of social media care teams and communication being to create loyalty—if the interaction is likely to damage or inhibit loyalty, another option should be considered.

The formation of social care teams and the adoption of social care as a philosophy by organizations indicate a maturation of social media in brand communication. Similar to social businesses being a model/ philosophy to support social media interaction, as discussed in the first chapter, social care teams represent another philosophical shift. Social care is another way that brands are making social media communication a natural and authentic outworking of their overall mission/vision as a brand. Rather than using it as a tool to only publicize or respond when there are issues, social care as a philosophy embraces the idea that social media is *the* platform that equalizes power between all publics and the brands that they are engaged with by facilitating dynamic, immediate interaction.

Never before has the public had such access to brands. Historically, legacy communication media such as newspapers, radio, and magazines were all one-way. The early days of social media illustrated the struggle brands go through when shifting from a one-way communication platform to a two-way one. Now, with increased expectations of brand accountability, accessibility, and advocacy, the public is watching to see which brands are transparent in their social media communication's intentions. That is why social care is critical: It is a tangible expression, both at an organizational structure level and at an applied interaction level, that the brand values, cares about, and is listening to the public.

The foundation of social care as a philosophy can help guide interaction throughout particular campaigns. But it is still important to understand best practices and standards in establishing quality campaign measurement and engagement. The first step is to create a content calendar.

CONTENT CALENDARS

A content calendar, as previously described in the general content calendar portion of a strategic plan for social media, helps develop purposeful interaction across all the platforms on which a brand is active. The goal of a campaign content calendar is to capture all the information that is needed in order to implement the campaign effectively, which requires it to have much more detail than the general social media content calendar. In addition, because it is a holistic calendar, it gives a 30,000-foot perspective of the communication occurring across all platforms, allowing a unified approach to engagement with online audiences. Put simply, *content calendars* are documents that contain all posts and all content that are to be posted in a given time period, for all platforms, and identify the way in which those posts support the campaign objectives.

Key Elements

There are several key components that should be present in a social media campaign content calendar. The areas to specify include: the date, platform, organizational objective being supported, specific campaign goal/objectives being supported, precise audience the message is created to reach, strategy that is being enacted, keywords or topic of the content, the action desired from the audience as a result of the content, and the actual content of each post. The ideal process is to create a content calendar for the entire campaign while also leaving flexibility for some adjustments to be made in real time. Although the content calendar will document the campaign delivery, it will not be able to capture the ways to respond to a social community, which is a key component of a social campaign. This live-time interaction behavior will be addressed later in this chapter. At this point, a social media campaign content calendar should simply be able to effectively reflect each strategy and tactic that was identified in the campaign design.

Figure 5.1 Content Calendar Elements

Meaning Making

A primary goal of developing a content calendar is to pay specific attention to understanding *when* it will be most meaningful to deliver a message to a particular audience.[6] As part of this, review the information gathered during the listening stage in order to identify the best days and times to engage with specific audiences on platforms. Although it is possible to find general information such as this online, it is always beneficial to compare those general studies with the research gathered on the specific social media community of the individual brand that the campaign is designed to engage. Next, consider whether there are any significant events or dates that are occurring during a campaign that should be kept in mind. Be sure to leverage certain holidays or events to enhance a message. For example, a non-profit brand may encourage giving or donations during Thanksgiving or Christmas, tying in to the general cultural communication of benevolent actions in the holiday season. Another area to identify is dates that the organization would want to avoid posting on or would develop a post specifically dedicated to the date, apart from any campaign messaging, in order to show respect, such as 9/11. Keeping in mind the social media community's engagement times and general events in the year, social media strategists are able to develop a holistic social media campaign calendar.

Integrating a Content Distribution Plan

Previously, a content distribution plan that identified the percentages of social media posts that would be dedicated to specific organizational objectives was created. It is important to reference this plan when developing a social media campaign content calendar. This will not only aid in designing posts that stay in line with the organizational goals, but also specifically support the campaign's objectives. For example, a brand may still end up with 45% of the posts driving traffic to the website, but now the traffic will be driven to the specific landing page that is the focus of the social media campaign, as opposed to the homepage that may have been the generic link used for social media posts not associated with the specific campaign.

Also identify whether any other, non-campaign-specific social media content will be posted during the life cycle of the campaign. To determine if this is the case, look at the general social media calendar for the department. It may be that, every Friday, LinkedIn has workplace tips for employees. That would be something to keep in mind when developing posts for the social media campaign content calendar. If, as part of the campaign, a change to that post topic needs to take place, that should be addressed with the social media director as well as the HR team, who would need to be notified so they are not caught off guard when the Friday workplace tip content is not posted during the campaign. However, it may also be possible to maintain certain generic posts while customizing them according to the campaign genre. If a social media campaign is focused on the ways the organization can enhance leadership training, for example, the Friday post for employees could be customized to describe how managers can effectively develop leaders in their departments. This would still stay on message with the campaign goal, but also resonate with the Friday focus on employees from HR.

Campaign Goals and Audiences

The next aspect to identify is which specific campaign goals or objectives are being supported by the post. For every post, on every platform, the ultimate purpose of the post within the big picture of the campaign should be clear. Be able to connect each post to a specific goal or objective to measure effectiveness. In addition, the audience for each post should be clear. It could be that, for the campaign overall, the audience is all the platform's users. Each post, however, may have segmented audiences to allow for stronger messaging. For example, if the organization is a university, the campaign may be specifically around recruitment. Audiences could include prospective students, parents, and incoming students. As the content calendar is created, identifying which audience is the focus of each post will help in the assessment of the campaign's message effectiveness.

Strategy

In this section, identify the exact strategy to which the post will relate. For example, if an advertising initiative was included in the campaign design strategies, be sure that each ad that is created and posted is labeled "advertising campaign." If a contest was launched on Instagram as a strategy, label posts that have content for the contest as "Instagram contest." As with the identification of the objectives, this will be a key way to assess effectiveness later on.

Message Creation through Topics and Keywords

Part of a social strategy is consistently optimizing social media posts so users who are interested in the same topic can easily find them. When designing a content calendar, reference the main keywords or topics identified in the listening stage. Classify every post by a specific topic or keyword that is being focused on so that it is easy to recognize which type of content effective posts have, which categories of keywords may need more posts, and which genres of content may need to have more strategic messaging in order to be effective.

Audience Response

Each post is tied to a specific outcome desired from the audience. Remember, every post supports a SMART, outcome-based objective, or something that the audience will *do* as a result of campaign activity. And each objective is tied to key audiences in order for it to be successful. To determine what audience response is needed for the post, consider what has to happen for the objective of that post to be reached. Perhaps it is sharing content, clicking a link and signing up for something, or an action as simple as hitting the like button. Be sure to carefully reflect on the specific action that the audience needs to take to help fulfill the objective that the post was designed to support within the campaign.

Content

Finally, the last portion is the actual content of the post. In this portion, it is important to reference the brand's social voice, key messages, and message map. This is the area where social strategists actually design and craft the messages that will go on each platform for each post. Include the exact wording for every tweet, post, snap, pin, vine, and video. Be sure the wording reflects the topic, is consistent with the brand's persona and tone, resonates with the target audience, and is of appropriate length for the platform. Also include any hashtags, tags, mentions, or other elements that should be part of the post. Finally, be sure also to place the exact image, video, and link that are needed as part of the post. Within this content section, review the post to ensure that every strategy, such as the launch of a social media advertising campaign, the initiation of a contest, or any other effort, is accounted for in the calendar. Be sure that all the details and information that need to be communicated are included in the content calendar. The aim is that the content section is a complete package of all the information needed to implement the entire campaign.

Review

As the content calendar is finalized, review it several times to ensure that it is on-message, supports the organization's overall communications, and is strategic for each audience. There are several steps involved in accomplishing this review.

First, connect with the marketing or PR department to review the organization's overall communication that will be happening via the website, blog, newsletter, or in person to ensure that the social media content calendar does not conflict with the timing of other communications from the brand. Ideally, not only will it not conflict, but the overall organizational messages will be *enhanced* as social media is used to support the mission of the brand.

Second, sort the content calendar by each platform. Review the content to make sure that multiple posts are not scheduled too frequently on any platform, that they are varied in content, and that the timing seems appropriate in light of any holidays, events, or activities that fall during the campaign.

Third, sort the content calendar by strategies. Be sure that every tactic is represented in the content calendar in order to accomplish the strategy that is being reviewed. For example, if the brand is running a contest, is there a post that introduces the contest and shares the rules? If there is a strategy that is about highlighting information and positioning the brand as a thought leader, are there enough posts to actually position the organization as a *leader* rather than something that only happens once or twice over the course of a campaign?

Fourth, sort the content calendar by topics/keywords. Review each post to make sure that the messaging is consistent. Be sure that the tone is engaging and relational, but also that the keyword or topic is clear within the message.

Finally, sort the content calendar by goals/objectives. Review the posts and ask: If the audience engages as intended with this post, will the goal or objective be met? If the answer is yes, it is time to move on

Date	Platform	Campaign Goal	Objective	Purpose	Audience	Strategy	Keyword/Topic	Content of Post
May 2	Facebook	Goal #1	Objective #2	Nvwsletter Signups	Young Professionals	Providing Free Resume Tips	Resume, Career, Young Professional	"3 tips to make your resume stand out to managers. Sign up for a full resume-review check-list today." PHOTO: Job Interview Candidate

Figure 5.2 Content Calendar Example

to the next step in the campaign. If the answer is no, it is important to review the content calendar, identify any holes, and create the appropriate content.

A word of caution: People generally assume a content calendar will be quick to produce. This could not be further from the truth. A well-thought-out, strategic content calendar is quite robust. A lot of work and expertise are required to craft an effective content calendar. Be sure to allow enough time between designing the campaign and the deadline for when the campaign must go live in order to create an excellent content calendar. Effective content calendars can be one of the most important tools throughout a campaign.

ENGAGING DURING A CAMPAIGN

The actual *launching* of a social media campaign is only the beginning of what social media strategists need to focus on during the live portion of a campaign. Throughout the course of a campaign, brands should engage with their social media communities and continually monitor their progress towards the SMART, outcome-based objectives of the campaign.

Responding and Engaging

Part of dedicating time to social media as a brand is recognizing that it is not a one-way platform but rather a dynamic conversation, which requires continual interaction. To foster relationships with the social media brand community, organizations need to be available and approachable. In light of this, whether the organization only has a few hours a week or an entire staff dedicated to social media, planning time for engagement with the social media community is crucial. There are several approaches to monitoring and engaging social media brand communities during a campaign that are helpful to consider.

Using Alerts

Social media platforms have the option to set up alerts when something happens on a brand's profile. For example, it is possible to receive a notification if someone mentions the brand on Twitter or if someone posts to the brand's Facebook page. Whoever is responsible on the social media team for engagement on a specific platform should customize the notifications so they are alerted when the community interacts. This is a quick and easy way to become aware of someone engaging with the brand online. Once an alert is received, be sure to respond. Remember, studies indicate that most people anticipate that a brand will respond within 1 hour.[7]

Listening Principles

Responding to notifications is a minimum requirement for brands that desire a strong social media community, and there are many more ways that are important to incorporate if there is the capacity within an organization. To begin with, it is helpful to implement the same paradigm as was used in the listening phase. Utilize social listening tools to monitor keywords and topics that are relevant to the brand. Also review social sites for common misspellings of the brand name just in case mentions or comments may be missing from the official platform alerts. Dedicate time each day to respond to these topics, even if the brand has not been directly tagged or mentioned. Be sure to interact in a natural, appropriate way. Remember that social media is about being relational—not being awkward and intruding on conversations that are not highly applicable or open to interaction from the brand.

In addition to engaging in general conversations, interact with the specific content being shared as part of the organization's social channels. If the brand is gaining new followers as a result of the campaign, be sure to thank them for following. If there are people who are commenting on an Instagram picture, be sure to respond. Social media is about being *social*. A campaign will not succeed, even with the best-designed content calendar, if there is no engagement with the brand's social communities once the initial post goes live.

Monitoring

Hand in hand with the launch of the content calendar on social media and engagement with the brand communities, the brand must also be proactive in monitoring social media communication. Rather than simply waiting to evaluate the effectiveness of a social media campaign until the very end, it is important to continually analyze the responses and interaction that are being gained as a result of the campaign. Ann Handley and C. C. Chapman[8] suggest that, "Good content always has an objective; it's created with intent. It therefore carries triggers to action."[9] The idea behind this is that each post created and used in the campaign has a purpose—and social media professionals should be able to watch the brand community and see that an action has been triggered as a result of the social media post.

Real-Time Marketing (RTM)

Along with social media content calendars and strategic planning for engagement, brands must be prepared to facilitate real-time communication. Chris Kerns[10] defines real-time marketing as "the practice of creating content inspired by a current topic, trend or event."[11] Essentially, it is the ability of an organization to adjust and participate in conversations organically, as they emerge in real-time. Although it can be tempting to just stick with programmed content, the ability of a brand to adjust within the moment is crucial. That is why monitoring is so essential in social media campaigns. Kerns[12] points out that, "if the brand wants to participate in the conversation, they'll need to create a memorable take on that current event and not just try to start a separate dialogue."[13] The ability to strategically design a campaign and also have expert insight into when and how to adjust and change content in light of current events is a sign of true expertise in social media.

Planning for the Unplanned

Brands should be aware that there will always be unplanned elements during the life cycle of a social media campaign. By recognizing significant events such as the Super Bowl, the Golden Globes, or an election, the brand can create some general content that acknowledges key components of those events. With research that is done ahead of time, premade posts can be crafted regarding certain elements such as the start time of the game or the background of a candidate. In addition, planning can be done by pulling data on the conversations from the past years when an event occurred and identifying information such as: What kinds of posts were most successful? What SOV did each group have during the event? Be sure to gather information beyond just the event itself and explore the implications for social interaction that occurred, such as which kinds of posts generated the highest engagement or involved influencers the most.

Once you have the background information from social media and the base level details for the event, it is important to remember that real-time engagement is powerful precisely because it is not something that can be premade. Dynamic connection happens when a brand engages

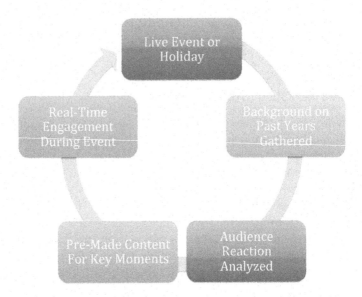

Figure 5.3 Process for Real-Time Engagement

in real-time social conversations—it is authentic, in the moment, and relevant. For example, responding to a touchdown play and tweeting the moment it happens is one way a brand could engage with real-time activity. As discussed previously, it can be hard to have the capabilities to perform with such live engagement because it requires the social team to be thoroughly familiar with the brand's voice, ready to engage in the moment, and to possess the authority within the organization not to have to run a post through multiple layers of approval before going live. Essentially, real-time engagement is when social media becomes most like a face-to-face interaction with the brand: It should be informed and represent the organization well, but be deeply humanized, interactive, and relevant to the conversation at hand. It is a fluid dialogue that captures the attention of the key audiences involved in the conversation. Kerns[14] summarized this nicely when he said, "Uncertainty is part of the social media world, and with RTM it's no different. When you know an event is coming, but can't be sure of all the details, it takes a unique approach and a large dose of patience."[15]

Key Metrics

In order to track triggering actions and social activity, carefully monitor each social post throughout a campaign. An effective way to do this is to use the same file that was designed for the content calendar with the addition of a few new columns: KPIs, influencers engaged, and time decay. Each of these new columns will come in very useful in the fourth step, when evaluating the effectiveness of the campaign.

First, record any social media engagement or actions that serve as KPIs for a brand; this helps identify movement towards the success of an objective. *Key progress indicators* (KPIs) are metrics that provide meaningful insight into the advance of a campaign toward reaching its goals. For example, the brand might record the following as KPIs for a given post on social media: 100 retweets, 340 favorites, and 25 replies. If the post being monitored is on Instagram, it would be important to record how many likes, comments, and mentions were garnered. Whatever metrics happened as a result of a post on a given platform would be recorded in this new KPI column on the content calendar.

Second, identify which influencers were engaged. Although everyone plays a valuable role in a social media community, social influencers carry a certain level of impact whenever they engage with social content. In the listening stage, influencers for the brand on various platforms were identified. It is helpful to record whether these influencers engaged with a specific post, what they did with the post, and the result of their engagement. For example, a brand might note that a specific influencer shared a post on LinkedIn, which resulted in 100 more likes, 20 shares, and a conversation that had 15 people participating on the influencer's LinkedIn profile.

Third, identify the time decay of the post. Depending on the detail of the organization, it might be best to list the total of social activities that took place on the first day, second day, third day, and by the end of the first week. If it is helpful to have more detail, and time allows, record the first day's activity by hours or hour blocks in order to provide details on when the community most engaged with the content and what kinds of activities happened throughout the lifetime of the post. Because the time-decay area can be quite complex, consider breaking this portion it into multiple columns so that it is easier to sort later on, labeling each column either by a day or time-block period.

At the end of this stage, review the brand's monitoring metrics to assess the impact of each post, strategy, objective, and goal. It is now possible to mine these data for the most effective times to engage with audiences and ways to increase interaction with influencers. More details of how to use this information during the evaluation of a campaign will be provided in the next chapter. However, before moving on to evaluation, a very crucial part of engaging and monitoring in social media is understanding how to handle a crisis while it unfolds on social media.

EXPERT INSIGHT

Leo Morejon

What do you think is one hallmark competency social media professionals need to succeed?

In order to do well in social media, you need to be able to sell your ideas and you need to be a trusted advisor. Social media is changing all the time, and in order to try new and different things (or even established things), you often will need more budget and resources for things that might not allow for a measurable return on investment right away. In order to reach and persuade the powers that be and stakeholders including clients, bosses, and team members, it is best to educate and be a trusted advisor.

What is an effective way for a brand to use a content calendar, but also be free to interact and be responsive in the moment?

I suggest that you build your content calendar with preplanned content and be ready to change it at a moment's notice. This can include changing content, optimizing, or stopping it all together to ensure you jump into a real-time contextual moment without sending mixed messages or over-messaging audiences. It comes down to being a good traffic cop, focusing on flow and avoiding traffic or accidents.

How can a brand effectively monitor and engage with social conversations taking place outside of the brand's official profile without appearing intrusive?

I generally focus on telling brands to be authentic, to add value during each engagement, to use their gut, and to always put themselves in someone else's shoes. While all that is still true, it's also true that it's a calculated risk, and there might be someone out there that will find it creepy or intrusive. For the most part though, most people won't find it intrusive/creepy; they expect it now, and it can mean a lot of great connections between brands and people.

What tips would you suggest for brands to keep in mind when engaging live in order to be authentic and interactive, but still on message with social media goals?

I advise brands to take chances while still understanding their own voice, the brand's mission, and its respective audiences.

In what ways, if any, does the information gathered from a social media campaign drive future strategy or engagement?

Every single campaign is a data point for the future. They're just that: data points. You need to know which data points are the right ones to focus on for the future and which to ignore. It's mostly about context. What was the past campaign about, and what are future campaigns about? It's not always apples to apples, in fact it's mostly apples to dogs.

What do you think the next big trends will be in social media for brands?

The next big trends will be about e-commerce and how it plays out from a marketing and executional perspective. Facebook and other platforms are bullish on developing and owning this space. While brands that can easily set up DTC (direct to consumer) pathways will be ahead of the game, other brands will soon follow.

Connect with Leo: Twitter.com/MoreLeo; www.linkedin.com/in/leonardom/; LeonardoM.com/

Leo Morejon is a successful marketing leader known for distinctions such as a Guinness World Record for Most Facebook Likes, pioneering real-time marketing while working on campaigns including the Oreo Super Bowl Blackout Tweet, and managing large international teams

SOCIAL MEDIA AND CRISES

A crisis, by its very nature, is substantial. It is an event, or the perception of an event, that damages the relationships between a brand and the public, resulting in a reduction in the organization's ability, or its inability, to continue to fulfill its mission. Freberg and Palenchar[16] explain that, "crises come in various forms and can impact an organization or individual at any time. In other words, crises are significant, disruptive events that often feature rapid onset."[17] Reynolds and Seeger[18] point out that communication during a crisis should "explain the specific event, identify likely consequences and outcomes, and provide specific harm-reducing information to affected communities in an honest, candid, prompt, accurate and complete manner."[19] Ideally, organizations are able to identify potential crises before they occur. But, as already explained, there are many times when a crisis will strike without warning, and there will be no possibility of diffusing it in advance.

Social media comes into play as part of the communication dissemination efforts during a crisis. Efforts to reply and provide accurate information during a crisis must be made in alignment with the organization's overall crisis plan. The integration with the organization's crisis response plan was explained in the social listening phase of campaign development. Owing to the highly uncertain nature of a crisis, it is important to provide needed information as quickly as possible to impacted audiences.[20] This communication is done by specifically crafting messages for the stakeholders who have been identified as being impacted and developing messages to get accurate and helpful information to key audiences.[21]

Although there are many categories of crises that an organization may face, in the context of the social media team it can be helpful to think in terms of two large genres: Crises that result from something outside social media and crises that result from activity or interaction via social media. It is important to explore not only how organizations can integrate social media effectively as a general part of their crises plans, but also how social media teams may best respond in the monitoring step of a social media campaign should a crisis due to social media emerge.

Crises External to Social Media

As defined above, crises can come about at any time and have dire consequences. Freberg and Palenchar[22] point out that a crisis can be both an event that has occurred as well as a *perception* of events. Pearson and Clair[23] explain the idea of crisis further by describing one as a "low-probability, high-impact event."[24] Crises, then, can be events actually occurring or rumors of things that may happen. Because a crisis impacts the organization and stakeholders, rumors can sometimes be just as damaging as events that have occurred. Elements that contribute to crises include the magnitude of the crisis, control over the event, the reactions of the public to the event, and the potential that the event (if perceived as a crisis) will be one that will actually happen.[25] Because of the variety of forms a crisis can take, including workplace rumors, natural disasters, human errors, accidents, and many others, it is helpful to categorize crises in order for communicators to effectively engage with audiences in meaningful ways.[26]

When an organization faces a crisis, utilizing social media to reach key audiences is helpful because it allows people to feel that they have more control over the crisis, as well as feeling like they are connected to a community.[27] The information that is posted by the organization, however, needs to be in line with the overall messaging from the crisis response team. Most crisis plans for organizations include sections on specific types of crises that may hit an organization—be it a product recall, natural disaster, violence, or some other potential impacting event. As part of the crisis plan, it is helpful to pre-craft how social media can be used during the event to provide timely, authentic, transparent, and relevant information to the social media community. If there is a product recall, for example, sample posts could be created that include general language on how to return products and what steps consumers should take. In preparation for a natural disaster, drafting information that includes where to go for shelter or tips on personal safety after an earthquake may be appropriate. It could also be that the organization will already have websites created with some basic information that will be black (not available) until a crisis happens. If that is the case, it is also possible to premake posts that reference the site, with the link, so that posts can go live immediately after a crisis hits. The goal is to have the social media strategy work in unison with other communication efforts, supporting the messaging strategies and responses of the crisis team.

Crises Caused within Social Media

The second genre of crises that a social media team should prepare for are those that originate within or because of social media. What exactly counts as a crisis in social media? It can be defined as: "a crisis issue that arises in or is amplified by social media, and results in negative mainstream media coverage, a change in business process, or financial loss."[28] These kinds of crises regularly make the news. An example of this is when a BBC reporter mistakenly reported that Queen Elizabeth II had died in a tweet that, despite being deleted quickly, had already been picked up by other news sources such as CNN and other publications.[29] Another example comes from KitchenAid, whose employee accidently sent an offensive tweet to President Obama about his dead grandmother. The brand quickly responded, apologizing and stating that the "tasteless joke in no way represents our values at KitchenAid, and that person won't be tweeting for us anymore."[30] Still another social media case study can be found in Papa John's response to a ten-word tweet from a customer that included a picture of the receipt from her recent order, which referred to the customer using a racial slur: "lady chinky eyes."[31]

Figure 5.4 Contributors to Crises in Social Media

These kinds of crises go straight to the center of the driving force behind a brand: The credibility and trustworthiness of the organization as perceived by the public. Coombs and Holladay,[32] leading crisis communication researchers, explained that social media crises are often reputational in nature: "Reputational concerns are important because an organizational reputation is a valued asset that must be cultivated and protected."[33]

In order to effectively respond to a social media crisis, there are three sources that may help determine the kind and nature of response required by the social media team.[34] Coombs suggests the three sources of social media crises are (1) organizational misuses of social media, (2) dissatisfied customers, and (3) challenges in social media.[35]

The first type of crisis, and possibly the most common type to make headlines, is organizational misuse of social media. This type of social media crisis can be defined as when an "organization violates the norms of behavior in a particular social media channel."[36] Crises such as these can often be prevented with additional training of employees, research carried out by organizations before they create content for social media, and a clear structure for addressing social media crises involving identified roles, responsibilities, and approval processes.[37] A strong example of a crisis caused by organizational misuse of social media is the classic example that occurred when DiGiorno decided to use the hashtag #WhyIStayed. The hashtag was a trending conversation that was a response to Ray Rice, an NFL player, being suspended after beating his wife. Women flocked to social media and used the hashtag #WhyIStayed to share their stories of what kept them in abusive and violent relationships. Without doing research or understanding the community having a conversation around that hashtag, DiGiorno used the hashtag and added three simple words: "#WhyIStayed you had pizza." Although this was a substantial debacle, largely criticized across social media platforms, DiGiorno's social media team did take swift action to actively engage with the crisis. After rapidly deleting the tweet and apologizing for its offensive nature, the brand began to individually apologize to each and every user who had engaged with it regarding the inappropriate brand tweet. Rather than cutting and pasting in automated apologies, each tweet was customized and showed a high level of remorse, authenticity, and transparency. This incident is a prime illustration of why brands should research before joining conversations, but is also a great example of an appropriate social response using individualized engagement through social media platforms.[38]

The second source of crises in social media is customer dissatisfaction. Coombs[39] explains that, "Dissatisfied customer social media crises are really a customer relations problem rather than a crisis."[40] However, social media is often used as a key part of public relations and, specifically, consumer or customer relations as it has the ability to foster two-way dialogue to resolve concerns. Key audiences have a higher likelihood of believing that an organization is trustworthy when there is two-way communication taking place.[41] In light of this, social media often becomes a primary platform for dealing with dissatisfied customers. In the airline industry, there are plenty of opportunities for this type of crisis to happen. JetBlue has become known as a leading example of a brand that uses social media to engage with customers and help resolve issues, minimizing crises due to dissatisfied customers. Back in 2010, JetBlue dedicated an entire team of people, 17 at the time, solely to interacting with customers on social media. This was highly unusual at the time, and it was one of the first airlines to make such a move.[42] Laurie Meacham, manager of customer commitment and social media for JetBlue Airways, explained that, for brands to be relevant and truly engage with customer needs on social media, the content has to be authentic and relational. The humanization is essential for organizational success:

There is a lot of vanity engagement happening out there. People talking about nothing and responding about nothing. We always recognize that as a brand, we are a guest in this community. Brands came in uninvited. We need to earn the right to be here.[43]

JetBlue has helped customers in sticky situations, such as one customer who tweeted about not knowing why there was a $50 charge to be on standby for an earlier flight home. JetBlue was able to tweet back and address the customer's concerns without it becoming a significant issue.[44] Although many brands have now followed this type of example, it is helpful to look at the trendsetters, and JetBlue is one such brand.

Sometimes, however, nothing will change the situation for key publics—in the case of JetBlue, flights will still be delayed or missed, and fees may still be incurred. When customers are upset on social media, and the brand's social media team cannot meaningfully engage or assist in the moment, it may be wise to wait to interact until there is more information or resources become available. Meacham refers to this type of situation as a DNE: Do not engage. "DNE is totally different from ignoring. We are taking note, and we will follow up where appropriate," she said.[45] The goal is not to ignore the customer or relationship, but to wait for the appropriate time to interact or directly contact them in a way that allows for follow-up that genuinely builds the relationship, rather than simply creating more social noise. It is worth noting that records of these types of interaction, whether they had a positive outcome or one that results in a DNE, are important for long-term planning on social media and crisis response.

The final genre of social media crises that originate within social media is called challenges, which is when key audiences believe an organization or brand has policies or behaviors that are inappropriate.[46] "The core of the challenge is that stakeholders argue that the organization is acting irresponsibly. Those charges can erode reputations."[47] There are three types of challenges that may come up within a social media crisis. The first is organic and occurs when the expectations of the online brand community are not met by the organization's behaviors. This often happens when a brand fails to maintain a strong grip on its online tribe's values, opinions, beliefs, and behaviors.

> If organizational behaviors do not change to mirror those of the stakeholders, stakeholders will perceive the organization as violating their expectations. The misalignment of expectations can be a natural process because organizations often lag behind stakeholder expectations (value and belief changes).[48]

A second type of challenge is an exposé, which arises "when stakeholders prove an organization's words are inconsistent with its actions."[49] This may happen when organizations claim to be environmentally friendly, but then information surfaces that show they are actually causing harm to the environment. Another example could be organizations that advocate for social justice, but then are found to be using sweatshops to produce their products.

Finally, the third kind of challenge is called a villain challenge, which, as the name suggests, is when groups make a claim that the organization itself is bad and needs to change. An excellent example of a challenge crisis can be found in the social media campaign launched by SeaWorld as part of its response to the documentary *BlackFish*, which accused SeaWorld of mistreating the animals, especially orcas, in its facilities. Because of the boycotts and impact on its bottom line that resulted from the documentary, SeaWorld created a multimillion-dollar campaign to repair its image by addressing public concerns and correcting misinformation presented in the film.[50] With more than 1 million people contacting SeaWorld through PETA's online website, the brand was looking for a way to directly engage with its key audiences. The social media element of the campaign was a Q&A session with the hashtag #AskSeaWorld.[51] Unfortunately, the campaign was critically received. Rather than the kinds of questions the brand may have been hoping for, it received questions from critics asking why SeaWorld would breed more animals in captivity when it is already overcrowded and criticizing its animal care and the death rates of SeaWorld orcas.[52] These kinds of responses represent villain challenges, as they were directed at the very core of the brand, claiming that the organization itself was unethical.

Organizations can respond in a number of ways to challenge crises, resulting in the potential to maintain trust and credibility in the eyes of the public. It is very important to consult the PR crisis plan and guide to determine proper responses to crisis situations, particularly if the nature of the crisis is a challenge, since it deals with the core reputation of the organization as a whole. Some ways in which professionals may decide to respond to challenges include (1) refuting the claims made in the challenge, (2) reforming the behaviors or actions of the organization to align with the key audience expectations, and (3) repenting by acknowledging the fault and harm done and explaining what will be done to rectify the situation.[53] Responding to a challenge in social media is the most complex of all the social crises with which a team may deal. Be sure to "carefully assess the nature of the challenge before selecting a response strategy. Organic, expose, and villain challenges have unique features that make different response strategies more or less effective."[54]

ORGANIZATIONAL SOCIAL FATIGUE

One final area to address in the monitoring step of a social media campaign, though an area that often receives very little focus, deals with social media fatigue. *Social fatigue* is when the level of interaction and repetitious nature of social media cause individuals to shut down or tune out.

Organizations experience fatigue in social media that can stem from having too many platforms and not enough resources to effectively engage or from lacking a clear vision for why social media supports the brand's vision. Just like individuals, brands should carefully consider their capacity to maintain authentic relationships on social media. Rebecca Lieb[55] points out the challenge to engaging strategically on social media:

> Like consumers, brands are challenged to make social channel choices. Spreading themselves too thin in an effort to be everywhere, for everyone, leads to challenges few brands are prepared to meet. The demands of continual parallel content creation. The ability to react and respond to earned media in multiple social channels.[56]

Essentially, brands must use discretion to avoid social media burn-out. Ted Coiné and Mark Babbitt[57] give three key ways brands can avoid feeding social media fatigue. First, be careful that the organization is not contributing negative content, or simply creating more social noise in an already over-saturated media environment. Make each post, tweet, and snap meaningful, having been designed with a purpose. Second, "deliberately be a relentless giver" on social media by highlighting others, being a resource, and genuinely interacting with people.[58] Finally, avoid being a "social echo chamber."[59] In other words, if the brand is simply reposting what has already been posted again and again and is no longer contributing original content to the social media community, take some time away. Give the brand space to be silent if there is nothing significant to contribute to the social world.

For brands on social media to be relevant, breaking through the relevance filters of users, they must stay authentically engaged. Content cannot simply be regurgitated because nothing new is available. Adding to the noise on social media does not help an organization stand apart or build stronger relationships. Rather, it should refocus on the purpose of social media, the ways for the brand to enhance relationships, and then develop interaction based on those elements.

KEY CONCEPT SNAPSHOT

1. Content calendars provide a way to harmonize communication on behalf of brands, developing a tapestry of unified interaction for the vision of the organization's values.
2. Crises on social media are going to happen—brands that are truly strategic in social media prepare for them *before* they occur, allowing a proactive approach to social media during crisis rather than a reactive one.
3. Social media is all about *relationships*. Monitoring and responding to people in social spaces shows authenticity and builds trust.
4. Relevance filters require brands to focus on creating meaningful and relevant content in social media in order to avoid social fatigue within its brand community.

NOTES

1   Kim & Freberg, 2020, p.14.
2   2016, para. 3.
3   2020.
4   p. 4.
5   Kim & Freberg, 2020.
6   Wilcox & Cameron, 2009, p. 156.
7   Baer, n.d.
8   2012.
9   p. 15.
10 2014.
11 p. 15.
12 2014.
13 p. 29.
14 2014.
15 p. 127.
16 2012.
17 p. 84.
18 2005.
19 p. 46.
20 Seeger, Sellnow, & Ulmer, 1998.
21 Heath, Lee, & Ni, 2009.
22 2012.
23 1998.
24 p. 60.
25 Freberg & Palenchar, 2012.
26 Freberg & Palenchar, 2012, p. 84.
27 Freberg & Palenchar, 2012.
28 Owyang, Jones, Tran, & Nguyen, 2011, p. 17.

29 Elgot & Plunkett, 2015.
30 Agnes, 2012.
31 Duke, 2012.
32 2014.
33 p. 23.
34 Coombs, 2012.
35 p. 23.
36 Coombs, 2012, p. 23.
37 Owyang, Jones, Tran, & Nguyen, 2011.
38 Sands, 2014.
39 2012.
40 p. 23.
41 Freberg & Palenchar, 2013.
42 Piazza, 2014.
43 Quoted in Piazza, 2014, "Speaking in one voice," para. 8.
44 Kolowich, 2014.
45 Quoted in Piazza, 2014, "Speaking in one voice," para. 16.
46 Coombs, 2012, p. 23
47 Coombs, 2012, p. 23.
48 Coombs, 2012, p. 25.
49 Coombs, 2012, p. 25.
50 Coffee, 2015.
51 Grisham, 2015.
52 Baker, 2015.
53 Coombs, 2012, pp. 25–26.
54 Coombs, 2012, p. 26.
55 2012.
56 "When to Invest Time in the New Things?" para. 5.
57 2014.
58 p. 221.
59 p. 221.

SUGGESTED READING

Freberg, K. (2018). *Social Media for Strategic Communication: Creative Strategies and Research-Based Applications*. Sage.
Kerns, C. (2014). *Trendology: Building an Advantage through Data-Driven Real-Time Marketing*. New York: Palgrave Macmillan.
Kim, C. & Freberg, K. (2020). Social Care and Professional Standards: Developing an Ethical Decision-Making Model. *Public Relations Journal*, 13(3), 1–24.

REFERENCES

Agnes, M. (2012, October 4). "KitchenAid: An excellent example of successful crisis management." *MelissaAgnes.com*. Retrieved from: http://melissaagnes.com/kitchenaid-an-excellent-example-in-social-media-crisis-communications/

Baer, J. (n.d.). "42 percent of consumers complaining in social media expect 60 minute response time." *Convince & Convert*. Retrieved from: www.convinceandconvert. com/social-media-research/42-percent-of-consumers-complaining-in-social-media-expect-60-minute-response-time/

Baker, D. (2015, March 27). "'Ask Seaworld' Twitter campaign chum in the water for critics." *The San Diego Union Tribune*. Retrieved from: www.utsandiego.com/news/2015/mar/27/ask-seaworld-twitter-campaign/

Coffee, P. (2015, March 24). "SeaWorld launched multi-million dollar reputation campaign." *PRNewser*. Retrieved from: www.adweek.com/prnewser/seaworld-launches-multi-million-dollar-reputation-campaign/111366

Coiné, T. & Babbitt, M. (2014). *A World Gone Social: How Companies Must Adapt to Survive*. New York: AMACOM, American Management Association.

Coombs, W. (2012). *Ongoing Crisis Communication: Planning, Managing, and Responding*. Thousand Oaks, CA: Sage.

Coombs, W. T. & Holladay, S. J. (2014). It's Not Just PR: Public Relations in Society. Malden, MA: Blackwell.

Duke, A. (2012, January 8). "Papa Johns apologizes for receipt's racial slur." *CNN*. Retrieved from: www.cnn.com/2012/01/08/us/new-york-papa-johns-receipt/

Elgot, J. & Plukett, J. (2015, June 3). "Rogue BBC tweet sparks global news alert about Queen's health." *The Guardian*. Retrieved from: www.theguardian.com/uk-news/2015/jun/03/queens-health-bbc-tweet-global-news-alert

Freberg, K. & Palenchar, M. J. (2013). Convergence of digital negotiation and risk challenges: Strategic implications of social media for risk and crisis communications. In Al-Deen H.S.N., Hendricks J.A. (eds) *Social Media and Strategic Communications* (pp. 83-100). Palgrave Macmillan, London.

Grisham, L. (2015, March 25). "'Ask Seaworld' ad campaign draws criticism." *USA Today*. Retrieved from: www.usatoday.com/story/news/nation-now/2015/03/25/seaworld-killer-whales-ad-campaign/70422606/

Handley, A., & Chapman, C. C. (2012). *Content Rules: How to Create Killer Blogs, Podcasts, Videos, Ebooks, Webinars (and More) that Engage Customers and Ignite Your Business*. Hoboken, NJ: Wiley.

Heath, R. L., Lee, J., & Ni, L. (2009). Crisis and Risk Approaches to Emergency Management Planning and Communication: The Role of Similarity and Sensitivity. *Journal of Public Relations Research*, 21(2), 123–141.

Kerns, C. (2014). *Trendology: Building an Advantage through Data-Driven Real-Time Marketing*. New York: Palgrave Macmillan.

Kim, C. & Freberg, K. (2020). Social Care and Professional Standards: Developing an Ethical Decision-Making Model. *Public Relations Journal*, 13(3), 1–24.

Kolowich, L. (2014, July 28). "Delighting people in 140 characters: An inside look at JetBlue's customer service success." *Hub Spot*. Retrieved from: http://blog.hubspot.com/marketing/jetblue-customer-service-twitter

Lieb, R. (2012, March 19). "How real is social media fatigue?" *Marketing Land*. Retrieved from: http://marketingland.com/how-real-is-social-media-fatigue-7665

Owyang, J., Jones, A., Tran, C., & Nguyen, A. (2011, August 31). "Social business readiness: How advanced companies prepare internally." *Altimeter*. Retrieved from: www.slideshare.net/jeremiah_owyang/social-readiness-how-advanced-companies-prepare

Pearson, C. M. & Clair, J. A. (1998). Reframing Crisis Management. *The Academy of Management Review*, 23(1), 59–76.

Piazza, J. (2014, July 29). "The secret of JetBlue's media success? Stay at home moms, cat memes—and a sense of humor." *Yahoo Travel*. Retrieved from: www.yahoo.com/travel/the-secrets-of-jetblues-social-media-success-93024204957.html

Quesenberry, K. (2016). *Social Media Is a Tool too Important to Be Left to the Marketing Department*. Retrieved from: https://hbr.org/2016/04/social-media-is-too-important-to-be-left-to-the-marketing-department

Reynolds, B. & Seeger, M. W. (2005). Crisis and Emergency Risk Communication as an Integrative Model. *Journal of Health Communication*, 10, 43–55.

Sands, K. (2014, September 9). "A lesson in crisis communications, courtesy of DiGiorno." *Huffington Post*. Retrieved from: www.huffingtonpost.com/katrina-sands/a-lesson-in-crisis-commun_b_5794122.html

Seeger, M. W., Sellnow, T. L., & Ulmer, R. R. (1998). Communication, organization and crisis. In Roloff, M. E. (Ed.) *Communication Yearbook 21*. Thousand Oaks, CA: Sage.

Wilcox, D. & Cameron, G. (2009). *Public Relations: Strategies and Tactics*. Boston: Person/Allyn & Bacon.

CHAPTER 6

Step 4: Evaluation

Showcasing Success and Growth Opportunities

> Social media experts should champion robust evaluation of each campaign as it not only provides evidence and support for the value of social media within a brand's overall communication efforts, but also because evaluation has a heuristic element that allows for future growth and greater expertise within the social world.

The final step in developing and managing social media campaigns is evaluating the effectiveness of the efforts. This step is critical in providing accountability and illustrating the value of social media for an organization. It is important, before developing the framework for evaluation, to understand the difference between *measurement* and *counting*. Unfortunately, people often oversimplify social media evaluation by viewing it as a simple set of numbers to be counted or gathered. The truth of the matter is that social media evaluation and measurement are much more rigorous than this. They require social media professionals to *apply* their expertise to the measurements that are gathered and then to develop meaningful applications from the data. Katie Delahaye Paine[1] explains it this way:

> *Counting* just adds things up and gets a total. *Measurement* takes those totals, analyzes what they mean, and uses that meaning to improve business practices. Measurement of your process and results—where you spend your time and money and what you get out of it—provides data necessary to make sound decisions. It helps you set priorities, allocate resources, and make choices. Without it, hunches and gut feelings prevail. Without it, mistakes get made and no one learns from them.[2]

There are a variety of metrics that are useful in the evaluation step for campaigns. To lay the foundation for understanding evaluation, it is helpful to reflect on the way data are used throughout a social media campaign. In addition, having a foundation of basic research practices and vocabulary can help clarify particular data analysis approaches in social media. Finally, the three levels to campaign evaluation will be explained: Preparation, implementation, and impact. Within each of these levels, specific processes and metrics that are important will be discussed.

DATA USE THROUGHOUT A SOCIAL MEDIA CAMPAIGN

Social media efforts should be driven by real-time activities: What audiences are doing, responding to, talking about, and engaging with all play a crucial role in social strategy. Data are gathered throughout a campaign to inform both decisions and strategies for brands. Sometimes, the data gathered are base metrics such as the number of likes, followers, comments, or mentions. However, as was discussed earlier, there are other kinds of metrics that are also helpful, including identifying influencers, measuring tone, and monitoring conversions. Although this chapter focuses on data collection, analysis, and interpretation in Step 4, evaluation, recognizing how a brand uses data throughout the entire campaign is an important competency.

Figure 6.1 Data Use through a Campaign

Social Listening

During the first step of the campaign, social media strategists gather formative data on the organization, current social media platforms, brand communities, and the competition. This social listening phase informs the entire design of the campaign in Step 2, strategic design.

Strategic Design

The formative research gathered in Step 1 allows social media professionals to craft engaging and dynamic campaigns, centered around SMART, outcome-based objectives. The entire strategic design phase is data-informed and data-driven in its creation.

Implementation and Monitoring

In the third step, implementation, strategists put into action the program that was created and designed for social media. In addition, data play a crucial role in this step because they drive informed engagement. In the world of social media, interaction with the publics should never be cut off from monitoring. As a brand monitors the campaign, measuring the reach, engagement, and impact of social media interaction, a wealth of information is gleaned. First, the brand understands what is working in the campaign. Second, the brand will also be alerted to when the brand community interacts, in what way the community is interacting, and the tone or intent of the interaction. This information informs how the brand should respond and who needs to be included in the response and ultimately helps define what type of communication the brand community is expecting from the organization. This kind of data monitoring during a campaign ensures that the social media campaign is achieving its intended purpose.

Evaluation

Finally, at the close of a campaign, social media professionals gather *summative* data. This information is used not only to evaluate whether a campaign was successful, but also to lay a foundation for the listening phase of future campaigns. Step 4 collects and interprets data in order to summarize what the campaign achieved.

The ability to gather information, which informs and helps develop business intelligence, through social media has revolutionized the ways organizations can apply meaningful data to strategic decisions and future activity.

Oliver Blanchard[3] identifies this powerful ability as the combination of velocity and specificity:

> The velocity with which organizations can collect specific data, gather business intelligence, and measure the impact of a particular activity at any given time by using social media is astounding. Two rarely discussed key benefits to emerge from the marriage of social media and business measurement are velocity and specificity. Velocity is important to the success of a social media program because the speed with which intelligence reaches a decision maker will impact the speed with which he can respond to a market opportunity.[4]

In other words, the ability to quickly gather data, have that information reach key strategists, and take action as a result of the specific detail empowers organizations to effectively engage with key stakeholders like never before in organizational history.

PRINCIPLES OF RESEARCH

Before examining the particular parts of campaign evaluation, it is useful to understand some key factors in research practices. Primary research, or original research as opposed to research from an outside source, can be broken down into two broad approaches: Qualitative research and quantitative research. *Qualitative* research "is an approach for exploring and understanding the meaning individuals or groups ascribe to a social or human problem."[5] Qualitative research is often called subjective, in that it is rooted in the opinions, perspectives, and thoughts of individuals.[6] Using qualitative research allows us to understand "issues in language and perspectives of stakeholders," as well as reasons *why* people feel the way they do about a particular subject or issue.[7] Some commonly used qualitative research approaches include interviews, focus groups, and case studies. *Quantitative* research, on the other hand, is often classified as more objective, meaning that the focus of this type of research is on testing theories or exploring the relationship between variables.[8] Rather than being about an individual's experience or thoughts, the goal is to understand generalizable data and the presence of factors, influences, and variables in particular scenarios. This type of research relies on using statistics and equations to make sense of the data and "provides researchers and professionals the ability to report their results with greater precision."[9] A common quantitative technique used among communication professionals is content analysis, such as when we examine types of media coverage. Other common methods are surveys and experiments. When researchers decide to use both qualitative and quantitative methods, it is known as *mixed methods* research.

An effective researcher will understand the value that each method brings and the particular insight that can be gained through qualitative or quantitative research. Thus:

> Qualitative and quantitative methods are not exclusive but work together, with quantitative methods used to harness and distill research so that public relations professionals may use qualitative methods to delve deeper into research issues and extract meaningful data that aligns with business objectives.[10]

In other words, as this chapter examines the various stages of campaign evaluation, keep in mind the importance of leveraging both quantitative and qualitative data in order to provide the most meaningful evaluation of a campaign.

While data are used throughout a campaign, the evaluation portion is particularly rich in measurement gathering and interpretation. Determining the effectiveness of a campaign is no small task, which is why it is valuable to understand the many elements that should be evaluated within a campaign.

COMPONENTS OF EVALUATION

Expert evaluation requires social media professionals to analyze every element of a campaign, from start to finish. For this to be accomplished, there are three main sections that should each be investigated to determine the total effectiveness of a campaign. These sections are: Preparation, implementation, and impact.[11]

- *Preparation* evaluates items from the listening and strategic design stages of the campaign. The goal is to assess whether, prior to the social media campaign being launched, proper information was in place and the strategic design was correctly developed from the data.
- *Implementation* evaluates the third stage of the social media campaign, examining whether information was delivered at the correct time, whether it reached the identified audiences, and the nature of the engagement that occurred as a result of the engagement.
- *Impact* relates to the specific objectives that were established for the campaign in order to achieve its overall goal.

Evaluation

Preparation	Implementation	Impact
• Formative Research Review • Strategic Design Analysis • Presentation	• Social Media Dashboard KPIs • Message Reach • Engagement	• SMART, Outcome-based Objectives • Consumption Metrics • Sharing Metrics • Actionable Metrics

Figure 6.2 Elements of Evaluation

What may already be apparent is that every social media campaign evaluation has a plethora of data to mine in order to provide an effective analysis. It is important to assess what is most critical for the brand to understand from the campaign in order not only to evaluate the campaign's impact, but to strategically move forward in future social media campaigns. That is why, within each of these areas, each brand will need to evaluate data based on its individual needs and values.

Some may argue that, essentially, the evaluation stage is solely to measure the impact, or ROI, of a social media campaign and the ultimate contribution to the organization, but this perspective fails to recognize the value that can be gained from an in-depth exploration of the entire campaign. In order for the full value of social media to be understood, it is helpful to have a more nuanced approach that allows social media strategists to articulate the multiple ways social media advanced the organizational goals and objectives.

Preparation

Evaluation of a social media campaign's preparation involves identifying whether everything was in place that needed to be prior to the launch of the actual campaign. A strong foundation, or preparation, gives life to a strategic campaign. On the other hand, a weak or incomplete preparation of a social media campaign is often the root cause of failures. Jim Sterne[12] points out the value of preparation by reminding strategists of the need for concrete planning before engaging in social media:

> Why are you even bothering with social media? If you don't know, you do not want to step in blindly. This is the realm of public opinion and customer conversations. You do not want to blunder onto the scene without a clear idea of why you are there and what you want out of it. Not only are you sure to make hash of it, anything you measure will be context free and worse than useless.[13]

Within the evaluation of preparation for a campaign, three main areas to consider are: the formative research that was gathered in listening, the program's strategic design, and the presentation content.

Formative Research

Formative research, which helps form the foundation of campaigns, is important as it helps identify key elements that, if missing or incorrect, could result in a less effective campaign. It is important, therefore, to consider whether, during the formative research, correct information was available to identify all the primary objectives of the campaign, key audiences, keywords, organizational structural needs, and other elements that were important to the success of the campaign. For example, were all the keywords and phrases that were used by the SEO team provided to the social media team to be integrated into the messaging of the social media campaign? Did the market research provide the necessary information to effectively develop audience profiles for the social media brand community? Did the information available regarding other communication from the brand during the campaign thoroughly explain times when it was effective (or ineffective) to communicate?

Next, identify if any assumptions or interpretations of the information were incorrect. For example, were the tones of the conversations in social media correctly identified, or was it later realized that some were much more positive (or negative) than originally thought? Perhaps it was assumed that certain social media users were influencers, only for there later to be a realization that they did not have a significant role within the social media platform the brand was using. Essentially, in this stage, each *application* of data that was made in order to determine strategy should be reviewed for accuracy and completeness.

Finally, there should be an evaluation of the documents that were available during the course of the social media campaign. It is important to identify, for the increased success of future campaigns, any documents that were needed but were not available. It could be something such as lacking the correct crisis response policy, which resulted in difficulties during the campaign. It could be that the web development team had no online user policies, and the social media team ending up being less efficient in meeting deadlines for campaign launches as a result. Whatever was not available, as well as the implication of not having these resources, should be noted. It is important to note that this final category is not a blame-placing section. It is simply an identifier of what might have delayed, inhibited, or influenced later results in the campaign.

Strategic Design

The next part of evaluating the preparation of the campaign is to review the strategic design. Begin by performing a top–down review of the campaign strategy:

- Was the goal appropriate for the organization's current need and purpose for social media?
- Were the audiences that were selected for each goal actually the ones that needed to be involved in ensuring the goal was met? Were there any that should have been removed or added?
- Was each objective SMART (strategic, measurable, achievable, relevant, and timely)? In addition, were the objectives outcome-based (reliant on an action that the online communities would take)?
- Did each strategy specifically relate to the direct success of the objective it was supporting? Were any of the strategies less effective or, potentially, would have had more impact if they had been used somewhere else in the campaign?
- Were all tactics identified correctly? Should any have been added or removed?

Next, it is important to return to the social media strategic plan and identify whether the social media campaign goal(s) supported the overall mission of the organization. Identifying how every campaign that is launched supports the overall vision of social media within the brand is a key part to program evaluation. In addition, review the purpose statement for each social media platform and evaluate whether the strategies and tactics that were implemented during the campaign supported those purposes.

Finally, evaluate the brand's persona and tone throughout the campaign. To do this component of the evaluation, review not only the posts from the content calendar, but also the engagement responses that were sent by the brand throughout a campaign. Review each tweet, post, reply, comment, and mention to determine if the organization's social voice was consistent with the brand's persona and tone and the purpose of the campaign. In addition to noting effective posts and content that were particularly relevant to the community, also identify anything that was not consistent and review what was missing or should have been added.

Presentation

The last component for evaluating the preparation for the social media campaign is to look at the creative pieces that were designed and the overall presentation of the brand throughout the campaign. Begin by reviewing the social profiles the brand used. Provide feedback on the quality of the profile's presentation, including the images used, the positioning of any information, such as in the "about" section, the nature of the social channel's connection to other properties of the brand (such as links to the website or other social media platforms), and the general impression of the brand that was given by each platform. Was it clear that the platform was the official presence of the brand on that social media channel? Was there anything that highlighted the current campaign on the profile, while keeping the general look and feel of the brand? Note any inconsistencies, strengths, or points of feedback.

Next, assess the quality of the creative content used throughout the campaign. The goal is that the quality of the content provided in videos, photos, infographics, memes, and so on would match the brand's persona and tone appropriately, while effectively delivering the intended campaign messages. Be sure to note any creative content pieces that were particularly strong and highly reflective of the brand, as well as those that were weak and did not stay true to the brand persona. In addition, comment on any pieces that seemed to effectively portray the campaign message, as well as those, if any, that were less suited to the purpose. For example, it might be noted that although a vine was professionally created and high quality, it was less effective at delivering a message for the campaign. Or, perhaps, an image that was designed carried a strong message but was pixelated. It is important to recognize that the evaluation is not only to identify opportunities for future growth, however, but also strengths. Make sure to identify specific elements of a campaign that had excellent presentation quality. Those can serve as models for future campaigns and initiatives.

Implementation

After evaluating the preparation that was involved in launching a campaign, it is helpful to evaluate the effectiveness of the actual implementation and engagement of the campaign. In this portion, the content calendar monitoring section will come in especially handy. The purpose of evaluating the implementation section is not only to analyze the actual flow of communication, but also to review key progress indicators (KPIs). As a reminder, KPIs are numbers that represent an organization's progress toward a given goal. They are the areas that are measured to illustrate whether, throughout a campaign, an objective is being achieved or the efforts are falling short. Eric Peterson[14] explains this by saying, "Key performance indicators are designed to summarize meaningfully compared data."[15] The purpose of KPIs is to allow large amounts of data to be explained in a simple, concise manner throughout the course of a campaign. Peterson suggests that KPIs are "a response to a general organizational fear of big, ugly spreadsheets and complex applications. The big idea behind KPIs is that you're taking technical data and presenting it using business-relevant language."[16] Each social media platform has a dashboard of information to review to begin the analysis of KPIs.

Message Reach

The goal of studying the message reach is to understand the exposure, or the potential audience size, a campaign message achieved. To help facilitate this evaluation of the message reach, reference the content calendar monitoring section where specific activities were recorded throughout the campaign and then review the messages in three different ways: individual posts, strategies, and objectives.

First, analyze each post and identify the reach, or how many people were exposed to the message. There should be a column next to each post in the content calendar that identifies this information—if it is missing, go into the social media platform analytics and retrieve it. Second, sort the content calendar by specific strategies. It can be helpful to compare across strategies to see if exposure was given proportionally to all strategies or if certain ones had an average reach that was greater than others. This could provide context for the reason why some may have been more effective and others seemed negligible. Third, do the same kind of comparison across objectives. The goal is to understand which specific posts and strategies had the strongest reach (and largest potential audience) and, ultimately, which objectives were given the greatest exposure.

EXPERT INSIGHT

Laurie Meacham

What do you think is one hallmark competency social media professionals need to succeed?

Humanity! Don't forget that social is exactly that: Social. People want to connect with brands in a personal way and feel like they're recognized as an individual.

What do you believe makes a social media campaign effective?

In one word: Engagement. If you're sharing content that your customers care about and want to engage with, your campaign is much more likely to be effective as it'll gain more reach.

How can social media professionals show the value of social media to an organization's bottom-line efforts?

Ultimately, the value created from social media efforts is one of loyalty.

With the increased scrutiny on vanity metrics for social media evaluation, what would you identify as key values within social media that show authentic ROI for a brand?

I believe it all comes down to loyalty. If you're able to connect with customers in a meaningful way and maintain their loyalty through the relationship you've built with them on social media, then you're getting an authentic ROI. Regardless of how many likes, shares, RTs, etc. you get, if your customers are doing more business with you and sharing their personal experiences with your brand with their network, then you're achieving success.

In what ways, if any, is it possible to assess the value added by social media to the quality of relationships with key audiences?

This is a hard thing to measure, but the important thing is to remain authentic to your brand. No one should be portraying their brand or business differently on social than they do at any other touch point and you also shouldn't sell yourself out for the sake of trying to achieve a viral campaign. All interactions should be reflective of the brand and social is just another channel where it's possible to engage and leave an impression. If those opportunities are genuine and used wisely, they'll add to the overall value of the customer experience.

What do you think makes social media evaluation or measurement so intimidating? Is there a way around this intimidation factor?

There's a tendency to look for reassurance that the effort being put into social media is a means to an end, but it's really an ongoing effort and an ongoing development of a relationship with your audience. Social media is a unique touch point where you not only have an opportunity to reach a large audience, you also can engage with your customers, often outside of a transaction. There's not always an immediate ROI and it can be hard to quantify success based on impressions, but when you look at human nature, patterns, and behavior, it all comes down to knowing that there's a unique opportunity here to humanize your brand and connect with people in a way that's meaningful to them. Keep in mind that there are many ways to define success when it comes to social media—and more than one could be right, in its own way.

What value does evaluation provide for a social media team and organization as a whole?

We know that what's measured gets managed and that's just as true with social media as it is for anything else you invest in. An organization should create meaningful KPIs for social media, collaborate with other teams, and keep the big picture in mind. We always ask the question: Are we doing the right things for the right reasons?

Connect with Laurie: @laurieameacham

Laurie Meacham is Manager of Customer Support for JetBlue and oversees the Social Media Team

Engagement

Although it is helpful to understand exposure, it means very little if an audience did not interact with the content or engage in the conversation on social media. Therefore, measuring the nature and depth of engagement is also crucial. To perform this evaluation, it is helpful to divide the social media posts by platform and save them in separate files or tabs within an Excel document for ease of analysis and interpretation. This allows brands to customize each report based on engagement types on a given platform. Next, add columns for each kind of engagement that can be measured on a platform, such as likes in Facebook or thumbs ups in YouTube or comments in Instagram. Be sure to include a "total engagement" column for the platform. As was done for message reach, evaluate the engagement for each post, each strategy, and each objective. Provide feedback on the most effective and least effective posts, strategies, and objectives by each platform.

Two-Way Dialogue Audit

In addition to understanding whether the content that was delivered reached the audiences and was well received, indicated by comments, sharing, and interaction, it is important to evaluate the implementation of two-way conversations by conducting a summative, two-way dialogue audit. Because social media is about a dialogue, brands should regularly evaluate the capacity and performance of brand engagement during a campaign. Chuck Hemann and Ken Burbary[17] suggest that there are two levels of measurement in the two-way dialogue audit: Conversations within the social media properties that a brand owns and conversations outside the direct social network of the brand. The necessary measurements and analysis for each of these levels will be discussed below.

Conversations in the brand's own social media platforms: Whenever content is posted onto social media, there is the potential that a member of the audience will comment, mention, follow, or share via their own social media channels. In order to have high levels of community interaction, therefore, a brand cannot simply post original content, but must also *respond* when the community interacts. Review posts to see if there are unanswered questions or comments, whether the brand replied to new members who joined as a result of the initiative, and whether there are any pieces of interaction that seem to have dropped. It could be that the level of interaction is far too high to reply to all community members. In this case, it is important to identify if there was a process in place to understand how dialogue would be handled: Were all influencers responded to? Were complaints addressed? Were questions answered? Identify the process for how the brand responded and then analyze the interaction based on the process.

Two-way dialogue audits should also review the social community's participation in the conversation or dialogue. There are several steps in effective community participation analysis. Four key components are recommended by social media expert Avinash Kaushik:[18]

1. conversation rate;
2. amplification rate;
3. applause rate;
4. economic value.

He suggested this model because he wanted to "propose a framework you can use to measure success using metrics that matter for one simple reason: They actually measure if you are participating in the channel in an optimal fashion."[19]

Measuring a *conversation rate*, the rate at which conversations happen on the social platform, provides a base estimate of the effectiveness of the engagement with a brand community. In order to measure the conversation rate, simply provide the number of comments, replies, or other conversation pieces per post. Anytime a social media community member generated original content in the conversation, it should be included as part of the conversation rate.

Next, evaluate the *amplification* of the conversation. This involves looking specifically at things that elevated the conversation to a wider audience, such as shares or retweets. Kaushik suggests that this type of activity helps break past the limitations of an online community size (for example, 50,000 followers on Twitter) and into a wider audience network of engagement. Over time, those people in the wider networks, which Kaushik identifies as second- and third-level networks, may become part of the brand's direct social media community having discovered relevant and meaningful content produced by the brand thanks to amplification by community members. Although this metric does not measure a two-way dialogue with the community, it does show amplification of a conversation that was being fostered in social media, which can eventually produce more two-way dialogues.

Third, *applause* is a way to measure the affinity of the community with a post. This involves likes, favorites, +1s, and other affirmation-based actions in social media. This is valuable as it allows the organization to identify what kind of content is most valuable to an audience. In addition, it builds the credibility of the content as users provide endorsements. This will help attract other users who are interested in the same content. Kaushik[20] identifies the value of this kind of interaction, saying, "Your selfless social media contribution comes back to assist you in driving valuable business outcomes."[21]

Finally, *economic value* should be calculated, and this will be discussed in greater detail later. It is worth noting that using social media for the sole purpose of driving bottom-line business revenue will not, necessarily, yield a strong social strategy. Social media is about being *social*. It involves developing relationships, contributing to conversations, and being an active participant in an online community that shares a mutual interest. But that does not mean that social media cannot support bottom-line initiatives. Kaushik argues, "Social media participation, done right, adds value to the company's bottom-line. Some of it can't be computed. That is okay. But some of it can be and it is your job, nay duty (!), to quantify that."[22]

Having analyzed participation in the conversation, it is important next to evaluate the increase in positive communication that occurred as a result of the campaign. To evaluate this, it is helpful to run a new SOV report that highlights activity during the social media campaign and compares it with the original SOV report that was developed in the listening phase. Remember, SOV involves looking at key competitors and calculating how much conversation relates to the brand versus competitor brands.

In addition to the SOV report, there are several more layers that can be analyzed in evaluation to understand the full impact of the dialogue throughout a social media campaign. For example, a "share of conversation" report could be developed. Chuck Hemann and Ken Burbary[23] define share of conversation as "a more accurate gauge of how aware people are of a product or campaign within a broader industry than share of voice. This metric tracks, typically in percentage form, how much conversation is happening versus the broader industry."[24] *Share of conversation* reports reflect what topics a brand community is talking about and how much of those conversations reference or mention the brand in any way, whereas an SOV report focuses more on a comparison of conversations that mention the brand with conversations that mention competition. In short, share of conversation focuses on topics and the brand, where SOV focuses on competition and the brand. The SOV takes a topic, such as fitness, and analyzes all of the conversations happening on a platform about that topic. Then, the brand calculates how much, if any, of the conversation about fitness relates to the brand.

Other dimensions to conversations that it can be helpful to evaluate include the sentiment of conversations taking place, the resonance (or how well the brand community is accepting a message), and the overall volume (or how frequently communication is occurring) of the brand's conversations on social media. To calculate any of these, a brand should analyze each post and interaction within a brand community, using many of the same tools discussed in the listening chapter. Then, beyond merely *counting* the mentions, comments, or replies, each one should be analyzed for the tone that the brand community had in the interaction, the resonance (indicated by the conversation rate, amplification, and applause), and the frequency of the brand's communication within the dialogue. These measurements can then be compared and contrasted to provide a fuller analysis of why certain strategies, tactics, or posts were successful in supporting the campaign objectives and others may not have been. For example, perhaps there was a high level of interaction around a post, but the tone was fairly negative. This may show why, despite having high scores in engagement, the strategy was not, in fact, supported through that interaction. Or, perhaps, the brand seemed to be strong (having a louder volume) sometimes within a campaign, but then was quiet for long periods in other places. That may have sent mixed messages to the community regarding the brand's intentionality with dialogue and genuine interest in conversations. These kinds of analyses help provide context and meaning for the overall impact of the campaign.

Conversations occurring outside the brand's own social media platforms: Throughout a campaign, there are often conversations that are relevant for the brand but they may not directly mention the brand or may incorrectly tag the organization. Review interactions that involved the brand during the campaign that were *unrelated* to a specific post by the brand, perhaps examining the brand's interactions around certain hashtags that were relevant or providing resources and answers to social media user questions that had nothing to do with planned posts from the content calendar. Look at these conversations to determine if the interactions seem well received. Determine this by asking questions such as whether the brand was perceived as helpful or intrusive, based on the response of the social media user. Were any actions triggered as a result of the communication with the person (such as liking a page, having issues resolved, etc.)? Ideally, the brand should join appropriate conversations outside the social media posts that the organization crafted itself. This second level of evaluation analyzes whether, throughout the campaign, the brand was able to appropriately join conversations that were user-generated within the social sphere and yet outside the original content posted by the brand for the campaign.

Conversation Check	• Did the brand respond to interaction on the brand's profile? • Did the brand interact with conversations that were applicable *beyond* the brand's profile?
Conversation Rate	• The total number of conversations for a post (replies, comments, mentions, etc.)
Amplification Rate	• The total engagement that extends a conversation on a post (shares, retweets, etc.)
Economic Value	• Anything that stemmed from a post and led to a sale or other form of financial gain.
Share of Voice	• Reveals the percentage of communication focusing on the brand versus competitors.
Share of Conversation	• Highlights the percentage of communication focusing on a brand in a given general topic.
Conversation Sentiment	• The tone or feeling of the communication between the brand community and the organization.
Conversation Resonance	• The reception or acceptance of key messages into the brand community throughout a campaign.
Conversation Volume	• The strength and consistency of communication from the brand throughout a campaign.

Figure 6.3 Components of Communication Audits

Advertising Metrics

Although this text largely focuses on running organic social media campaigns, the integration of paid strategies is a reality for many social media initiatives. When a campaign integrates paid placement, it is essential that evaluation of those placements occurs. As was mentioned above, many social media platforms offer comparative evaluations between organic and paid posts on a site. In addition, social media advertising platforms offer deeper analytics that relate to various pricing and interaction methods such as cost per click, cost per impression, cost per view, or cost per action. Each advertising platform provides different combinations of these pricing methods. As an advertising strategy is implemented, analysis should be provided on the effectiveness of the placement, the value of the clicks or followers that are gained through the advertising efforts, and feedback on whether such efforts should continue, be adjusted and then continue, or be discontinued as part of the ongoing support to reach a campaign's objective. For the final evaluation, review the total contribution of the paid placement efforts in social media to the success of the objective the strategy was designed to support. It is helpful to analyze what percentage of the success should be attributed to paid efforts versus organic efforts.

A word of caution should be noted about using *advertising value equivalency* (AVE) in research. Essentially, AVE is about associating a dollar amount with earned media by equating that presence with how much it would cost to "buy" that placement. For example, in social media, some people may report how much the reach, engagement, or impression would have cost if it was purchased through social media advertising instead of organic campaign efforts. To do this, they would look at similar costs on the social media platform to advertise and report the AVE in their evaluation. However, as this chapter has emphasized, robust social media evaluation is an examination of the impact and reaction of people, whereas AVE "is a rigid construct that lacks the flexibility and depth to factor in things such as audience perception, message credibility and audience attention."[25]

Impact

The final level of evaluation has to do with the end results of the campaign. This portion involves returning to the SMART, outcome-based objectives that were established at the beginning of the campaign and analyzing whether or not these objectives were accomplished. This is why it is so crucial that each objective is designed to be specific (so brands know what to measure) and measurable (so brands know what change they are expecting to see in metrics). In addition, the time elements of the objective allow brands to know when the measurement should take place. For each objective, provide the exact social metrics that confirm success or show the need to improve. Sometimes, the data that are needed to determine whether an objective was met are unavailable as part of the typical social media dashboards. This requires social media professionals to review information from the website analytics of an organization, often integrating platforms such as Google Analytics into the evaluation.

Integrated Social Media Measurement

As previously mentioned, there are some metrics that are housed outside a social media platform, and yet they are crucial for knowing the value of social media initiatives. Often, these types of metrics involve conversion behaviors that are ultimately tracked on the website of an organization. To find and mine this type of data, coordination with the website team is required.

A critical part of the process of designing campaign budgets is to assign values to specific activities. For example, if lead generation was the focus of the campaign, how much is each name worth? Or perhaps the campaign was designed to generate awareness of a topic or cause. How much value is assigned to each person who received or is exposed to the information? Typically, the marketing department would be able to provide these values. If those values had not already been established, the social media team should coordinate with the marketing department to determine the value before launching the campaign. The question then becomes, how to attribute an action on a website, such as gaining a lead for a sale, to social media engagement.

To address these kinds of questions, use the organization's website analytics. There is a wealth of information and data that the website analytics should be able to provide, including the ability to track user paths, traffic sources, and conversions. Perhaps one of the most valuable competencies that a social media professional can apply to this final stage of the campaign is recognizing which data are helpful and which are a distraction. Lars Lofgren,[26] KISSmetrics marketing analyst, argues,

> Not all data is helpful. Some of it is worse than worthless because it tricks us into believing we have answers when we don't. But when you focus on data that helps you make decisions, everything else in your business gets easier.[27]

The goal is to identify actionable metrics that inform decisions and future strategy.[28] Jay Baer[29] suggests that the types of numbers, or metrics, that matter can be classified into four genres:

1. Consumption metrics, which are the engagement data points gathered from social media dashboards such as watched videos, reach, or visits.
2. Advocacy and sharing metrics, also gathered from social dashboards, which indicate that the content was shared through actions such as retweets, share buttons, or direct quotes.
3. Lead-generation metrics, which indicate that someone wants to learn more or is considering a purchase.
4. Sales metrics, which indicate that revenue was earned as a result of an action taken.

While consumption metrics and advocacy/sharing metrics are easier to find and are, therefore, regularly highlighted by organizations, it is also critical to dive deeper into the data in order to measure the lead-generation and sales metrics.[30]

Recognizing that analytics will give far more data than is useful, it is necessary for the social media team to identify the specific information that is required to measure objectives. In many analytic programs, a customized dashboard can be established that will track specific data, which have been identified as useful, from social media sources. These filtered data will help the social media team to collect and track the most important data pieces that relate to their campaign. Be thoroughly familiar with the analytic data available prior to beginning evaluation in order to correctly assess what data will be most meaningful and actionable.

One helpful feature in analytics is customization of a URL so that it can be tracked and associated with specific efforts. Some people use third-party apps to shorten and track URLs, such as Bitly and Ow.ly. These services allow brands to shorten a URL and then track whether people end up clicking the link. One thing that these services cannot do, however, is tell a brand what a user does *after* clicking the link. Although it may not seem to be crucial information, it really is valuable insight, particularly when people are driven from a brand's social media platform to the brand's website. The ability for the social media team to definitively answer what social media brand community members do when they visit the website helps support the claim that social media engagement has resulted in lead-generation or sale metrics on the brand's website.

To develop a customized URL that can be tracked by analytic software, brands identify specific data pieces to include in the URL so that the analytics system knows to track the information. A brand can identify a specific medium from which the link was sending people, the campaign with which the link was associated, the source where the link was located, and the type of content or term that was included to drive an individual to visit a brand's website. Analytic platforms make the process of creating custom URLs quite easy. Google Analytics, for example, provides a page to help brands generate custom URLs that will be tracked in Google Analytics and provide reports on that activity. On this page, brands can simply copy and paste the URL that they want to put onto social media, such as a link to a product that is on sale or a free trial to sign up for, and then enter the exact information they want to track (such as the name of the campaign or the source, such as the social media platform, that will be driving the traffic). Google Analytics will then generate a custom URL for the social media team to use, track, and analyze.

A custom URL a brand might develop, for example, could be for all links that will be posted on Facebook with the intention of driving people to sign up for a free trial of a product. The website analytics would then track what those users who click the link on Facebook do when they arrive on the brand's website. Social media strategists will be

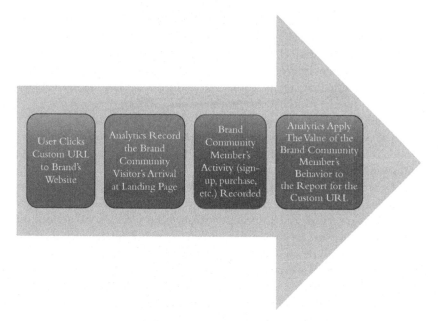

Figure 6.4 Custom URL Data Tracking Process

able to know whether the users sign up for the trial, whether they look at the page and immediately leave, or if they end up signing up and also looking around at other pages. This kind of information helps a social media team gain much more insight into a social media brand community's behavior. In addition to monitoring the activity of people who click to visit the website from Facebook, the team may also opt to create another custom URL that is used only for Instagram. This new custom URL would also drive people to the free trial, but would be customized with tracking information to identify that those individuals came to the website from Instagram as opposed to Facebook. In the evaluation, then, the team could compare the effectiveness of Instagram versus Facebook in driving sign-ups. It would be possible not only to understand which platform drove the most sign-ups, but also which platform was most likely to send users who viewed other pages on the website, people who would spend longer on the website, and those who were not interested in the content and immediately left.

This concept of creating custom URLs to track the behavior of users from social media could be applied across platforms, such as Pinterest, Instagram, or YouTube, or even incorporated to test specific *types* of posts on a platform. By creating two custom URLs, the social media team would be able to measure whether video posts in Facebook or photo posts in Facebook drove more sign-ups. Similarly, it would be possible to compare whether videos posted in TikTok, Instagram, or Facebook were most influential. Therefore, using separate custom URLs across platforms and for different post types allows the brand to compare and contrast the effectiveness of posts in actually producing tangible results such as lead generation or sales on the brand's website.

Whether brands use custom URLs for each social media platform (such as one for TikTok, one for Facebook, one for LinkedIn), have custom URLs for each *type* of post analyzed by platforms (such as Facebook links with images, Facebook links with videos, etc.), or even if custom URLs are generated for specific strategies, to determine which is most effective, this method of tracking allow brands to analyze every user who clicks on a link and accurately measure their behavioral actions on the brand's website. In conclusion, the goal at this level of analytics is to: (1) identify the type of action or behavior that needs to be tracked on social media; (2) develop the back-end process to track the action (customized URL, analytic report, etc.); and (3) pull the data at the end of the campaign to directly attribute concrete actions that resulted as part of a social media campaign effort.

Outcome-Based Objectives and Reporting

Whether using proprietary analytic software, Google Analytics, or a mixture of paid and free social and web analytics tools, the ultimate goal is the same: Identify meaningful data, apply the information to the campaign objectives, and evaluate the effectiveness of the campaign. Having SMART, outcome-based objectives should allow for precise evaluation of the success or lack of success of an objective. It is also important for a social media professional to dive deeper into the data and apply *context* to the success or failure of the objective. This occurs when each of the three layers of evaluation (preparation, implementation, and impact) are considered.

Additionally, because analytic and reporting platforms offer automatic downloads of many of the reports, it is quite tempting to simply export those reports, compile them, and send them as one document to management. It is best, however, for a social media strategist to customize reports and provide the appropriate context. Although automated reports can provide useful additions to a social media report for a campaign, a strategist should fully review each level of the evaluation (preparation, implementation, and impact), provide KPIs from those key areas, and then offer a comprehensive analysis of the campaign's effectiveness as a whole. It is helpful to include a one- or two-page executive summary at the beginning of a social media evaluation report so that those who are unable to dive into all the information can still assess the value of the social media campaign. It is also equally important for the report to break down each stage of the campaign, highlighting strengths, identifying weaknesses, and ultimately reflecting on the goals being met. Finally, each evaluation of a social media campaign should include recommendations, lessons learned, and key take-away points that can be applied for a better strategy and more effective campaign design in the future.

THE FUTURE OF SOCIAL MEDIA CAMPAIGNS

The nature of social media is that it is constantly changing, evolving, and moving. Being effective in social media requires that brands regularly adapt. Social media compels professionals to be bold, willing to attempt new processes and adopt new platforms and strategies. The four steps to a social media campaign provide a framework that professionals can apply to brand initiatives in the ever-shifting social world. The value of listening, understanding the culture of a brand and the current social media climate, is paramount for any campaign. This in-depth information infuses life into the efforts and activity of the brand. Meaningful data are precisely how brands develop strategic campaigns—they form *out* of research that seeks to understand the social media brand community. The strategic design step marries the science of data with the art of relationship, drawing together all of the information into a creative and engaging roadmap that guides the social media efforts of the brand. After the creation of this social masterpiece, the third step, implementation, orchestrates the tapestry of engagement, weaving together all the strategies and tactics into a harmonious dialogue with key stakeholders.

It is in this step, the implementation of a campaign, that many brands struggle to understand how interaction can ever be scripted. After all, social media requires flexibility and adaptation. The beauty behind data-informed strategic designs, however, is that they are not developed from a static, boring room full of people who are bent on pushing messages in front of the public, but rather grow as a direct result of understanding *who* the brand community members are, what they *value*, and the conversations they *want* to be having with the brand. Campaigns developed from this type of relationally informed data are anything but scripted—they are, in fact, *reactive*, responding to the needs and communication of the brand community connections. In addition, the third step of a campaign involves not only sharing content from the brand that was developed around a rigorous understanding of the audience, but also *actively* responding to the live-time interaction, discussions, and questions that occur throughout the life of a campaign. Strategic design is preparation for dynamic conversations and thriving relationships in brand communities, not staunch parameters that stifle the relational dimension of social media.

Finally, the fourth step evaluates all of the efforts of a campaign, analyzing everything from the smallest piece of information to the overall impact. This analysis not only provides insight into the impact of the campaign, elements that supported that success and areas that hindered it, but also affords rich data for future social media use. In this sense, social media campaigns are heuristic in nature, in that each campaign reveals new information about the brand community and the relationships that key stakeholders have with the brand. This valuable insight should not be lost by being used solely to evaluate a single campaign and then filed away. Rather, it should also be used to apply strategic insight into future campaigns.

The relationships in social media with the brand community do not end with each campaign. They are, ideally, long-term, ongoing relationships that will span the course of many campaigns, initiatives, and efforts. Losing the insight gained about these relationships, the ways people interact and respond, tactics that are particularly helpful in building meaningful dialogue, and the methods which the brand community has developed over the course of a campaign would be tragic. Rather, this wealth of information should be carefully secured and purposefully integrated into future campaigns. Not only is this simply a smart move on the part of a brand, giving it a wealth of information for the next campaign, it is also a sign of the value that the brand community holds. If these relationships matter, genuinely, to the brand, then it is a disservice to disregard every conversation and interaction at the end of a campaign, to simply begin again. Authentic relationships are a continual dance of communication, interaction, and engagement.

The core component of social media relates to people: Understanding them, interacting with them, and developing relationships with them. Ultimately, the goal of strategic social media use is to encourage purposeful engagement in the midst of a dynamic platform that fosters unscripted, two-way dialogue. Thus, although there are four steps to a social media campaign, and this framework provides a structure to have robust and authentic relationships in social media, the truth is the four steps never stop—instead, they form a continuous process, devoted to thriving relationships and authentic communication. Once evaluation concludes, the brand should already begin again, listening, seeking to understand, and preparing meaningful communication with its brand community.

BEYOND EVALUATION: STEWARDSHIP IN SOCIAL MEDIA

As explained above, the real heart of any social media campaign is to create a more loyal brand community that engages and interacts far longer than any single campaign. This is the exact issue that all communication campaigns really face as they work to make "communications cyclical rather than episodic."[31] This is where *stewardship* comes into the picture, as organizations seek to maintain and cultivate long-term relationships with stakeholders. The purpose of stewardship is to "establish the means for continued communication that will help to preserve their interest and attention to the organization."[32] Scholarship suggests that there are four dimensions to stewardship:[33]

- *Reciprocity*, which involves public and personal acts of appreciation between the organization and its stakeholders (such as videos thanking donors on social media).
- *Responsibility*, which is about the work an organization is doing to fulfill its role as a good citizen in culture and to accomplish the organization's mission. "At the core of demonstrating responsibility is keeping promises, being a good citizen, and acting in a socially responsible manner."[34]
- *Reporting*, which involves clear communication that the organization is meeting legal and ethical requirements.
- *Relationship nurturing*, which is "concerned with keeping supportive publics at the forefront of the organization's awareness, maintaining open channels of communication with stakeholders and providing communications reinforcing that the involvement is wanted."[35]

Scholars have suggested that the focus on embedding stewardship into the ethos of public relations and strategic communication efforts will provide the opportunity to shift organizational communication toward a consistent and continual relationship management cultivation act rather than a series of disconnected communication campaigns.[36] In the world of social media, this concept is critical, as brands envision the maturation of social media to be more than simply a communication tool. Rather, brands are catching the vision that social media is a relational function which creates authentic and transparent connections with stakeholders. This is the essence of a social brand philosophy: It is about brands that adopt a commitment to maintaining communication using an organization structure that facilitates consistent and authentic interaction between brands and *all* publics (such as described in the social care section of this text), dedicated to authentically listening to, responding to, and stewarding these stakeholder relationships. And this is where an organization has the potential to experience the very best results of social media in its brand communities: Loyalty, trust, credibility, and commitment that will help sustain and propel the organization to fulfill its mission and vision while providing meaningful value to the public and society.

KEY CONCEPT SNAPSHOT

1. Evaluation contains many components that are designed to explore the total impact and effectiveness of each element of a campaign. While evaluating the SMART, outcome-based objectives should be the key measurement of success, professionals should also analyze all elements included within the preparation, implementation, and impact to understand what contributed to or hindered the overall effectiveness of a campaign.
2. Many brands rely on vanity metrics to illustrate the value of their social presence. Rigorous evaluation demands that social media professionals analyze KPIs that have a direct connection to the purpose of the campaign and the two-way engagement being sustained within social media.
3. Social media evaluation is not something that happens in a vacuum. Often, coordination with the marketing, IT, and web team will be required for a truly holistic understanding of the impact of social media within an organization.
4. Evaluation is never the end of social media interaction—rather, it serves as the start of the process for the next campaign. Relationships are continual, as is interaction in social media. Strategic design recognizes the value and contribution past campaigns make to future social media initiatives.

NOTES

1   2011.
2   p. 5.
3   2011.
4   "Building Velocity and Specificity," paras. 4–5.
5   Creswell & Creswell, 2017, p. 4.

6   Men, Robinson, & Thelen, 2019, p. 120.
7   Men et al., 2019, p. 120; Michaelson & Stacks, 2011.
8   Creswell & Creswell, 2017, p. 4.
9   Men et al., 2019, p. 122.
10 Men et al., 2019, p. 121.
11 Broom & Sha, 2013.
12 2010.
13 p. xxvii.
14 Peterson, 2006.
15 Peterson, 2006, Slide 8.
16 Peterson, 2006, Slide 7.
17 2013.
18 2011.
19 para. 6.
20 2011.
21 "3. Applause Rate," para. 15.
22 "Economic Value," para. 10.
23 2013.
24 p. 21.
25 Men et al., 2019, p. 119; Men & Bowen, 2016.
26 n.d.
27 para. 3.
28 Lofgren, n.d., "Actionable Metrics."
29 2013.
30 pp. 174–181.
31 Pressgrove & Harrison, 2019, p. 141; Kelly, 1998.
32 Greenfield, 1991, p. 148.
33 Pressgrove & Harrison, 2019.
34 Pressgrove & Harrison, 2019, p. 142.
35 Pressgrove & Harrison, 2019, p. 142.
36 Pressgrove & Harrison, 2019; Ledingham, 2003; Kelly, 1998.

SUGGESTED READING

Hemann, C. & Burbary, K. (2013). *Digital Marketing Analytics: Making Sense of Consumer Data in a Digital World.* Indianapolis, IN: Pearson Education.
Kelly, N. (2013). *How to Measure Social Media: A Step-by-Step Guide to Developing and Assessing Social Media ROI.* Indianapolis, IN: Que.
Khan, G. F. (2018). *Creating Value with Social Media Analytics: Managing, Aligning, and Mining Social Media Text, Networks, Actions, Location, Apps, Hyperlinks, Multimedia, & Search Engines Data.* Seattle, WA: CreateSpace.
Waters, R. D. & Feneley, K. L. (2013). Virtual Stewardship in the Age of New Media: Have Nonprofit Organizations Moved Beyond Web 1.0 Strategies? *International Journal of Nonprofit and Voluntary Sector Marketing, 18*(3), 216–230.

REFERENCES

Baer, J. (2013). *Youtility: Why Smart Marketing Is About Help Not Hype*. New York: Portfolio/Penguin.

Blanchard, O. (2011). *Social Media ROI: Managing and Measuring Social Media Efforts in Your Organization* [E-reader version]. Indianapolis, IN: Que.

Broom, G. & Sha, B. L. (2013). *Cutlip and Center's Effective Public Relations*. Boston: Pearson.

Creswell, J. W. & Creswell, J. D. (2017). *Research Design: Qualitative, Quantitative, and Mixed Methods Approaches*. Sage.

Greenfield, J. M. (1991). *Fund-Raising: Evaluation and Managing the Fund Development Process*. New York: John Wiley.

Hemann, C. & Burbary, K. (2013). *Digital Marketing Analytics: Making Sense of Consumer Data in a Digital World*. Indianapolis, IN: Pearson Education.

Kaushik, A. (2011, October 10). "Best social media metrics: Conversation, amplification, applause, economic value." *Kaushik.Net*. Retrieved from: www.kaushik. net/avinash/best-social-media-metrics-conversation-amplification-applause-economic-value/

Kelly, K. (1998). *Effective Fund-Raising Management*. Mahwah, NJ: Lawrence Erlbaum.

Ledingham, J. A. (2003). Explicating Relationship Management as a General Theory of Public Relations. *Journal of Public Relations Research*, 15(2), 181–198.

Lofgren, L. (n.d.). "Metrics, metrics on the wall, who's the vainest of them all?" *KissMetrics*. Retrieved from: https://blog.kissmetrics.com/vainest-metrics/

Men, R. L. & Bowen, S. A. (2016). *Excellence in Internal Communication Management*. Business Expert Press.

Men, L. R., Robinson, K., & Thelen, P. (2019). Measurement and evaluation in public relations. In Kim, C. M. (Ed.) *Public Relations: Competencies and Practice*. New York: Routledge, 115–128.

Michaelson, D. & Stacks, D. W. (2011). Standardization in Public Relations Measurement and Evaluation. *Public Relations Journal*, 5(2), 1–22.

Paine, K. (2011). *Measure What Matters: Online Tools for Understanding Customers, Social Media, Engagement, and Key Relationships*. Hoboken, NJ: Wiley.

Peterson, E. (2006, January 1). *The Big Book of Key Performance Indicators*. Retrieved from: http://design4interaction.com/wp-content/uploads/2012/09/The_Big_Book_of_Key_Performance_Indicators_by_Eric_Peterson.pdf

Pressgrove, G. & Harrison, V. S. (2019). Stewardship. In Kim, C. M. (Ed.) *Public Relations: Competencies and Practice*. New York: Routledge, 141–154.

Sterne, J. (2010). *Social Media Metrics: How to Measure and Optimize Your Marketing Investment*. Hoboken, NJ: John Wiley.

Index

Page numbers in **bold** refer to figures.